The Rise and Fall of Adolf Hitler

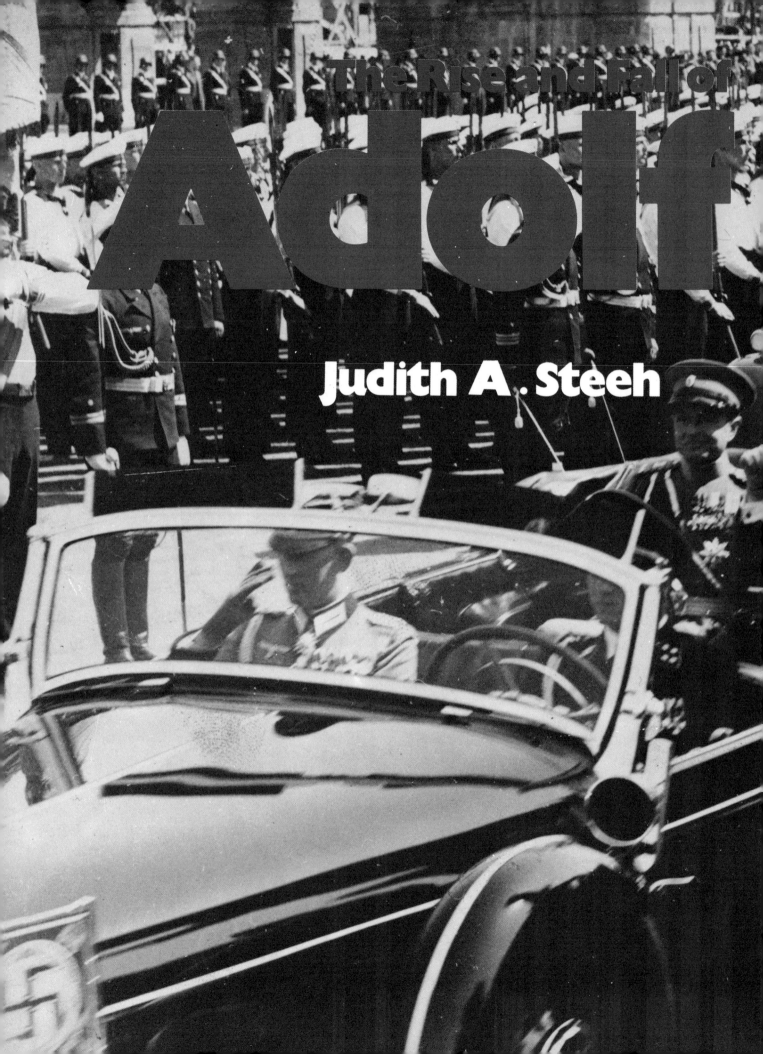

The Rise and Fall of Adolf

Judith A. Steeh

Hitler

HAMLYN
LONDON · NEW YORK · SYDNEY · TORONTO
A BISON BOOK

Contents

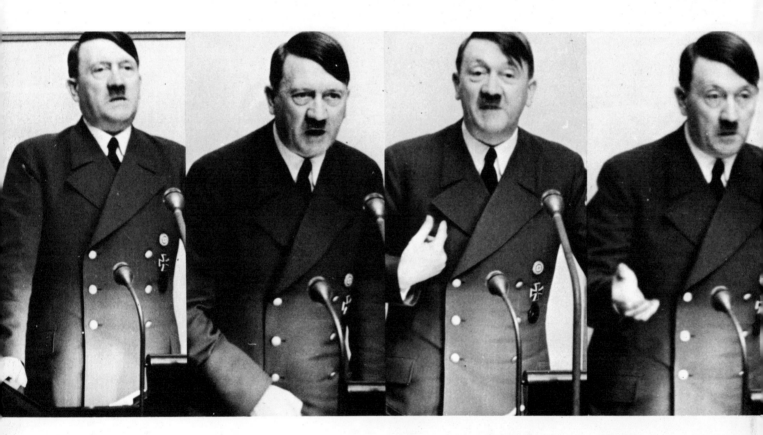

Published by
The Hamlyn Publishing
Group Limited
London New York Sydney
Toronto
Astronaut House, Feltham
Middlesex, England

© Copyright Bison Books
Limited 1980

Produced by
Bison Books Limited
4 Cromwell Place
London S W 7

ISBN 0 600 341526

First published 1980
All rights reserved. No part
of this publication may be
reproduced, stored in a
retrieval system, or
transmitted, in any form or
by any means, electronic,
mechanical, photocopying,
recording or otherwise,
without the permission of
The Hamlyn Publishing
Group Limited and the
copyrightholder.

Designer: Mike Wade

Editor: Catherine Bradley

Indexer: Susan de la Plain

This book is dedicated to
Robert Di Giovanni with
many thanks for his careful
and critical reading of the
manuscript.

Printed in Hong Kong

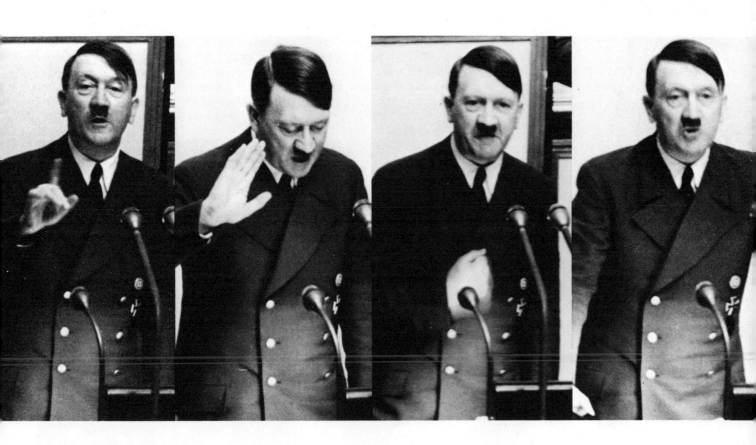

The Early Years

Far right:
An exhibition of 'The Wonders of Life' had a display illustrating Hitler's origins.

At 0630 on a gloomy Easter Sunday evening, 20 April 1889, Adolf Hitler was born. The place was a modest inn, the Gasthof zum Pommer, in the Austrian town of Braunau am Inn on the Bavarian border.

As the son of an Austrian customs official, it is not surprising that he was born on a frontier, but the fact was to assume great importance in years to come. He early formed the conviction that there should be no border between those two German-speaking states. In fact, *Mein Kampf* opens with a commentary on the symbolic significance of his birthplace:

> ... it seems to me providential that fate should have chosen Braunau am Inn as my birthplace. For this little town lies on the boundary between two German states. ... [and] seems to me the symbol of a great mission.

Hitler rarely spoke about his origins, even to his few confidants, and regarded any attempts to delve into them as an unwarranted intrusion on his privacy. In *Mein Kampf* the biographical information is sketchy and often misleading. This supports the suggestion that the Führer deliberately and systematically attempted to detach himself from his background—not because he was ashamed of it, but because he wanted to appear as the very incarnation of the German people.

Hitler's ancestry is firmly rooted in the Waldviertel, a district in Lower Austria which lies between the Danube and the Bohemian border. It is a hilly, heavily wooded region of small villages and rather wretched farms—poor, remote, and somewhat cut off from the mainstream of Austrian life. The name Hitler in various forms (Hitler, Hiedler, Huetler, Huettler)

Center right:
Klara Pölzl, Adolf's mother.

Right:
Hitler's first photograph and attached, a newspaper clipping announcing births in Braunau. Adolf Hitler's birth is mentioned last.

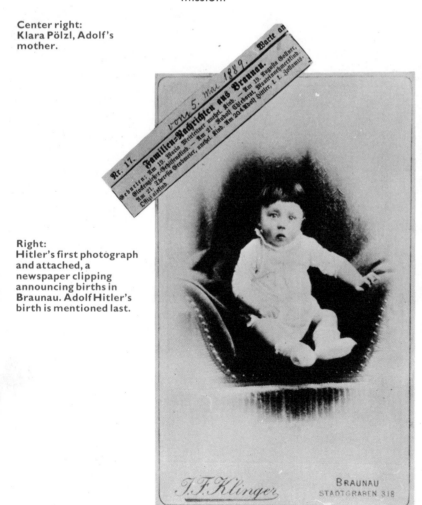

Wichtige Lebenstage

20.4.1889	Geboren in Braunau a./Inn
9.11.1918	Blind durch Gasvergiftung in Pasewalk
24.2.1920	Hofbräuhaus München, Programm
10.1922	erster SA-Aufmarsch in Coburg
9.11.1923	Umsturzversuch in München
1.4.1924	Antritt der Festungshaft, Landsberg a. Lech
4.6.1926	erster Parteitag in Weimar
14.9.1930	von 13 auf 107 Mandate im Reichstag
31.6.1932	230 Mandate im Reichstag
30.1.1933	Machtübernahme
21.3.1933	Tag von Potsdam
2.5.1933	Auflösung der Gewerkschaften
30.1.1934	Gleichschaltung aller Länder
2.8.1934	Führer und Reichskanzler

Schichlgruber Jakob Bauer — 20

Schichlgruber Johann Bauer — 10

Gögenbauer Gertraut — 23

Pfeisinger Johann Bauer — 22

Pfeisinger Theresia — 11

Silipp Theresia — 21

Schichlgruber Anna Maria — 5

Eva Maria — 19

Göschl Leopold Bauer — 18

hitler Alois — 2

Göschl Anna Maria — 9

hiedler Johann Georg — 4

Neugschwandtner Anna Maria — 17

Mutterstamm

Pölzl Johann Bauer — 24

Pölzl Laurenz Bauer — 12

Ledermüller Theresia — 25

Pölzl Johann Bauer — 6

Adolf hitler Führer und Reichskanzler des deutschen Reiches

Braunau a./Inn — München — Nürnberg — Berlin

hüttler Martin Bauer — 8

Vaterstamm

hiedler Johann Bauer — 16

Wally Julianna — 13

Pölzl Klara — 3

Wally Franz Anton Bauer — 26

Spauner Anna Maria — 27

hüttler Johanna — 7

Göschl Anna Maria — 29

Dekker Eva Maria — 15

hüttler Johann Bauer — 14

Dökker Josef Bauer — 30

hinterlechner Theresia — 31

hüttler Martin Bauer — 28

Die Ahnentafel zeichnet sich durch folgende Eigentümlichkeiten aus:
1. Frühzeitiges Auftreten von Alpenerblast
2. Landschaftliche Geschlossenheit
3. Gesellschaftliche Geschlossenheit

☐ Bauer ☐ Männer
☐ Beamter ○ Frauen
☐ handwerker

has been common among the peasants of the districts since the mid-fifteenth century. As late as the second half of the nineteenth century intermarriage was frequent and illegitimacy common (as high as 40 percent in some remote areas).

Thus it occasioned little comment in 1837 when Maria Anna Schicklgruber, an unmarried peasant woman from the village of Strones, gave birth to a son. It was perhaps more unusual that this thrifty, shrewd—and determined—woman should refuse to name the father of her child, who was finally entered in the parish register with her maiden name, Alois Schicklgruber.

Five years later Maria married a wandering miller named Johann Georg Hiedler—the man who, almost 35 years after, would be named Alois's putative father and, thus, Adolf Hitler's presumed grandfather.

Despite the fact that Alois Schicklgruber became Alois Hitler in 1876 through a bit of scarcely legal rustic intrigue (probably instigated by the uncle who raised him and compounded by a spelling error on the part of the parish priest), his parentage remains shrouded in mystery. There is little evidence to show that Hiedler really was his father. It is possible that Hiedler's brother, Johann van Nepomuk Hiedler, who raised the boy, actually fathered him as well. Other candidates, ranging from various illiterate peasants to the son of a Jewish family named Frankenberger, cannot withstand serious investigation.

Young Alois left his uncle's home at the age of thirteen to become a shoemaker's apprentice in Vienna, but at the age of eighteen, he joined the border guard of the Austrian Customs Service. Nine years later he was promoted to the Customs Service itself, and was able to marry. His first wife was Anna Glass-Hoerer. Although the marriage was childless and not at all happy (Anna was fourteen years his senior and in bad health, while Alois always had a roving eye), it lasted for sixteen years before the pair separated. Three years later, in 1883, Anna died.

The next month Alois (by now known as Alois Hitler) married again – this time a young hotel cook named Franziska Matzelberger. Their liaison was already several years old; she had borne a son, also called Alois, in 1882, and within three months of the wedding had produced a daughter, Angela. Within a year, however, Franziska too was dead of tuberculosis.

This time Alois waited six months before remarrying, on 7 January 1885, for the third and last time. His new bride was 25-year-old Klara Pölzl, from the ancestral village of Spital. Part of the delay might have been caused by the need to get special permission from Rome to marry, since the two were second cousins. Four months later their first child, Gustav, was born. He died in infancy as did the second, Ida. Adolf—third child of a third marriage—was fol-

lowed by Edward in 1894 (who lived only six years) and Paula in 1896 (who outlived her famous brother by some twenty years).

Contrary to his mother's descriptions of him as sickly and delicate, a former housemaid remembers the young Hitler as a healthy, lively child. Contrary to his own descriptions of himself as the child of poor but proud laborers, the family enjoyed a comfortable prosperity.

In the spring of 1895, Alois retired and the family settled in Hafeld-am-Traun, a small farming community about 30 miles southwest of Linz. Soon Adolf, now six, and his half-sister Angela were enrolled in a small Volksschule (primary school) in the village of Fischlham, more than an hour's walk away.

Remembered as 'very alert and obedient, but lively,' the youngster enjoyed school. At home, life was less pleasant. Alois did not take gracefully to retirement; he became increasingly irritable, took to drinking heavily, and was often violent. His main target was the younger Alois, who finally left home at the age of fourteen—feeling mistreated by his father, neglected by his stepmother, and deeply resentful of her favorite, his half-brother Adolf.

After Alois's departure the family spent the next several years moving from one village to another in the vicinity of Linz, while the father's hand fell most heavily on Adolf. At one point things got so bad that the youngster decided to run away, but his father got wind of the plan and locked him in his room. Adolf took off his clothes and was trying to wriggle through the bars that covered the window, when he heard footsteps on the stairs. Hastily he pulled back

Above:
The house in which Hitler was born was converted into a shrine once the Nazis came to power.

Left:
The view from the courtyard of Hitler's birthplace in Braunau. His family were comfortably off but did not live in great style.

and draped himself with a tablecloth. But Alois, instead of whipping him, broke into laughter, calling to Klara to come up and see the 'toga boy.' The ridicule, Hitler confided later, hurt him more than any switch would have done.

Both in and out of school, Adolf was a leader among his friends. He was virtually obsessed with the western stories of James Fenimore Cooper and his German imitator, Karl May, while the Boer War fed his patriotism and provided yet another game. Day after day the peaceful meadows became battlefields where cowboys chased Indians and Boers pursued the unfortunate English for hours on end.

Later, while the family lived in Lambach, Adolf sang in the choir at the Benedictine Monastery, took singing lessons at the choir school, and contemplated a life in the church—a plan that was rather shortlived.

Finally Alois acquired a modest house in the village of Leonding, south of Linz, and in September 1900 the eleven-year-old began classes at the Linz Realschule—a high school designed to train boys for technical or commercial careers. It was not inexpensive, but Alois was anxious for his son to follow in his footsteps in the civil service—an ambition Adolf most definitely did not share.

The determination with which the boy opposed his equally determined father is recounted at great length in *Mein Kampf* and was, or so we are led to believe, one of the earliest demonstrations of the fierce drive and stubbornness that would carry him in future years over all who stood in his way. Far from wanting to spend the rest of his life in an office—a prospect he says made him feel sick to his stomach—Hitler had a quite different dream. He wanted to become an artist, a painter—a prospect which filled his father with dismay.

How much of this dramatic conflict was real and how much an excuse for academic failure is a moot point. Certainly rebellion against his father was a factor in his sudden decision to stop studying. However another reason was an inability to cope with a larger, impersonal institution after the friendly, comfortable village school, and also, as some critics have suggested, sheer laziness.

Whatever the reason, that failure rankled; even during the last years of his life Hitler would be fond of expounding on the shortcomings of his teachers—they were 'distinguished by unparalleled ignorance,' 'absolute tyrants,' or even 'somewhat mentally deranged.'

During his second year in Linz his grades improved and he again became a leader among his peers. The games of cowboys and Indians continued (by this time he had learned to throw a lasso), and at recess he lectured his comrades on the Boer War, passing out sketches of the gallant Boers. At that time German nationalism was popular among the schoolboys, but Hitler seemed to take it more seriously than the others—perhaps because his father was a staunch supporter of the Habsburgs. His Pan-Germanism was given an extra boost when he saw his first Wagnerian opera—*Lohengrin*—at the age of twelve, and found himself 'captivated at once.'

Soon his schoolwork started slipping again, but this was soon overshadowed by another

Right:
Hitler's classroom in the village school at Fischlham, which Hitler attended when he was six years old.

Steyr, 25 miles away. He soon came to detest both the town and the school, and would go to ridiculous lengths to avoid doing his schoolwork. Though he finally managed to graduate he could not face any more schooling. Despite his mother's desire for him to continue, he managed to persuade her to let him drop his studies.

The sixteen-year-old youth now embarked on a solitary two-year escapist existence— reading, drawing, visiting the opera and the

crisis. On the morning of 3 January 1903, Alois took his usual walk to the local inn, sat down, ordered a glass of wine—and collapsed. Within minutes he was dead, of a pleural hemorrhage. Contrary to many accounts, he did not leave his family in poverty. In fact, they were quite comfortable, and the absence of tension after so many years improved life tremendously.

To save the long journey back and forth from Leonding, Adolf was soon sent to live in Linz, where he and five other boys boarded with an elderly woman named Frau Sekira. For the rest of that desultory school year he continued to ignore academic subjects in favor of drawing. The last year followed the same pattern. Only one history professor, Leopold Poetsch, was able to break through to him, with colored slides of ancient Teutons which made an indelible impression on the young man.

His marks became so bad that Adolf was not allowed to return to Linz for the Final Form. Instead, he had to attend the Realschule in

and his friend Kubizek, he seems to have been almost entirely cut off from society.

This self-imposed isolation extended to members of the opposite sex, even though the young man had fallen in love. The object of his devotion was one Stefanie Jansten—a tall, slim blonde whom he saw daily in the streets of Linz as she promenaded with her mother. Despite the attraction (which was wholly one-sided), Hitler refused to even speak to her. Theirs, he told Kubizek, was to be an idyllic relationship,

museums. He had only one friend during this period: August Kubizek, son of a Linz upholsterer, whose great ambition was to become a famous musician. It was a pleasant, bohemian life, with days and evenings filled with art, music, explosive conversation and grandiose dreams. Home with Klara and Paula was a warm, happy place, geared mainly to his comfort.

It is little wonder that Hitler later described those years as the happiest of his life. Perhaps the best thing about them was freedom from the need to work for a living. The prospect of a regular job was still distasteful, even though his mother was ill and was having trouble making ends meet—and it would remain so for the rest of his life.

At this time Adolf Hitler was a pale, lanky youth—usually shy and retiring, but subject to sudden fits of hysterical anger against anyone who disagreed with him or whom he thought opposed him in any way. Except for his mother

in which the partners would communicate with their eyes alone. At one point, he decided that Stefanie was angry with him and devised an elaborate mutual suicide scene, complete with dialogue for both parties. Through all of this Stefanie remained oblivious, and she was greatly surprised when she was told of it many years later.

Soon, however, these pleasant fantasies were replaced by a growing obsession with architecture. Never one to do anything by halves, Adolf was soon busy redesigning the entire city of Linz; he and Kubizek wandered the streets for hours while he talked and sketched, remodeling building after building.

A short visit to Vienna in May and June 1906 had filled him with enthusiasm for that romantic old city with its music, art and architecture. A year later he determined to enter the Academy of Fine Arts there. Poor Klara, already gravely ill with cancer, was now besieged on all sides. Adolf pleaded passionately on one side, while on the other his brother-in-law, Leo Raubal, and his guardian, Josef Mayrhofer, argued that it was high time he settled down and chose a respectable profession.

Of course Adolf won. Klara gave in, as she had done so often before, and he was allowed to withdraw his patrimony from the bank. On a morning in late September 1907 he left Linz with 700 kronen in his pocket—enough for a year's tuition, room and board. During his first trip to the capital he had deluged Linz with post cards, so after ten days had gone by without a word Kubizek went around to Klara's apartment for news. But he was greeted by a tired, sick old woman whose first words were, 'Have you heard from Adolf?' Without her son, she seemed to have completely let herself go.

In Vienna, meanwhile, Hitler had found lodgings in an apartment near the Westbahnhof. He took the stiff Academy entrance examination with confidence and passed. The next stage, however, was evaluation of a portfolio of sample drawings, and these were judged unsatisfactory. After several days of deep depression he came to a decision; painting was only a hobby—architecture his true vocation. He spent the next week reading, or walking the streets pondering his dilemma. In order to enter the Academy School of Architecture he needed a diploma from a building school—which in turn required a diploma from a Realschule.

At home, Klara was dying. In response to a letter from the postmaster's wife Adolf rushed back to Linz, and for the next two months he devoted himself to his mother. Although she lived in constant agony Klara was proud and happy to have her boy home again, while Kubizek could not believe the change in his friend. During those months Hitler 'lived only for his mother.' He was never cross or impatient, and even began to take a more parental interest in little Paula, scolding her when she did poorly at school. (Alan Bullock maintained in *Hitler: A Study in Tyranny* that this is a fiction and that Hitler only returned to Linz after his mother's death.)

Finally Klara passed away, early in the morning on 21 December 1907. Her Jewish doctor, Eduard Bloch, recalled, 'In all my years of practice I had never seen a young man so broken with grief and bowed down by suffering as young Adolf Hitler on that day.' Though while his mother was ill Hitler had occasionally railed against her doctors and their inability to help her, the gratitude he later expressed to Bloch was genuine. Thirty-three years later the doctor was able to write in *Colliers*, 'Favors were granted to me which I feel were accorded no other Jew in all Germany or Austria.'

Settling Klara's estate did not take long and soon Hitler was ready to return to Vienna, despite pestering from his family. After all the bills were paid and the estate divided up, Adolf—who had given his share to Angela, while Alois gave his to Paula—was left with his orphan's pension and what was left of his patrimony. He was not rich, but neither was he poverty-stricken, as he liked to claim in later years.

In February 1908 he was on his way to the capital for the third time. In his pocket was a letter of introduction to Professor Alfred Roller, Director of Scenery at the Royal Opera, which he had obtained through his mother's landlady. He found a room at 29 Stumpergasse with a Polish landlady, Frau Zakreys. Here he was soon joined by his old friend Kubizek, whom he had persuaded to leave Linz and share the gay life of Vienna.

The two young men found themselves in a brilliant, cosmopolitan city with some two million inhabitants—a melting pot, with not even a common language. At the turn of the century Vienna's gaiety and charm were unique among the great cities of the world. The middle classes were cultivated, light-hearted, and pleasure-loving. A great part of their lives was spent waltzing, making light conversation in coffee houses, listening to music, enjoying the make-believe of theater, opera, and operetta, flirting, and making love. The massive buildings on the Ringstrasse, erected during the late nineteenth century, reflected their confidence and prosperity. Vienna was not only the greatest industrial center in eastern Europe, but also the capital of a polyglot empire of 50 million people that stretched from the Rhine to the Dniester, and from Saxony to Montenegro. The Empire had to be governed, the army and navy maintained, goods manufactured, and business transacted.

The masses—the lower middle and industrial working classes who lived around the factories and in the poorer streets on the outskirts—controlled the city politically. Labor

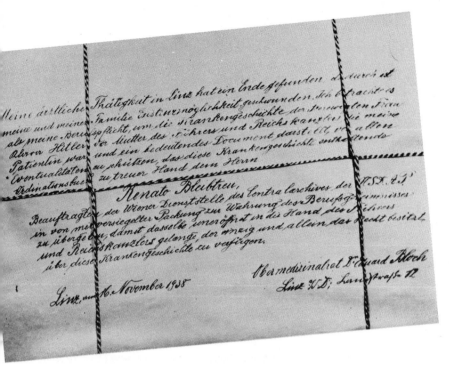

was organized into trade unions and even had its own political party, the Social Democrats. As their growing power began to challenge the autocracy of the Habsburgs, opportunity for education and culture opened up to the masses.

Vienna was a city of contradictions—of glamorous balls and sordid slums, culture and commercialism, rigid conventions and radical intellectual experiments. Hitler's reaction—mingled love and disgust—was common to many who knew the city during that period.

Hitler and Kubizek were soon settled in comfortably. Since their small room could not possibly hold two people plus Kubizek's grand piano, Hitler had persuaded Frau Zakreys to give them her large room in exchange for their little one, and the furniture was carefully arranged to give Hitler room to pace. Within two days Kubizek passed the entrance examination for the Academy of Music, but his friend feigned lack of interest.

Although his own work was going well, Kubizek soon began to fear that Hitler was unbalanced. He would fly into a terrible rage at the slightest provocation and seemed according to his friend, to be 'at odds with the world. Wherever he looked he saw injustice, hate and enmity.' He was incapable of systematic work; he drew a little, wrote a bit more, even dabbled in music, but he still spent much of his time dreaming or brooding. His life was as solitary as it had been in Linz, and though he talked at great length about his determination to succeed he never took his work to Professor Roller for an evaluation. Several times he made it to the professor's door, portfolio in hand, but he never had enough nerve to knock. Finally he tore up the letter to remove temptation—and it is impossible to tell now whether he was motivated by the fear that his work was not good enough, by an unconscious desire to fail, or if he was simply in awe of Roller's reputation.

The two friends took every opportunity to go to the opera or to concerts, economizing on food in order to buy tickets. Hitler never tired of Wagner, who provided 'an escape into a mythical world which he needed in order to endure the tensions of his turbulent nature.' Although he allowed himself to be persuaded to see several Verdi operas, the only one he liked was *Aida*—and he much preferred second-rate Wagner to first-rate production of anything else.

It was the golden age of music and opera in Vienna. Gustav Mahler had just left the Royal Opera for the Metropolitan Opera in New York but his magnificent productions—many done in collaboration with Roller—were still being performed. Hitler was to see their inspired production of *Tristan und Isolde* almost once a month for the next five years.

Hitler also began developing a taste for symphonic music since Kubizek, as a student at the Conservatoire, got free concert tickets. He especially liked the Romantics—Schubert, Mendelssohn, Weber and Schumann, as well as Beethoven, Bruchner and Grieg.

At one point he even attempted to write a musical drama about Wieland the Smith, after Kubizek remarked that an unfinished work on the subject had been found among Wagner's papers after the composer's death. During the day he composed the music (naturally enough, it was imitation Wagner, but some of the themes were reasonably good). In the evenings he worked on designing the scenery and costumes, while Kubizek orchestrated and transcribed the music.

Spring came and the two young men spent several Sundays on picnics in the Wienerwald, or taking day trips on steamers down the Danube. They often discussed sex, love and marriage, but lived a monastic life. Hitler in-

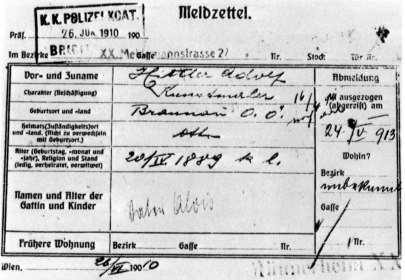

sisted he had to remain chaste to keep the 'Flame of Life' pure—echoes of his Catholic upbringing. He would also talk angrily for hours about prostitutes and their depraved sexual practices.

In July Kubizek finished the year with excellent marks and conducted the end-of-term concert, in which three of his own compositions were featured. With congratulations from both the head of the Conductors' School and the Director of the Academy ringing in his ears, he went back to spend the summer in Linz.

Hitler seemed proud of his friend's success, but was silent about his own plans. For the rest of the month he stayed in Vienna, lonely and bored in the hot, bug-ridden room. In August he left for his own holiday in Spital; the clean country air was pleasant enough, but his family—still pressuring him to give up, come home, and get a real job—made it an uncomfort-

Above:
A police registration card issued in Vienna, when Hitler moved to the Meldemannstrasse hostel at the end of July 1910. Despite the fact that Hitler had failed to gain admittance to the Academy of Art his profession is described as fine artist.

able time. That summer marked the end of his youth—no longer could his family or the little village serve as refuges from the life he had chosen.

In mid-September he tried again to gain admittance to the Academy of Art, but this time the drawings he submitted were so poor that he was not even allowed to take the examination. Now, with his money gone, he faced the problem of survival. His first economy was on rent. In mid-November he gave Frau Zakreys notice, paid up his share of the rent, and left—without even leaving a note for Kubizek, who was expected at any moment. He moved to a gloomy apartment overlooking the railroad yards, on the other side of the Westbahnhof.

When Kubizek arrived in Vienna he looked around the station expecting to see his friend. Surprised and puzzled, he hurried home to find Hitler gone, and no message. When weeks passed without a word he contacted Hitler's older sister Angela—but she knew as little as he did. Hitler for whatever reason—wounded pride, perhaps, or an inability to bear the comparison between Kubizek's success and his own failure—had cut himself off completely from friends and family.

For the next five years (1909–13) he buried himself in obscurity. Later he would say that they were the unhappiest years of his life. But as we will see, they were also in many ways the most important, as the formative years in which his character and opinions took on a definite shape. Those who knew him at this time describe a thin, pale youth with sunken cheeks and staring eyes that dominated his face. His hair was brushed low over his forehead and hung down over his collar, and he always looked as though he needed a shave.

On one level he lived the life of a tramp. For the first year his orphan's pension and what was left of his father's money kept him afloat, but by the fall of 1909 his patrimony had been exhausted. For the next few months, echoing his father's ceaseless wanderings, he lived in a series of furnished rooms, each dingier than the last. But he was never desperate enough to find a full-time job. He still had a great fear of sliding back into the great mass of manual laborers—just like all the underpaid, half-forgotten white-collar workers who would flock to the Nazi banner in the years to come.

Soon Hitler was reduced to sleeping on park benches and in doorways. In October, when the weather turned cold, he moved to bars, coffee houses, or dismal flophouses. Vienna, the City of Dreams, had become a nightmare of misery and filth.

In December, just before Christmas, he walked for two and a half hours to get to Meidling, on the outskirts of the city. His destination: the Asyl für Obdachlose, a shelter for the destitute supported by a family of Jewish philanthropists.

As such institutions go, it was not at all bad. The large, modernized building had been fitted out with many showers, toilets, and other amenities. The dormitories were also large, airy, and clean. The food was plain, but good and substantial. But no matter how well-meaning the administration, the regimentation and lack of privacy in such an institution cannot help but be depersonalizing—and are especially painful to anyone as proud and as private as Hitler.

In the shelter, he was soon befriended by one Reinhold Hanisch who, having spent some years tramping around Germany and Austria, was able to take him in hand and show him how to survive in the streets. Together the two would leave the Asyl early in the morning and make the long walk into Vienna to get something to eat at a charity kitchen. They would then spend a few hours in a warming room or a hospital, and be back at the Asyl again when the gates

were opened at dusk. In between they would sometimes pick up a little money doing odd jobs—shovelling snow, carrying baggage at the Westbahnhof, or beating carpets. Hitler even tried begging, but turned out to have little talent for it.

The comrades in misfortune became fast friends. Hitler would listen, enthralled, to Hanisch's stories of life in Germany while Hanisch, for his part, was fascinated by Hitler's talent, education, and articulate conversation. Soon Hanisch, who was nothing if not enterprising, came up with a scheme whereby Hitler would paint pictures and he would sell them, dividing the proceeds equally.

But the Asyl was no place to work, so early in February 1910 Hitler moved across town to the Mannerheim, a large men's hostel on Meldemannstrasse. Although it was an institution, at least a man could have his own cubicle, and

Above:
One of the water-color sketches which Hitler probably sold in order to make up his living allowance in Vienna. It shows Ratzenstadt in the old part of Vienna and was drawn before war broke out.

there was a large, sunny common room where residents could gather to talk or indulge in their hobbies. Soon he was turning out picture postcards, copying photographs or paintings of street scenes, which Hanisch then sold at taverns in the Prater (Vienna's famous amusement park). When Hanisch decided there would be more money in larger works Hitler began doing paintings about twice the size of the postcards, turning out about one a day.

Within a few months the two had a comfortable system in operation, and survival was no longer a pressing problem. Hitler enjoyed the easygoing camaraderie of the hostel common room. It was a new experience for him, and he soon became the leader of a group that gathered to discuss politics—discussions that grew quite heated at times, of the Social Democrats' corruption or the promise of Karl Lueger (the anti-Semitic Christian Social Party leader). Even when he was working Hitler would fly across the room at the hint of an argument, paintbrush waving and hair flying. As his interest in politics grew his desire to paint waned, much to Hanisch's dismay.

While Hitler claimed in *Mein Kampf* that he learned to hate Jews in Vienna, August Kubizek remembered him expressing anti-Semitic views many years earlier in Linz. Hanisch, on the other hand, says he never heard Hitler deride Jews during the discussions at the Mannerheim, or even in private, and that he even expressed gratitude to the Jewish charities that had helped him. In fact, his other friend at the Mannerheim was a Jew—a Hungarian named Josef Neumann who was a part-time art dealer, and who gave him a long black coat to replace one he had been forced to sell the previous winter.

The truth is that for most of his stay in Vienna Hitler was probably no more anti-Semitic than the average citizen of that city. The deep, all-consuming hatred came later, perhaps following some personal confrontation. There is some evidence that he did read some of the trash literature that filled the bookstalls at the time—magazines like *Ostara* that combined mysticism and virulent anti-Semitism with erotic pictures of blonde beauties being ravished by hairy, ape-like creatures.

The coming of spring found Hitler still less inclined to keep his nose to the grindstone. In June, tired of Hanisch's constant nagging, he and Neumann disappeared on a five-day spree through Vienna's streets and museums, finally returning with scarcely a cent between them. The break was long enough to let him get back to work, at least in spurts.

At the beginning of August 1910 Hitler and Hanisch had a falling-out. Hitler had painted a view of the Viennese Parliament which he thought was worth 50 crowns, but which Hanisch sold for 10. Furious, and sure he had been cheated, Hitler brought a lawsuit against his former friend, who was found guilty and sentenced to seven days in jail.

In September Hitler tried again to enter the Academy of Art, and again failed. Professor Ritsche, whom he had asked for help, was not impressed with his work, though he did think the drawings showed remarkable architectural precision.

For a time life was difficult without Hanisch to sell the pictures, despite a windfall in the form of a reasonably large sum of money from his Aunt Johanna in Spital. But Hitler still managed to eke out a living. In addition to his postcards and small paintings he turned his hand to producing advertising posters for small shops. In some of the few that survive we see two postmen discussing the merits of Teddy's Perspiration Powder, the tower of St Stephen's cathedral rising majestically over a mountain of soap, and a Santa Claus selling candles.

But after about a year Hitler's life began slipping gradually into a more stable routine. He painted more and argued less—and when he did discuss politics he was less flamboyant and tried to persuade rather than antagonize his opponents.

As he established a fairly regular market for his pictures, his work improved. The paintings are technically competent and quite professional—except for the human figures, which he never learned to draw. Even his appearance improved; he shaved off his beard, cut his hair, and cleaned his clothes, so that at length the eccentric young bohemian looked so respectable that his old friends would hardly have known him.

Hitler himself has said that Vienna provided the school of hard knocks in which he became a man. In *Mein Kampf* he writes, 'A world picture and a philosophy took shape within me which became the granite foundation for all my acts. Since then I have had to learn little and I have altered nothing.' The ideas he gained, then, from his voracious reading as well as his experiences in Vienna bear closer examination.

The set of basic beliefs that lie beneath Hitler's political theorizing has been described as the 'philosophy of the doss house.' Certainly the outcast who must live by his wits can easily come, as Hitler did, to see life as a struggle in which only the strong can win and the weak must lose; to condone any trick however ruthless, any weapon however treacherous; to view any hint of trust or loyalty to another as weakness. But 'social Darwinism,' which theorized about 'the struggle for existence' and 'survival of the fittest,' was enormously popular among the intelligensia of every political persuasion at the turn of the century—until it was finally adopted by the Right. Soon it was extended to cover a deliberate population policy—including the elimination of undesirable organisms, various ways to 'measure' genetic superiority and many others.

Many of Hitler's attitudes were based on contempt—the belief that men were only motivated by fear, greed or lust. Politics, he claimed, was simply knowing how to manipulate those motives for one's own purposes.

He especially despised the working classes, and the misery in which many laborers lived evoked no sympathy. In fact he had more regard for the rogues and beggars he met in the hostel than for labor organizations and trade unions with their call for solidarity, which he probably viewed as a threat. At one point he even wondered if trade unionists deserved to belong to the great German race—finally concluding that their minds had been poisoned by the leaders of the Social Democratic Party as part of a Jewish plot.

Neither Hitler's philosophy nor his political theories were original, but were picked up wholesale as he watched the Austrian scene from the sidelines. What he did best, however, was to clearly see the strengths and weaknesses of the various political movements, remember them, and put them to use years later.

Ever since the mid-nineteenth century the German-Austrian hold on the Empire had been weakening: Italy had broken away in the early 1860s, and in 1867 the Hungarians had been made equal to the Germans under the Dual Monarchy. By the early 1900s the Slavs (Czechs, Slovaks, Serbs, Croats) were demanding equality too. The political revolt was exacerbated by a social revolution, and when the working classes were given the vote, German domination of the Habsburg Empire (where they made up one-third of the population) was effectively ended.

Hitler, of course, was bitterly opposed to all these developments and hated the Social Democrats (one of the three major political parties in Vienna) for their 'hostile attitude toward the struggle for the preservation of Germanism.' But his dislike could not blind him to the reasons for their popularity, which he later narrowed down to three: they knew how to create a mass movement, they understood the art of propaganda, and they made full use of what he called 'spiritual and physical terror.' Spiritual terror he described as 'unleashing a barrage of lies and slanders against one's adversaries until the nerve of the attacked person breaks.' This last observation was probably occasioned more by a vision distorted by prejudice than by logical analysis, but it nevertheless became one of Hitler's prime tactics in years to come.

There were two political parties that attracted the young man. The first, the Pan-German Nationalist Party, was founded by Georg Ritter von Schönerer who came from the same region (near Spital) as Hitler. The Pan-Germans were desperately trying to make one last bid for German supremacy with a program that combined a violent nationalism and a passionate desire for union with Germany with virulent anti-

Semitism, anti-Socialism and opposition to both the Habsburgs and the Church. Though Hitler enthusiastically endorsed their program he could also see the reasons for their failure.

The biggest problem he saw was the Pan-Germans' inability to understand either the psychology of the common people or the social problems besetting them—which lost them the support of the militant masses. He also felt that their entry into Parliament robbed them of their impetus and burdened them with all the bureaucratic weaknesses of that institution, while their opposition to the Catholic Church meant that many, who otherwise would have supported them, were lost. In addition they made little effort to get the support of other powerful organizations like the Army or head of State.

The Christian Social Party was led by Dr Karl Lueger, the Mayor of Vienna. Although the two never met, Lueger was truly Hitler's mentor; the Führer was later to describe him as 'a statesman greater than all the so-called "diplomats" of the time.' Party membership was mainly drawn from the ranks of the discontented white-collar workers and stressed a strident anti-Semitism. Lueger—a big, genial, fundamentally decent man—never let his party's official stance stop him from being friendly and helpful to Jews on an individual basis. Hitler deplored this attitude; he also thought Lueger was far too tolerant and that he should abandon his loyalty to the Catholic Church and the Habsburgs in favor of Pan-Germanism.

But he had to admit that Lueger was a genius when it came to understanding the problems of the masses and gaining their support. He was adept at using backing from the Church and any other possible institution to his best advantage, and was a master of propaganda and oratory. It was at this time that Hitler began to practice his own public speaking, which he would eventually develop into a formidable talent.

Hitler's originality, then, lay not in his ideas, but in his being first to apply those ideas in post-World War I Germany—first gaining the support of the masses and then of the Army, big business, and the President of the Weimar Republic.

On 24 May 1913 (not in the spring of 1912 as he claims in *Mein Kampf*) Hitler left Vienna; the following day he was in Munich—Germany at last! He confided in no one and we do not know why he chose that particular time to leave. In *Mein Kampf* he speaks rather vaguely of being repelled by Vienna ('the embodiment of racial

17

desecration') and of wanting to find a place with more scope for his political studies. In fact, his main reason for moving was probably to avoid being drafted into the Austrian Army, for which he had been eligible since 1910.

He chose as his new home a city with many of the same qualities he had first enjoyed in Vienna. Prewar Munich had a reputation throughout Europe as a charming, humane, light-hearted center of the arts and sciences–in distinct contrast to the noisy, modern, prosaic capital, Berlin. Munich was an intellectually restless place where originality was welcomed and where the most bizarre idea had its place. Lenin had lived there, as had Hitler's idol, Wagner. Thomas Mann had recently completed *Death in Venice* and Oswald Spengler was writing *The Decline of the West*; poets Stefan George and Rainer Maria Rilke held court, while painters like Paul Klee opened new dimensions in art.

Most of this intellectual and artistic ferment passed Hitler by. The awkward, brooding, sallow 24-year-old had taken a third-floor room in the apartment of a tailor named Popp on the Schleissheimerstrasse. Here, in the suburb of Schwabing where the bohemians–artists, anarchists, revolutionaries–mingled and endlessly

argued over the cafe tables, Hitler led the same solitary life he had in Vienna.

He continued to support himself with postcard views of Munich–faithful reproductions of every roof tile, brick and blade of grass, not affected by any of the experimentation in painting that was going on all around him. According to Frau Popp he was an insatiable reader, but we do not know much about what he read; later he claimed that many hours were spent studying socialism–the 'doctrine of destruction'–and trying to think of ways to master it.

But apart from a little socializing with the Popps and their friends, most of his free time was spent in taverns where he was just another eccentric and where he could find the casual acquaintances and chance conversations over a glass of beer that he felt most comfortable with.

In January 1914 the Austrian authorities finally caught up with him; an officer of the criminal police appeared on his doorstep, arrested him, and carried him off to the Austrian consulate. Draft dodging was a serious charge and Hitler knew it–but his evident fright convinced both the consul and the Munich police of his sincerity and honesty. He managed to concoct an explanation which, though flimsy, was enough to enable him to escape being charged with any crime. Two weeks later he appeared before a draft board in Salzburg, where he failed the physical examination due to his run-down condition. Immediately he returned to Munich.

Archduke Franz Ferdinand was assassinated on 28 June. On 28 July Austria, after much urging from Germany's Kaiser Wilhelm, declared war on Serbia and the entire network of entangling alliances was brought into play. Russia mobilized against Austria, and on 1 August the Kaiser announced the beginning of Germany's mobilization against Russia.

Hitler, along with the rest of the population of Europe, was caught up in the war fever, seeing the conflict as an opportunity to escape the boredom of normality, and exulting in the almost religious feeling of community that swept Germany.

On 3 August, the day war was declared on France, he petitioned Ludwig III, King of Bavaria, for permission to volunteer for a Bavarian regiment despite his Austrian citizenship. Despite appearances, this does not contradict his earlier draft-dodging in Austria; peacetime military service would have seemed to him pointless coercion; war meant liberation from the aimless emptiness of his life and an opportunity to be part of the powerful German Army he had admired from childhood.

The very next day the answer arrived, accepting him as a volunteer. On 16 August he reported to his first choice, the Bavarian King's Own Regiment, only to find it filled. He was accepted by his second choice, the 1st Bavarian Infantry Regiment. A few days later he was trans-

Hitler im Felde

ferred to the 2nd Bavarian Infantry Regiment and began basic training; within a week he had been permanently assigned to the 16th Bavarian Reserve Infantry Regiment—also known as the List Regiment after its commander, Colonel List.

The period he described as 'the greatest and most unforgettable time of my earthly existence' had begun. It began prosaically enough with basic training—mainly drilling, marching, and bayonet practice—in Munich. On 8 October, after a solemn swearing-in ceremony, the regiment marched to Camp Lechfeld, about 40 miles west of the city.

The next twelve days were a strenuous round of still more training exercises. Finally, on 20 October, the recruits were loaded on trains for the Front, and in just over a week found themselves heavily engaged against the British in the First Battle of Ypres. Hitler, by now a regimental dispatch runner, was spared injury in this battle, but his unit was decimated. In a letter to Herr Popp he reported that the regiment had been reduced from 3500 to just over 600 men and only 30 officers.

As the Ypres offensive stalled and degenerated into trench warfare, life at regimental headquarters became relatively quiet. Hitler, who had been awarded the Iron Cross

Second-Class for his bravery during the battle, even found some time to paint. He was to continue to serve as a dispatch carrier for the rest of the war. Though he was not actually in the trenches it was still dangerous work, and he would be at the Front or just behind it for most of the next four years.

By the end of the summer of 1915 Hitler had become known as someone who could be relied upon to get his messages through—an important task, since the telephone lines between Headquarters and the battalion or company command posts were down as much as they were up. The other runners admired his apparent lack of fear and his skill; he could crawl up to the trenches as stealthily as he had worked his way around the meadows near Linz when he played cowboys and Indians as a child. He was also rather self-righteous; he would often volunteer to take difficult messages for other runners, and his sense of duty seemed somehow excessive. But time and again he delivered his messages and returned safely to headquarters through a deadly barrage until it seemed to many, including himself, that he led a charmed life.

His luck ended October 1916, during the Battle of the Somme, when a shell exploded in the entrance to the headquarters. Hitler was hit in

the thigh; despite his protests he was evacuated to a field hospital and thence to a military hospital outside Berlin.

After two months he was released and sent to a replacement battalion in Munich, where he soon became indignant and disgusted at the state of affairs on the home front. Wherever he looked he saw low morale, lack of discipline, all the accouterments of civilian life during a war—shirkers, grumblers, profiteers, the black market, and (to his eyes) Jews, Jews, and more Jews. Thoroughly upset, he wrote to his old commander, and on 1 March he was being welcomed back to the 16th Regiment at a special dinner prepared in his honor. He felt that he had come home again.

That summer the regiment participated in the last part of the Battle of Arras and in the Third Battle of Ypres, which was as deadly as the first. Winter was quieter, but still difficult; food was in short supply, and the men were reduced to eating cats and dogs. The situation was

Above:
The official document issued by Pasewalk Hospital, registering Hitler's disability resulting from gas poisoning.

equally bad on the home front for both Germany and her allies. In January 1918 hunger and disappointment over Germany's failure to make peace with the new Russian government led to a general strike, with workers demanding not only peace, but also representation in the peace negotiations, increased food rations, the abolition of martial law, and a democratic government. At the Front opinion was almost equally divided between those war-weary souls in sympathy with the strikers and those who felt betrayed by their own countrymen. Hitler, predictably, took the latter view, calling the strike 'the biggest piece of chicanery in the whole war.'

During the spring and summer of 1918

Above left:
German flame-throwers advancing along a trench on the Marne, 1918.

Hitler's regiment was in the thick of the fighting during the last great German offensive, on the Somme, the Aisne and the Marne. At one point he captured several prisoners single-handed – (the actual number varies from four to fifteen, depending on the report), armed only with a pistol. On 4 August he was awarded the Iron Cross First Class – a decoration hardly ever given to common soldiers – for 'personal bravery and general merit.'

How good a soldier was Adolf Hitler? An excellent one from all accounts; if nothing else, the fact that he received four other awards in addition to his two iron crosses would confirm his bravery and devotion to duty. The reasons for his remaining a corporal, despite such gallant service, were much debated during the early thirties when he was making his bid for power. One reason, according to one of his former officers, was that he was judged to lack the 'capacity for leadership.' Another might well have been his bearing, which continued to be eccentric – he tended to slouch around, had little regard for niceties such as keeping his boots shined, and refused to snap to attention at the approach of a superior officer. There was probably some element of choice involved too: there were no positions as messengers open to sergeants and if he had been promoted he would have had to give up a job he enjoyed and did well.

He was not unpopular, though his comrades thought him peculiar and sometimes found him well nigh intolerable. He never got letters or food packages from home, and often ended up buying extra food from the kitchen staff, thus earning a reputation as the unit's biggest glutton. He showed no interest in women, and never indulged in the soldier's favorite pastime – complaining about the mud, filfth, lice and stench of the front line. He had little sense of humor and was always especially serious about Germany's war aims and manifest destiny. Periodically he would leap from his quiet corner and run around the room, excitedly claiming that Germany's 'invisible foes' – Jews and Marxists – were a far greater danger than the enemy's guns.

Still, he was generally liked. The cartoons he drew on postcards of the lighter incidents in camp life livened many a dull moment. More important, his companions knew that he was absolutely reliable in a crisis – he never turned down a dangerous job or abandoned a wounded comrade.

For his part, Hitler found the discipline, excitement, and closeness of life at the front far more enjoyable than the obscurity of his peacetime existence. He was not alone in this feeling; many others who felt similarly would later join the Nazis, the Freikorps or a score of other extremist groups.

It soon became obvious that the Ludendorff

offensive of 1918 had failed, and morale, even among the older soldiers, plummeted. Desertions multiplied and disorder often approached rebellion. Ludendorff called it 'the black day of the German Army' in World War I.

On the morning of 14 October, while his regiment was under heavy British bombardment during the third Battle of Ypres, Hitler was caught in a mustard-gas attack. Blinded, he and his comrades stumbled to a first-aid station where they were put on a train heading east. He ended up in a hospital in Pasewalk, in Pomerania; after several weeks of pain and despair he gradually began to regain his sight.

Meanwhile the Marxist revolutions that had begun on the day he was gassed were threatening the very structure of Germany, and the fact that they were for the most part very orderly revolutions with almost no casualties did not make them any the less terrifying. Open revolt broke out in the navy, and in Kiel the sailors took over the city. The rebellion spread to garrisons and factories throughout the country. In Munich revolutionaries seized the city, forcing Ludwig III to flee.

On 9 November news of the Munich uprising reached Hitler in Pasewalk. Suddenly his newly regained eyesight was gone and everything went black. He was convinced that Germany was doomed and that he himself would never see again.

News of Germany's surrender on 11 November was a still greater blow, but then, suddenly in the night, what he later described as a 'supernatural vision' came to him, and he heard voices summoning him to save Germany. Miraculously his eyesight returned, and then and there he vowed to become a politician. Perhaps the greatest political force of the twentieth century had been born.

Above:
Hitler at a field hospital recovering from the gassing he suffered during the Battle of Ypres.

II The Road to Politics

Die deutsche Friedensdelegation

Prof. Schücking   Giesberts   Landsberg   Brockdorff-Rantzau   Leinert   Dr. Melchior

6612

Above:
The German delegation at Versailles. Although the military leaders had actually advised the German government to surrender, the news of the military defeat came as a shock to the German people. In their eyes the German Army had not collapsed but had been betrayed by the politicians.

Hitler was not alone in the shock and despair he felt at the news of Germany's surrender – his feelings were shared by the Army and the entire German people. Nothing had prepared them for the news. Only a few months earlier they had seen victory almost within their grasp. In March the Treaty of Brest-Litovsk had marked Russia's capitulation and in May the Treaty of Bucharest sealed Rumania's defeat, ending the 'war on two fronts.' Early summer saw the beginning of the Ludendorff offensive – a series of attacks in France which drove the British and French Armies back to within 40 miles of Paris.

But in August the great offensive, having taken an enormous toll in terms of men and supplies, ground to a halt. The Allies not only were able to stabilize the front after each breakthrough, but soon passed over to counter-

attack. Ludendorff had put everything on one throw – victory or defeat – and had lost.

For several months, however, the news was kept from the German people, who continued to see ultimate victory just around the corner. Even the political leaders of the Reichstag were not informed about the true military situation until 2 October, when Ludendorff summoned them to demand an immediate armistice.

America refused to deal with Kaiser Wilhelm, and the German Empire finally ended on 9 November 1918, when Wilhelm relinquished power to the moderate socialist leader, Friedrich Ebert. To Ebert's government, then, fell the task of accepting the armistice two days later – despite the fact that German forces still stretched across France in an unbroken line. Thus was born the myth of the 'November

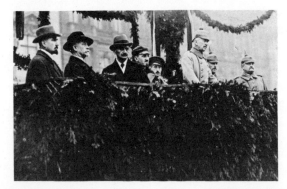

openly and bitterly declared that loyalty to the Fatherland required disloyalty to the Republic.

When Hitler was discharged from the hospital in Pasewalk, still unable to see very well, all his old problems reappeared. He had to make a living, but had no inclination to look for a job—and little chance of finding one in any case.

Ordered to report to the replacement battalion for his regiment in Munich, he was disgusted to find on his arrival that the Türkenstrasse barracks had gone over to the Communists and were under the control of a Soldiers' Council.

criminals' who stabbed the nation in the back. The sudden disillusionment of the German people led to a growing tendency to deny reality and look for scapegoats, in order to escape the miseries of the truth.

Throughout Central and Eastern Europe the end of the war meant years of unrest and insecurity. The great empires—Romanov, Habsburg, Hohenzollern, and Ottoman—disappeared; political and social structure were in chaos.

In Germany, where the reaction was intensified, the new Republic immediately found itself threatened on all sides. On the left extremists agitated for a Communist-style revolution. The right, who were considerably more dangerous, considered signing the Versailles Treaty in June 1919 a betrayal; it was

There was no discipline, the facilities were filthy, and worst of all, no one had any respect for the front-line veterans. After about two weeks, he and an old comrade, Ernst Schmidt, answered a call for volunteers to act as guards at a prisoner of war camp at Traunstein, near the Austrian border. There they stayed until January 1919 when the prisoners were sent home and the camp closed.

On their return to Munich—a city where the political atmosphere had always been unstable and exaggerated—they found that violence had become a part of daily life. The leader of the November revolution, Kurt Eisner, was assassinated in February 1919, and a Socialist government under Johannes Hoffmann took over. On 6 April a Soviet republic was proclaimed in the city, partly in response to the formation of the

Above:
At the height of the fighting during the Spartacist Uprising government troops man the barricades. The Army used *Freikorps*, new units of reliable volunteers, to put down the uprising.

Right:
The Allied leaders at Versailles dictated the terms of the peace to the Germans. From left to right: Woodrow Wilson, Georges Clemenceau, Lord Balfour and Premier Orlando of Italy. David Lloyd George is the major figure missing.

Hungarian Soviet Republic. Within a month the revolutionaries too were overthrown, this time by the Whites—a coalition of regular troops and Freikorps volunteers. So many were killed in the wave of repression that followed that the bodies littering the streets became a health menace, and had to be hastily buried in shallow trenches. Though Hoffmann's government was eventually restored, politics in Bavaria had made a definite move to the right.

Catholic Bavaria had always resented being governed by Protestant, Prussian Berlin. During the unsettled years between 1919 and 1923, as the power of the central government weakened, Bavaria was to operate more and more as an autonomous unit, following the orders of the Reich government only when it was convenient.

In June 1919, the Treaty of Versailles was signed by the Allies and reluctantly ratified by Germany. The terms were harsh, humiliating, and in several instances blatantly hypocritical; in addition to assigning sole responsibility for the war to Germany and forcing her to assume a crippling debt for reparations, great chunks of territory were taken away, Allied troops were to occupy the Rhineland for fifteen years, and a strip, 30 miles wide, on the right bank of the Rhine was to be demilitarized. Finally, the Germans were forbidden to have submarines,

military aircraft, or a standing army of more than 100,000 men.

But the new army (the Reichswehr) immediately became a force to be reckoned with. One of its first steps was to organize a Political Department to investigate subversive activities among the troops and also to infiltrate various workers' organizations. Hitler soon found himself a job with the department, in the Press and News Bureau for the VII (Munich) District Command.

First step for new agents was a course of political instruction at the University of Munich where one of the instructors soon noticed that Hitler—with his 'unsoldierly flowing lock of hair, close-cropped mustache, and remarkable large light blue eyes that shone fanatically'—had a natural talent for oratory. This led to his appointment as an Instruction Officer, assigned to a Munich regiment as a lecturer.

In addition to speaking to soldiers in squad rooms and transit camps, he also helped investigate the many radical organizations that had sprung up in Munich. In September he was ordered to check on a small group called the German Workers' Party (*Deutsche Arbeiterpartei*).

The German Workers' Party, which at the time consisted of little more than a six-man committee, had been founded in March 1918

Below:
Pro-Communist
demonstrators in
Munich mourn the death
of Karl Liebknecht and
Rosa Luxemburg, who
were killed in
mysterious
circumstances during
the Spartacist Uprising.

Above:
Government units
patrol the streets of
Berlin in January 1919.

by a Munich locksmith named Anton Drexler. Drexler, like Hitler, had seen that the middle-class parties were out of touch with the masses, who were coming increasingly under the influence of the various antinational, antimilitaristic groups. Drexler and his deputy, Karl Harrer, wanted to create a party that was both working class and nationalist.

When Hitler attended that meeting on 12 September in a little beerhall on the Herrenstrasse he found the group unprepossessing and rather dull. But toward the end of the evening his fifteen-minute rebuttal of a speaker who had advocated the secession of Bavaria from the Reich and union with Austria impressed Drexler and led to an invitation to attend the next committee meeting.

He hesitated, but in the end he went—and came away still unimpressed with what he had seen. After two days of hard thinking, however, he decided to join as the seventh member of the committee—mainly because he saw that he had more chance to play a leading role in a small, obscure party.

Soon he was channeling all his energy and ambition into pushing the GWP forward from a discussion group to a viable political organization. He sent invitations, took out advertisements, hired larger halls. When he spoke for the first time at the Hofbräuhaus the audience numbered almost a hundred and his half-hour, emotion-packed speech brought down the house.

The meetings became more frequent and the numbers rose steadily. By the beginning of 1920 Hitler, who had been placed in charge of propaganda, had already established a party office, hired a full-time business manager, and was making plans to completely overhaul the organization. At a mass meeting at the Hofbräuhaus on 24 February his oratory (along with the rubber truncheons and riding whips of his sup-

Below:
Hitler attends a
National Socialist Party
meeting in Salzburg in
August 1920. The
Bavarian branch co-
ordinated with groups in
Austria and the
Sudetenland. Hitler is
above the X on the
3rd row.

porters) swept the crowd of almost 2000 along to practically unanimous agreement with the party's new 25-point program. He also took the opportunity to announce the party's new name—the *Nationalsozialistische Deutsche Arbeiterpartei* (NSDAP) or National Socialist German Workers' Party.

The party also adopted a flag: a swastika against a black, white, and red background. The swastika itself originated as a Sanskrit word meaning 'all is all.' In ancient times it was a symbol of the cycle of life; both in Europe and

Above:
Hitler joined the
German Workers' Party
in September 1919. This
is his membership card
for 1920. Note that he
was Member number 5.

for some American Indian tribes. Later it was used by the Teutonic Knights and then, in Germany; by various National Socialist parties and several Freikorps units. The brilliant colors and striking design were specially chosen to outdo the flaming red Communist flag. Although Hitler did not invent the symbol, as he claims in *Mein Kampf*, he immediately grasped its usefulness as an almost magical symbol, and made it an obligatory emblem.

He carried his concern with form and pageantry even further, introducing *Heil* as a greeting, and personally overseeing the solemn ceremonies and rituals of the meetings. Heraldry and symbolism absorbed him and he spent hours searching in reference books for the official party eagle. Later he would design standards for the stormtroops—an idea taken from the Fascists in Italy.

In March 1920 a coup d'état, carried out with the support of the Reichswehr, ousted Johannes Hoffmann and the Social Democrats in favor of a right-wing government under Gustav von Kahr. Bavaria thus became the focal point for the disaffected forces of the right who opposed the Weimar Republic. They included not just the former rulers—nobles, Junkers, industrialists, and big businessmen—but also white-collar workers and ex-servicemen who found it easiest to blame the Republic for their personal grievances—unemployment and/or their inability to make the transition between wartime life and a placid peacetime existence. The atmosphere of agitation and conspiracy against the government, which often included violence, was perfect for Hitler's purposes—and he was to exploit it to the hilt.

Not unnaturally, then, Bavaria was the focal point for elements of the Freikorps as well. This illegal army of volunteers had been formed under the auspices of the Reichswehr, ostensibly to protect the eastern frontier, but actually to circumvent the provisions of the Treaty of Versailles. They were the young men who had seen the Great War as an opportunity to spring into action for the Fatherland, finding the same brotherhood in the trenches as they had felt around their campfires. Now they saw themselves as New Men, as storm soldiers—'a completely new race, cunning, strong and purposeful.' The Freikorps became what Alan Bullock has aptly called 'training schools for the political murder and terrorism which disfigured German life up to 1924.'

In addition to their support from the Army (especially officers like Major General Franz Ritter von Epp and Captain Ernst Röhm), the Freikorps had powerful friends in civil government. Typical supporters were Wilhelm Frick, Assistant to the Police President of Munich, who later became Hitler's Minister of the Interior and Franz Gürtner, who would become the Nazi Minister of Justice. Whether military or civilian, all dreamed of overthrowing the Republic in order to restore the Army to its pre-eminence in Germany and Germany to its position in continental Europe.

For the NSDAP, too, the support and encouragement of the Army were vital to the Party's growth during its early years. This was achieved primarily through the good offices of Captain Röhm, who had joined the German Workers' Party before Hitler—for many of the

same practical and philosophical reasons. As Hitler began to build up the party, Röhm was able to supply a steady stream of ex-Freikorps members and servicemen to swell its ranks; they formed the first strong-arm squads that 'kept order' at meetings, and became the nucleus of the SA. As Hitler's meetings got rowdier, and the clashes between his supporters and detractors more frequent, Röhm was able to get the Army (the ultimate authority for main-

Major General Franz Ritter von Epp.

Hitler and Captain Ernst Röhm.

Wilhelm Frick.

The Battalion flag of the 1st SS Regiment 'Julius Schreck.'

taining public order) to overlook and sometimes even support his methods of incitement and violent intimidation.

Most of the credit for Hitler's success should not be attributed to his backers, but to his own vitality and political ability. Those first years in Munich, when he argued night after night before every kind of audience in every kind of hall, gave him a tremendous store of practical experience. He gained a working knowledge of the German mind that was unsurpassed by his political opponents; he learned to hold his audience's attention, to sense what was in their minds, to find the soft spots in their sensibilities and hammer at them until the group was completely won over. Most of all, his genius lay in his almost instinctive feel for the potential of propaganda and the best ways to use it.

On 1 April 1920 Hitler resigned from the Army in order to devote all his time to the party. By the end of the year he had managed to boost NSDAP membership to almost 3000 and was becoming fairly well known; he had been the featured speaker at about 80 mass meetings, many of them outside Bavaria, had traveled to Berlin in March to meet with General Ludendorff and a few right-wing groups during the Freikorps' Kapp Putsch, and had spoken to a

Below:
The NSDAP's
headquarters in
Corneliusstrasse in
Munich in 1921.

combined international conference of National Socialist parties in Salzburg.

In December 1920 a financial crisis at the *Völkischer Beobachter*, the anti-Semitic, anti-Marxist paper which had first published the spurious 'Protocols of the Elders of Zion,' gave him the opportunity to establish a wider forum. Röhm persuaded General von Epp to part with about 60,000 marks from secret Army funds and this, along with other contributions including a sizeable sum from the eccentric author Dietrich Eckart, allowed the NSDAP to purchase the paper.

It was soon clear that the party was moving further and further away from the original ideas of Drexler and his co-founder, Karl Harrer. Harrer had already resigned in protest and in July 1921 the rest of the Party Committee, who resented being pushed aside in Hitler's attempts to build his own mass following, tried to regain control. Hitler, who had been meeting with some northern nationalist groups in Berlin, returned to Munich immediately—and announced his resignation. This was not at all what the Committee had intended, for they all knew who had been responsible for the phenomenal growth of the party so far. The old-fashioned theorists had no weapons to match his energy

28

and unscrupulousness coupled with his obvious success. They could not afford to let him go, and so in the end Hitler—far from being put in a weaker position—was able to demand and get dictatorial powers over party policies and actions. It was the first manifestation of his belief—gained during the war—in the principle of absolute obedience.

Hitler set to work as never before to consolidate his position. Max Amann, an ex-sergeant major from the List Regiment, was installed as the new business manager of the Party. Eckart, who had put up half the money for the *Völkischer Beobachter*, was made editor of the paper. In August the Gymnastic and Sports Division of the Party was established. Originally billed as a means to organize the 'younger members' of the Party into a 'powerful organization . . . at the disposal of the movement,' it was a uniformed, paramilitary unit. While Hitler saw it as a group that would be able to keep order at meetings and simultaneously impress the public, its leader, Captain Röhm, already considered it a private army. On 5 October its name was changed to the more descriptive *Sturmabteilung* (SA, or Storm Section). In November they fought a pitched battle with the Communists during a Nazi meeting at the Hofbräuhaus. Though badly outnumbered the SA managed to rout its enemies, and the 'battle' soon became a party legend.

While his practical political education was advancing rapidly, Hitler began to develop strong views on foreign policy. Although it was still tentative, he began by making remarks in speeches that identified his friends and enemies: 'We do not fear a war with France,' and 'For us the enemy lies across the Rhine, not in Italy. . . .' He also began attacking Jews publicly for their internationalism.

His political philosophy too was developing rapidly, based in large part on his hatred of the Jews which was an obsession. The feeling had been in evidence to a greater or lesser degree since his early days in Vienna and had come to fruition during the revolutions that followed the last days of the war. It was basically a personal anti-Semitism, but in his speeches Hitler was able to give it an historical and philosophical tone. Since medieval times, he claimed, Jews had been polluting society; it was time to remove them from the midst of the German people. Some of his ideas, such as the Jewish international conspiracy to undermine the nations of Europe, came from the writings of the Thule Society and famous anti-Semites like Luther, all of which supported his own observations of Marxism in action. But many other ideas and much of his polemic came straight from the gutter press, which he had been avidly reading since his Vienna days.

It is important to understand, however, that Hitler did not appeal only to racist fanatics.

Above:
Dietrich Eckart was a journalist, poet and playwright. He spread his racist views through the *Völkischer Beobachter*, of which he was editor.

Many of his closest associates, as we will see, failed to show his paranoiac hatred of Jews. They and many others could overlook it, however, because anti-Semitism had been, to some degree, an accepted part of the European consciousness for so many centuries. Their task was made easier because so many of his other beliefs and prejudices were shared at a basic level by so many respectable, hard-working, middle-class Germans—white-collar workers and front-line soldiers who were disconsolate over their country's defeat in war, who were horribly frightened by the specter of Marxism and Red Revolution, and who were being hardest hit by Germany's continuing economic difficulties.

During 1921 and 1922 the situation in Germany continued to worsen. The Allies demanded increased reparations payments and, when they were not immediately forthcoming, threatened to occupy the Ruhr Valley. Poland was awarded part of Upper Silesia—the part that contained most of the region's mines and heavy industry. On Easter Sunday, 1922, Foreign Minister Walther Rathenau signed a treaty with the Soviet government—an act which infuriated the right, who failed to see the many advantages Germany gained from the agreement.

Above:
The scene in Berlin by the Brandenburg Gate during the Kapp Putsch. Whereas the Kapp Putsch failed to overthrow the Berlin government, in Munich a coup succeeded. Gustav von Kahr established a right-wing government after 14 March 1920.

On 4 June 1922 Rathenau was shot down in the street by two former Freikorps members. On the same day Hitler entered Stadelheim prison to begin serving a three-month sentence for disturbing the peace—a sentence imposed by a Bavarian government finally coming under pressure to clamp down on the violence that filled the streets.

After not quite five weeks he was released, to find Bavaria in an uproar over the Law for the Protection of the Republic—issued by the Weimar government in an attempt to stop

right-wing terrorism. His enforced 'retreat' had given him time to rest and reorganize his ideas into a more cohesive form. On the day he was released he delivered one of the most telling speeches of his career—ostensibly an attack on the new law, but in reality a bitter denunciation of Jews and the alleged Jewish plot to conquer the world. The speech ended with a direct call for physical violence, couched in idealistic, self-sacrificing terms that roused his audience to a frenzy.

Later that September, Hitler became interested in the techniques of Benito Mussolini and his Italian Fascist movement and sent a recent convert—a young, self-styled sophisticate named Kurt Ludecke—to Italy as his emissary. Ludecke returned to Munich with an enthusiastic report; Hitler was especially interested in Mussolini's use of brute force to take over towns and gain political power. The methods seemed fairly simple, and he determined to try them himself.

An occasion soon arose when Hitler was invited to bring 'a few companions' to a German Day celebration in Coburg, some 160 miles north of Munich. Interpreting the invitation after his own fashion he set off on 14 October 1922 with more than 600 stormtroopers, armed with rations for two days, knives and rubber truncheons. Their number had swelled to about 800 by the time they disembarked at Coburg, formed into orderly ranks, and marched toward the center of town. First came eight husky Bavarians in leather shorts, armed

with alpenstocks, followed by a row of flag bearers carrying large red and black banners. Then came Hitler and seven companions in civilian dress, a brass band playing military marches and the ranks of the SA.

Coburg was a stronghold for Socialists and Communists, and a crowd soon gathered to shout insults, but the Nazis ignored them and kept marching. No one attacked them physically, however—and since the expected riot had not started, Hitler turned his men around and marched back again. This time there was no music—only drum rolls. Finally the cobblestones started flying. At a signal from Hitler the SA turned on its attackers, and after a series of short skirmishes retired victorious.

Next day the left called for a series of mass demonstrations against the Nazis. But instead of the expected 10,000 people, only a few hundred eventually appeared in the city square—while Hitler and the SA marched again through the streets, this time with the sound of friendly crowds in their ears, past hundreds of imperial flags that had been resurrected and hung in windows. All in all, Coburg had been a great success; later a special medal would be designed for those who had taken part in the march.

During those early years, which Hitler always remembered with justifiable pride, his companions—like the members of the party as a whole—came from every class and every sort of background. Two things held the disparate group together: nationalism and fear of Marxism.

Top:
Rudolf Hess.

Above:
Hermann Göring.

Below:
Bavaria was the focus of right-wing, nationalist groups in the 1920s. It was a perfect place for Hitler to build a power base. This photograph shows how a small Bavarian village turned out en masse to greet Hitler and the SA.

The contributions that Ernst Röhm made to the party have already been discussed. The fact that he was a homosexual was outweighed by the bonds between him and Hitler—two front-line soldiers who shared an intense German nationalism. A short, stocky man with close-cropped hair and a deep scar on one cheek, he was totally devoted to the military—and remained so even after he was forced to resign his Army commission in 1923.

Rudolf Hess had served with Hitler in the List Regiment for a time, before becoming a pilot. Though he could look quite frightening with his square face, heavy black eyebrows, tight lips and intense stare, he was really shy, unassuming and modest. He was also humorless and rather stupid, all of which combined to make him the perfect disciple for Hitler. After the war he had joined the Freikorps and also entered the University of Munich, where he won a prize for an essay on the topic, 'How must the man be constituted who will lead Germany back to her old heights?' He found that man in Hitler, becoming his secretary and devoted admirer in 1921.

Hermann Göring was quite a different type; a buoyant, exuberant extrovert who was also a fighter ace—the last commander of the famous Richthofen Fighter Squadron. With his impos-ing bearing and Nordic good looks, he was the perfect picture of the German war hero—and had, in fact, been awarded the *Pour le Mérite*, Germany's highest decoration for bravery under fire. Like Hess he was enrolled at the university. He joined the NSDAP in 1922 and Hitler, who recognized a man of action when he saw one, immediately made him commander of the SA. Göring was no anti-Semite, at least by Hitler's standards. In fact—like Hess—he had a number of Jewish friends. He had joined the party because it was revolutionary, not because of what he called 'the ideological stuff.'

Dietrich Eckart was another important figure during those early years. A tall, husky, bald man with a raffish air, Eckart was a well-known Munich eccentric who dabbled in poetry and drama, but who got most satisfaction from intellectual coffeehouse conversation. He was an ardent Pan-German, violently anti-Semitic, anti-clerical and anti-democratic. He ran his own weekly newspaper. He had a lot to do with polishing Hitler's rough edges; he lent him books, corrected his grammar, and—most important—introduced him to influential people in Munich. Richard Frank, for example, who had made a fortune in wheat, was to give Hitler the money to keep the *Völkischer Beobachter*

running in 1923. Helene Beckstein, wife of the wealthy piano manufacturer, was another admirer who gave parties for him, raised money for him, and even visited him in prison.

Through Eckart he also met Alfred Rosenberg, a fanatic anti-Semite and anti-Marxist. An Estonian of German descent who had been forced to leave Russia to escape the Revolution, he was, like Hitler, a fanatic Pan-German. He had been trained as an architect, which impressed Hitler, but it was his theory that Communism was a Jewish plot to conquer the world that really cemented their relationship. Hitler soon came to regard him as the philosopher and prophet of the Party. He also became the editor of *Völkischer Beobachter*, the Party newspaper, when Eckart died.

attention, not only from the Bavarian Government, but from the Central Government in Berlin and even from the Allies.

An American, Captain Thomas Smith, was sent to investigate the party in November, 1922. He came to the conclusion that Hitler had a big part to play in future German politics; as he left Munich he asked a friend, Ernst Hanfstängl, to have a look and send him his impressions. Hanfstängl, half-American and Harvard-educated, was a six-foot four-inch giant appropriately nicknamed 'Putzi' (little fellow) whose family owned an art publishing house in Munich. At the first meeting he attended he found himself impressed by most of the party program (though he did not agree with its anti-Semitism) and fascinated by Hitler. The

Above:
Alfred Rosenberg was the Nazi Party ideologue. He became the temporary leader of the Nazi Party when Hitler was imprisoned.

Above right:
Hitler surrounded by those who helped build the Nazi Party in the early days. From the left: Putzi Hanfstängl (with belt), Julius Schaub, Hitler, Rudolf Hess, Walther Darré, Julius Streicher and Adolf Hünhlein.

Another follower who surpassed even Hitler in the depth and violence of his anti-Semitism was Julius Streicher, surely one of the most unsavory characters in the history of the Third Reich. A sadist who was always seen in company with his whip, he reveled in excesses of every kind, at table as well as in bed. His notorious weekly magazine, *Der Stürmer*, was filled with obscene stories of Jewish sexual crimes and 'ritual murders' that even disgusted many Nazis—including Hitler himself. But at the same time, he enjoyed Streicher's blind, unquestioning loyalty and admired his apparently limitless energy.

Despite its initial successes, at the end of 1922 the NSDAP was still a small provincial movement, with no support or organization outside Bavaria. Still, it was beginning to attract some

two became friends; Hanfstängl would play the piano for Hitler (Wagner was the favorite, of course) and even composed several marches for the SA in the style of American football fight songs. He began to devote more and more time to the party, giving Hitler advice (which he says was rejected more often than it was accepted) and even money to turn the *Völkischer Beobachter* from a weekly into a daily paper.

Hitler became a frequent visitor at Hanfstängl's home, where he also grew fond of Putzi's American wife Helene and their two-year-old son Egon. Helene would say later that he enjoyed the cozy, friendly atmosphere, playing with Egon (who called him Uncle Dolf) on the floor or gossiping with the adults.

He probably relished the change from his own life, which at that time was pretty drab. He lived in a dingy, barely furnished room in 41 Thierschstrasse, alone except for his dog Wolf. It was a place to sleep and keep his few belongings—nothing more. His real life was lived in the cafes and beer halls of Munich where he could chat with other regulars and watch the world go by. Helene Hanfstängl was convinced he was 'a neuter'—that politics took the place of sex in his life. But Emil Maurice, who was his chauffer, said that the two did occasionally go girl-chasing together, and that Hitler sometimes entertained ladies in his room.

On 11 January 1923 French troops occupied the Ruhr valley—the industrial heartland of Germany. For a time the German people were united behind their government as it called for a campaign of passive resistance that soon spread to the occupied areas of the Rhineland as well.

None of this was to Hitler's liking, since he was in no position at the time to exploit a feeling of national unity. But the French move also made certain the total destruction of the mark, which had long been on the brink of collapse. The resulting inflation did more to destroy the very fabric of German society than any war or revolution could ever have done. In their misery and despair, the starving Germans were ready to listen to Hitler's violent denunciations of the corrupt Jew-ridden economic system that had reduced them to their present state.

Hitler had two main goals in 1923: to unify the various nationalist organizations in Bavaria and to gain the support of Gustav von Kahr's Bavarian government and of General von Lossow, the Bavarian Reichswehr commander. But the government and the Army were not wholly on his side. Though Kahr and Lossow disliked the central government as much as Hitler did, their ultimate goal was the separation of Bavaria from Germany—precisely the opposite of Hitler's. On the one hand he and the NSDAP were a danger to law and order and a threat to their authority; but they thought that they could control Hitler and use him for their own purposes.

When the NSDAP began laying plans for their First Party Rally at the end of January the authorities decided to take a strong line, and banned the proceedings. Hitler was first furious and then in despair; he seemed to see his whole political future in ruins at his feet. But at that point Röhm and his superior officer, Ritter von Epp, convinced Lossow to meet with Hitler, and the General—after extracting some concessions regarding the size and number of rallies to be held—convinced the civil government to lift the ban. Hitler had won, and he knew it. Triumphantly he held all twelve mass meetings, reviewing battalions of SA troopers, most of whom were now in uniform. His sheer nerve impressed many people, and the party began to grow steadily. Between February and November the Nazis enrolled 35,000 new members, and the SA would grow to almost 15,000.

At about this time the conflict which had been simmering for some time between Hitler and Röhm began to boil up. Röhm, the complete military man, saw the SA and other paramilitary groups primarily as a supplement to the regular army, to be used for an attack on France as soon as the time was right. This was the entire purpose behind his enormously successful training and expansion program. Hitler, on the other hand, saw the SA as *political* troops who would help him gain power within Germany—a necessary prerequisite to any conflict with other nations. He was beginning to see that too great a dependence on the Army could actually be detrimental to his plans.

Still, at the beginning of 1923 he was in no position to choose his allies. By February he managed, with Röhm's help, to make an alliance

Top:
Rhenish separatists beat up a German policeman in Dusseldorf 1923, as French cavalrymen look on. The French hoped to aid the movement for autonomy in the Rhine valley.

Above:
From left to right: Putzi Hanfstängl, Hitler and Göring. Hanfstängl was the son of a rich Munich family of art publishers and provided the money to make *Völkischer Beobachter* a daily.

with several other Bavarian patriotic leagues. He was established as political leader, and a Lieutenant Colonel Kriebel was named military commander of the organization.

At the end of April the Nazis decided to follow up a series of confrontations designed to force a further split between the Bavarian government and Berlin by staging a mass right-wing demonstration on May Day–the traditional union and socialist holiday. On 30 April orders went out to the SA and other units throughout Bavaria ordering them to report to Munich, while Hitler visited Lossow and asked for arms–in case of a Communist revolt. Lossow categorically refused, adding that the Army would have orders to fire on anyone who disturbed the peace, whatever their political

affiliations might be.

Röhm solved the problem by collecting a detachment of stormtroopers, bluffing his way into a barracks, and taking whatever arms he wanted. Next morning, while the Socialists paraded in the center of Munich, the Nazis gathered at a parade ground on the outskirts. All morning they waited. Finally, just before noon, something happened: a detachment of regular army troops and police appeared and surrounded the field. With them was a chastened Röhm, who had spent some hours being forcibly reminded by Lossow of his responsibilities as an officer. He told Hitler that the arms had to be returned and Hitler, despite arguments from some of his companions, complied with the order.

The whole operation was a fiasco that cost the movement many followers, but it turned out to be an even worse defeat for the government. For when Hitler was threatened with prosecution he insolently replied that he would be more than happy to have an opportunity to present his case in open court. The last thing the government wanted was to give him that kind of publicity, and the matter was dropped.

After 1 May, Hitler, Röhm and several others went on vacation to let things cool off; Hitler went to Berchtesgaden, a resort town on the

Below left:
An SA motorcyclist and escort patrol the streets during the year of the Hitler Putsch, 1923.

Below:
A French officers' club in Mainz, 1923. The French occupation of the Ruhr aggravated the already precarious German economy. Businessmen, officials and workers all pursued a policy of nonco-operation with the French, which meant the central government had to foot the bill.

Austro-German border, near Salzburg. Even after he returned to Munich he kept a low profile for some months–a fact that was misinterpreted by many observers as the beginning of the end for the Nazis.

It was early September before Hitler made an attempt to regain his lost prestige. The occasion he chose was a German Day celebration in Nuremburg on 1–2 September. More than 100,000 nationalists–the largest number of them from the NSDAP–crowded into the city, and the streets were festooned with Nazi and Bavarian flags. On the first day Hitler addressed several mass meetings, his speeches marking his public return to his old rabble-rousing tactics. On the second, the German Battle League (*Deutscher Kampfbund*) was formed. Though it

troublemaker. Kahr refused to back down.

The following weeks, during which the various parties jockeyed for position, each trying to outmaneuver the others, were confused. Hitler's own position was clear; he wanted a nationalist march on Berlin. He realized that if it was to succeed it had to be backed by the political and military authorities in Bavaria, but his ultimate goal was the establishment of a new regime for all Germany. Berlin's position was clear too: with the backing of Seeckt and the Army, the Central Government was determined to stop all separatist or revolutionary movements within Germany.

What confused the issue was the attitude of the Bavarian government, which had become in effect a triumvirate consisting of Kahr, Lossow

was ostensibly an association of several nationalist organizations, most of the Kampfbund officers were Hitler men and its platform—based on opposition to Marxism, pacifism, and international Jewry—came straight from Hitler's speeches. The Kampfbund had two avowed goals: the overthrow of the Republic and the destruction of the Treaty of Versailles.

By 26 September tension between the Bavarian and the Central governments reached breaking point with the announcement by Chancellor Gustav Stresemann that passive resistance in the Ruhr was ended and that reparations payments would be resumed. Nationalists and Communists alike were furious. But Stresemann had anticipated their reaction and immediately had President Ebert declare a state of emergency, placing executive power in the hands of the Commander of the Army, General Hans von Seeckt, and the Minister of Defense, Otto Gessler.

Seeckt, a nationalist himself, fully realized his powerful position. For the time being, however, he opted to support the Republic—not because he believed in republican principles, but because he saw it as the only way to save Germany from civil war and ultimate dissolution. Thus his first acts were to suppress a series of uprisings by both the right and the left.

The Bavarian government, in no mood to adopt any Central Government solution, had declared its own state of emergency. Alarmed by Hitler's increasingly strident calls for violent revolution, they appointed former Minister President Gustav von Kahr—a well-known rightist and monarchist—as State Commissioner with dictatorial powers and specific instructions to suppress Hitler's activities.

One of Kahr's first acts was to ban fourteen simultaneous mass meetings planned by the Nazis for 27 September. Hitler was absolutely furious. With the formation of the Kampfbund he had come to see himself as equal with the government; now it seemed that Kahr was reducing him to the status of a loud-mouthed

(head of the Army) and Hans von Seisser, Chief of the Bavarian State Police. Their goals were probably not even clear to themselves, beyond a general antagonism to Berlin. Kahr was alternately attracted by the idea of obtaining a more autonomous position for Bavaria under a conservative central government and by breaking away from the Republic completely. While both Kahr and Hitler realized they were pursuing incompatible goals, each hoped to use the other for his own ends, with a doublecross after the event.

Both sides, then, devoted the beginning of October to preparations for a confrontation with Berlin. Under heavy secrecy plans were laid, weapons collected and military exercises held. Slogans and counterslogans appeared on walls throughout Munich and the cry 'On to Berlin!' became the magic solution to all problems for the nationalists, just as 'Away from Berlin!' was the rally cry for the separatists.

Meanwhile inflation had been spiraling at an almost unbelievable rate; by October it took 6,014,300 marks to equal the value of one pre-war mark. A housewife could have purchased 30,000,000 eggs in 1913 for the price of one in October 1923. Life was rapidly becoming in-

Below left:
Alfred Rosenberg and Hitler at a meeting in Munich in 1923.

Bottom left:
The SA parades past Hitler and Streicher (center of picture) during German Day in Nuremberg, 1923.

Below right:
The SA flag of the unit from Regensburg.

tolerable. To hold on to money for an hour was to see its value reduced by half. At times the situation bordered on farce, as in the story of the woman who left a basket of money in the street and returned a few minutes later to find her money in the gutter and her basket stolen. Anyone lucky enough to have his own small potato patch had to be ready to defend it against marauders. Of course, some benefited. Debtors could pay off their obligations in worthless paper. But the real killings were made by foreigners and profiteers who had their money in hard currencies and could buy huge estates and valuable heirlooms for a fraction of their real value.

By mid-October plans for the march were beginning to take on a definite shape, and it became obvious that the time for a confrontation was drawing closer. Lossow had ignored orders to curb Hitler and shut down the *Völkischer Beobachter*, and when Seeckt dismissed him for insubordination, Kahr had immediately made him Commander of the Bavarian Reichswehr—an act of direct defiance. Kahr himself had publicly attacked Berlin and called for the overthrow of Stresemann's government. But Hitler was becoming increas-

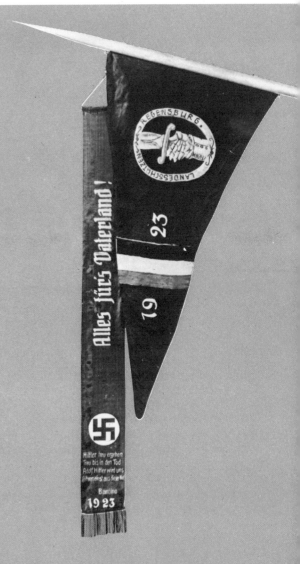

ingly afraid that the Bavarian triumvirate would use the SA and other Kampfbund forces for the march and then use the opportunity to declare Bavaria a separate state.

He decided to act on 6 November when he discovered that he had been excluded from a meeting between the government and representatives of several nationalist organizations. Kahr had stressed at the meeting that the overthrow of the national government had to be accomplished in concert, not independently–a clear reference to Hitler, who then had little choice in what to do next. He knew that any appearance of compromise would destroy his credibility in the eyes of his followers. He knew too that his stormtroopers, who had been on alert for weeks, were becoming restless and angry at their continued inaction.

So the next day the leaders of the Kampfbund set 11 November–the fifth anniversary of Germany's surrender to the Allies–as the date for their own putsch. But that afternoon, 7 November, Kahr unexpectedly announced that he would hold a mass 'patriotic demonstration' at the Bürgerbräukeller on the following evening. Fearing that he planned to announce a Bavarian break with Berlin then and there, the Kampf-

Below:
The SA marches past Hitler during German Day in Nuremberg in 1923. Hitler is above the X. Police estimated that 100,000 people took part in the event.

bund devised another plan: to forestall the announcement by appearing at the meeting, 'escorting' the triumvirate to another room, and convincing them to go along with Hitler's plans.

The next morning of 8 November was windy and bitterly cold. During the day SA and Kampfbund units were hastily mobilized. At a few minutes past eight Hitler, dressed in an old black tailcoat, arrived at the beer hall, and took up a position near a pillar in the jammed meeting room. Just after 0830, armed Nazis surrounded the building, greatly outnumbering the bewildered municipal police, while Captain Göring and his special Brownshirt bodyguard unit, armed with machine pistols, pushed their way into the hall.

That was the signal. With a dramatic gesture Hitler took a last swallow from his stein of beer, dashed it to the floor, and marched into the hall at the head of his squad. Pandemonium reigned as furniture went flying and men dived for cover. Then Hitler climbed onto a chair and fired a single shot into the ceiling. In the shocked silence that followed he announced, 'The national revolution has begun. The hall is surrounded by 600 armed men. No one may leave the premises.'

PERNET   Dr. WEBER   FRICK   KRIEBEL   LUDENDORFF   HITLER   BRÜCKNER   RÖHM   WAGNER

Kahr, Lossow and Seisser were ordered into an adjoining room where Hitler tried to convince them that their only option was to go along with him—with a singular lack of success. Descriptions of the posts they were to occupy in the new government and threats of death if they failed to comply left them equally indifferent. Shaken, Hitler returned to the hall, where the crowd was beginning to get out of hand. When he appeared there was a cacophony of whistles, catcalls and insults, punctuated with shouts of 'Theater!' or 'South America!' He pushed his way to the platform, engulfed by the din and stood quite still for a moment. Then he shouted, 'If silence is not restored I will order a machine gun placed in the gallery!' In the silence that followed, recalls Hanfstängl, the comical little man in the ridiculous cutaway became a superman—a maestro conducting a huge orchestra. He began to speak, and within a few minutes the mood of the crowd was completely reversed.

His task accomplished, Hitler dashed back into the anteroom as cheers echoed round the hall. In the meantime General Erich Ludendorff, with whom Hitler had been working for some months for various nationalist causes, had arrived. Though he was angry about not having been told of the plot beforehand, he still agreed to help and immediately began to try to convince the three politicians to agree to Hitler's plan. Impressed by his rank and prestige, they finally did so; soon all returned to the platform

Above:
Ludendorff, Hitler and the other conspirators who took part in Munich Beer Hall Putsch.

in apparent unity and Kahr, stiff and pale, announced that he would serve Bavaria as Regent for the monarchy.

Next came Hitler, who met the wild cheers of the crowd with equal passion, 'Now I am going to carry out the vow I made five years ago when I was a blind cripple in the Army hospital: to neither rest nor sleep until the November criminals have been hurled to the ground, until on the ruins of the pitiful Germany of today has risen a Germany of power and greatness, of freedom and glory!' Ludendorff, still angry, rose to assure the audience that though surprised at its suddenness, he placed himself at the disposal of the German national government at this turning point in history.

As the meeting started to break up Hess began rounding up 'enemies of the people,' including Prime Minister Eugen von Knilling, Police Commissioner Mantel and other ministers. Then Hitler, drunk on the drama, the cheers, and the action, made a grave tactical error.

Receiving word of a minor emergency outside the Engineers' Barracks, he decided to deal with it himself, leaving Ludendorff in charge at the beer hall. The moment he was out of the building Lossow bade Ludendorff a comradly farewell and departed, saying he had to go to his office and issue orders to the troops; Kahr and Seisser were hard on his heels. When Hitler and one of his principal advisers, Max von Scheubner-Richter, returned a half-hour later

they were appalled to find that the three had been allowed to escape. Ludendorff's only reply was to look down his nose at the former corporal and icily forbid him to doubt the word of a German officer.

But when the leaders went to Lossow's office at the military command post to set up their own headquarters he was not there—nor were they able to find the other members of the triumvirate, who in fact had already put into action a series of countermeasures. Lossow had met with his officers and, in the face of their menacing opposition to the putsch, had assured them that he had never had any real intention of carrying it out. Kahr had not only issued a statement denying everything he had said in the Bürgerbräukeller, but had published an edict dissolving both the Nazi Party and the Kampfbund, and had ordered that no Hitler sympathizers were to be allowed to enter Munich.

In the city gangs of jubilant youths were keeping guests in downtown hotels awake with their songs and shouts of triumph, while elsewhere SA units searched out opponents of the putsch and Jews—whom they identified by going through the telephone book—and pulled them from their beds. One unit broke into the offices of the *Münchener Post*, the Social Democratic newspaper, intent on smashing the presses.

Back at headquarters Hitler began to realize that he had been tricked and went through a violent series of moods, ranging from depression through despair. But when the facts were

finally confirmed at about five that morning he was calm again. Leaving Röhm and his men to hold the building he, Ludendorff, and their staff returned to the beer hall. Orders were issued to all not manning strongholds to return there.

The morning was damp and cold as the Putschists gathered in the clammy, smoke-filled hall of the Bürgerbräukeller for a breakfast of cheese, bread and coffee. All were unshaven, unwashed and rather depressed after the excitement of the previous night.

In a private room upstairs their leaders were debating the next move. A proposal to withdraw to Rosenheim and reorganize was put forward and rejected; the discussion dragged on through the morning, becoming progressively more acrimonious. The arguments were brought to a sudden halt by the news that Röhm and his 150 men were being besieged in the military district command building by a vastly superior force of military and state police troops.

'We march!' roared Ludendorff, convinced that in a face-to-face confrontation the officers and men of the Army would never fire on the legendary hero of World War I. Within an hour 2000 men were lined up behind the standard bearers with their swastikas and black-white-red party flags. First came the leaders: Scheubner-Richter, Hitler, Ludendorff, Colonel Kriebel, Hitler's bodyguard Ulrich Graf, the head of the Bund Oberland, Friedrich Weber, and Göring—his black leather coat open to show the *Pour le Mérite* on his breast. Then came the crack SA troops: Hitler's 100-man bodyguard with their steel helmets, carbines, and grenades, alongside the tough Munich Regiment and the Bund Oberland troops. Bringing up the rear was the rank and file—military cadets, businessmen, students, shopkeepers. Their only uniform was their swastika armband, but almost all were armed with rifles or pistols.

After a brief march the force met a detachment of state police at a bridge over the Isar River. The police hesitated just long enough to allow themselves to be overrun; by 1230 the Putschists were in the narrow streets of the old city, singing as they marched. As they drew nearer their goal, Hitler linked arms with Scheubner-Richter, anticipating trouble.

It was not long in arriving. As the parade approached the Odeonsplatz they met yet another police cordon. The police moved forward but the Putschists stood firm, with fixed bayonets. Suddenly a single shot cracked, and a police sergeant fell. For a split second everyone seemed frozen—then the police opened fire and the Putschists returned it as both marchers and bystanders ran for cover.

First of the Putschists to fall was Scheubner-Richter, fatally wounded in the lungs. As he fell, he dragged Hitler down with him. At the same moment Ulrich Graf, who had leaped in front of his Führer to protect him, also went down –grabbing Hitler's arm so hard that he dislocated it.

As the volley ended Ludendorff, who had dropped flat to avoid the hail of bullets like the battle-seasoned soldier he was, rose and marched arrogantly through the police line, brushing aside the carbines that were levelled at him. He was placed under arrest.

Göring was picked up from the pavement with a bullet in his thigh and carried to a nearby house, where his comrades asked for shelter. The owner, Robert Ballin, allowed them to enter, administered first aid, and allowed the wounded man to stay until he could be moved to safety. Ironically, Ballin was a Jew.

Hitler, convinced he had been shot, moved painfully away from the battlefield. Together he and Dr Walter Schultz, head of the Munich SA Medical Corps, found a car and headed south. They ended up at Putzi Hanfstängl's country home in Uffing, where Helene Hanfstängl took them in and Hitler's arm was set. That evening and the following day were anxious times. Hanfstängl (who had never thought of going home and was on his way to Austria) had not returned; the car Hitler had attempted to get in order to continue his escape did not arrive; they all knew it was only a matter of time until he was traced to Uffing. At about five in the afternoon they were warned that the police were on the way. When Helene told Hitler he grabbed a revolver from a nearby cabinet: 'Now all is lost! No use going on!' But he only lost his nerve for a moment, and giving the gun to Helene (who hid it in a flour barrel), he began to dictate instructions to his followers. A few minutes after he finished the police arrived; at 2145 on 12 November he was arraigned at the district police office in Weilheim and sent by car to prison at Landsberg, some 40 miles west of Munich.

Meanwhile, as foreign newspapers hurriedly put together garbled stories about the abortive Munich Putsch, the rest of the conspirators were either captured or in flight. Göring, Hess, and Hanfstängl made it safely to Austria; Röhm surrendered; and the rank and file were rounded up by the hundreds. Ludendorff, who had marched so bravely through the police cordon, was released on his own recognizance after assuring the authorities that he had really been little more than an innocent on-looker.

Ludendorff's conspicuous bravery in front of the Feldherrnhalle has often been compared to Hitler's quitting of the battlefield – usually to the latter's discredit. But Hitler, unlike the General, had realized that the Putsch was a failure long before that first shot rang out. In fact, it was over when Kahr and Lossow took sides against it. He had known all along that he had no chance of succeeding without the backing of the political and military authorities –

that was why no adequate plans had been made to seize obvious positions like police headquarters, the central telephone exchange, the power station, and the railroad terminal. He had never thought of violence as an option and had agreed to the march only because he thought there was a slim chance it might swing the Army back to his side. For Hitler, therefore, the shots fired at the Feldherrnhalle meant not only the end of three years of phenomenal progress, but also the sudden destruction of his entire system of tactics.

While the world press was writing his political obituary Hitler was in Landsberg brooding on the fiasco and refusing to eat. Anton Drexler, Hans Knirsch (founder of the National Socialist Workers' Party in Czechoslovakia), Frau Bechstein and Helene Hanfstängl all claim credit for talking him out of his fast.

In early December he had a visit from his half-sister Angela who came away impressed not only with his spirits, but with the continued loyalty of his followers and friends. The nationalist movement had lost little of its momentum, and in many circles Hitler was a hero. His allies were reforming into groups like the Völkischer Singing Club, the League of True German Women, or the German Rifle and Hiking League. Despite his disapproval, Röhm – operating out of Stadelheim Prison – was reviving the Kampfbund under a new name – Frontbann.

Though the NSDAP had been formally banned, underground operations were being directed from Munich by Alfred Rosenberg. The activities consisted mainly of feuding, especially between Rosenberg and the exiles in Austria – Esser, Streicher, Amman and Hanfstängl – who considered him an incompetent. In Hitler's eyes, however, Rosenberg had two overriding virtues: he was absolutely loyal and, since he had neither friends nor followers, he could not be a threat.

By 26 February 1924 when his trial began, Hitler was ready, both mentally and physically, to turn disaster into triumph. Nine others were beside him in the dock: Ludendorff, Ernst Pöhner, Wilhelm Frick, the three other leaders of the Kampfbund (Röhm, Friedrich Weber and Colonel Kriebel), and three active SA leaders (Wilhelm Brückner, Wagner and Pernet). Kahr, Lossow, and Seisser appeared as witnesses for the prosecution.

Because of his eminence Ludendorff was listed first on the transcript, and it was clear the government wished to spare him as much as possible. This suited Hitler very well. From the very start he was on the attack, assuming all responsibility for what had happened (which thrust him forward as the leader of the whole racist movement), and denying he was a criminal. How could he be accused of high treason when all he had been doing was to voice

„Mögen schuldig des ewi Geschich Antrag und das zerreiße uns frei

Above:
A postcard commemorating Hitler's trial quotes the leader: 'You may pronounce us guilty a thousand times, but the goddess of the everlasting court of History will smilingly demolish the brief of the State Prosecutor and the sentence of this court. For she pronounces us free.'

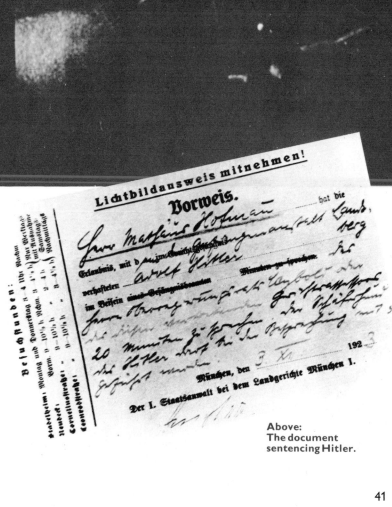

e uns tausendmal
rechen, die Göttin
n Gerichtes der
vird lächelnd den
s Staatsanwaltes
teil des Gerichtes
denn sie spricht

Adolf Hitler
'or dem Volksgericht 1924

opinions and seek goals already agreed upon with the three prosecution witnesses? In any case, there could be no such thing as treason against the criminals of November 1918—and if there was, then Kahr, Lossow, and Seisser should be in the dock with him.

His aggressive tactics were so unnerving that only Lossow retained the ability to fight back, contemptuously describing Hitler as 'tactless, limited, boring ... and unquestionably inferior.' The insults these and similar remarks provoked from Hitler brought no rebuke from the bench.

Throughout the trial the Court was extraordinarily sympathetic to Hitler—so much so that the presiding judge had great difficulty getting the three lay judges to arrive at a verdict

Above:
The document sentencing Hitler.

Left:
The garden of Landsberg prison. The fortress was in the valley of the Lech and did not have a repressive regime. Hitler was allowed many visitors but spent most of the time dictating *Mein Kampf*.

Below:
The day of his release, 20 December 1924, Hitler posed for his photographer, Heinrich Hoffmann, outside Landsberg.

of guilty. They were only convinced after being assured that he would not have to serve his full sentence. They were so obviously biased that many observers found it difficult to believe they were seeing a trial; one German journalist called it a 'political carnival.' Many particuarly objected to Hitler being allowed to harangue the court for hours on end and to insult the prosecution witnesses with impunity.

The court room was crowded on the day the verdict was to be read, with many of the women carrying flowers; another large crowd was gathered outside the building. Ludendorff, as expected, was acquitted. Hitler, also as expected, was found guilty and sentenced to five years in Landsberg prison. The sentence—which many considered ridiculously light for treason and armed insurrection—still honored him. It stressed his 'purely patriotic and honorable intentions' and was scathing to Kahr, Lossow, and

Left:
Hitler was allowed as many books and newspapers as he wanted in jail.

Seisser, who should have either 'clearly said "No" to Hitler's demands' or co-operated with him. The judges also refused to deport him to Austria, since he was so obviously 'a man who thinks and feels in such German terms.' Hitler appeared once at the window to wave to the cheering crowd before he was hustled back to Landsberg and his familiar Cell 7.

The Gefangenenanstalt and Festungschaftanstalt Landsberg were light gray buildings surrounded by high stone walls, on a hill overlooking the Lech River. The complex was divided into two sections—for ordinary and political prisoners.

Hitler was in the latter section where his life was, if not ideal, at least pleasant enough given the circumstances. Cell 7 was a large, sunny room on the upper floor. Kriebel was in 8 and Dr Weber, leader of the Bund Oberland, was in 9; Hess (who had voluntarily returned from Austria to share his Führer's imprisonment), Max Amann, and Emil Maurice were among the other 40 National Socialists in the prison.

The men ate well (Hitler grew almost fat) and were allowed visitors, books and papers as they wished. Food packages were allowed too, and Hitler had a steady supply. His favorite was poppy seed strudel which a group of National Socialist women brought him every Friday. Gifts of ham, sausage and bacon, however, usually went down to his comrades on the ground floor. Most of the prisoners, including Hitler, wore leather shorts and Tyrolean jackets. The men spent a lot of time outdoors in the garden.

Hitler was the acknowledged leader in the prison, by the authorities as well as the men, and was not required to participate in work details or physical fitness programs. He reigned supreme at the midday meal underneath a large swastika banner; the entire room would stand at attention until he was in his place, and then all would file up and present their respects before beginning the meal.

From July on, Hitler spent less time with his companions and more in his room dictating *Mein Kampf*, first to Maurice and later to Hess. Despite its original title–*Four and a Half Years of Struggle Against Lies, Stupidity and Cowardice* (shortened later by Amann to *My Struggle*)–there is little autobiographical material in it. Most of the book is a wordy, often boring description of Hitler's ideas. Though it is fascinating and invaluable for anyone trying to understand his thinking, it is such difficult going that even many loyal party members could not bring themselves to plow through it.

But perhaps more of the six million people who bought the book between 1925 and 1940 should have read it carefully–Hitler's writing style may have been turgid, but at least he was honest. *Mein Kampf* contains a clear outline of precisely the sort of state he intended creating if he had the chance, and also presents Hitler's own *Weltanschauung* (point of view, or philosophy of life).

Through all the extraneous material in the two-volume work–the almost random discussions of art, literature, sex, movies, the comics or whatever–comes a picture of Hitler's vision of the Third Reich: all Germans, including those outside the present frontiers, organized into an absolute dictatorship according to the *Führerprinzip* (leadership principle), with a network of subordinate leaders ruling under direct orders from the Leader himself.

One of the Reich's first priorities would be to deal with France–'the inexorable mortal enemy of the German people.' Another would be the search for *Lebensraum* (living space), probably at the expense of Austria, the Sudetenland, Western Poland, and Russia.

Hitler's *Weltanschauung*, which he shared with many other German philosophers and generals throughout history, can be seen as a kind of crude Darwinism: all life is a never-ending struggle in which the strong rule and only the fit survive. The 'strongest in courage and industry' is the Aryan–who has unfortunately fallen from his high estate and allowed himself to become 'submerged in a racial mixture.' The obsession with race becomes the basis for the 'folkish state'–a mystical union which would grow and prosper until the 'highest race' became 'master people . . . supported by the means and possi-

bilities of an entire globe.' The concept of the 'folkish state' is extremely difficult to understand; the German word *Volk* not only denotes people or nation, but also carries the connotation of a deeper, more primitive community rooted in blood and the soil.

Though many of the ideas in *Mein Kampf* seemed preposterous, even in Germany at the time, it held a vision of a glorious German destiny that captured the imagination of millions during those difficult years.

In mid-December 1924, after just over a year, Hitler's imprisonment in Landsberg came to an end. His release was unexpected; though several of his comrades had been sent home earlier in the year, his own requests for parole had been denied. But on 19 December the Bavarian Supreme Court ordered his immediate release. Prison warden Leybold personally delivered the news the next day, as the inmates were putting up their Christmas decorations.

As Hitler stepped outside the gates he was met by his printer, Adolf Müller, and his photographer, Heinrich Hoffmann, who had arrived with a touring car. Part way back they picked up an escort of Nazi motorcyclists; soon they were pulling up in front of Hitler's apartment building in Munich where Herman Esser, Julius Streicher, and other party faithfuls were waiting to welcome him with flowers, food and drink. He had come home for Christmas.

Above:
At the Nuremberg rallies the Blood Flag used in the Beer Hall Putsch was always prominently displayed. The 16 who died in the Putsch were reburied in 1935 in a new memorial.

III The Rise to Power

From Landsberg Hitler re-entered a world that was greatly changed, both politically and economically. The stabilization of the mark by a financial genius named Dr Hjalmar Schact, Currency Commissioner, had revived the people's faith in the foundations of their society. Stresemann's policy of reconciliation with the Allies showed results too: the Dawes Plan was easing the burden of reparations; and the influx of American capital was hastening German economic recovery. The French were beginning their withdrawal from the Rhineland, and discussions that were expected to lead to a general European security treaty and even to Germany's entry into the League of Nations had started. The stabilized economy and the settlement with France removed two of Hitler's prime themes at a stroke.

In the Reichstag elections in December 1924, two weeks before his release, the 'November criminals' had increased their vote by 30 per-cent, while the Nazis and other folkish groups lost more than half their support. It looked as though Germany was finally beginning to return to normal.

It was this upswing in German affairs that had made Hitler's release possible; no one thought that there was anything left to fear from either him or the Nazi Party. The NSDAP was still banned, and the right-wing had degenerated into a set of squabbling splinter groups. But from Hitler's point of view the situation was not as bad as it appeared on the surface. His deportation to Austria, which had been strongly urged by the Bavarian State Police, had been stopped by Gürtner, the Bavarian Minister of Justice, who was no doubt aided in his decision by the fact that Austria refused to have Hitler back. Despite the results of the December elections, the racist movement had been growing rapidly—and since no strong rival had appeared since 1923 to take his place, the way was open for Hitler to take control and gain a national position as the personification of freedom and racial purity. The middle classes, who had been hardest hit by inflation, were still angry and afraid; they tended to blame their troubles on the Marxists and the Jews, and thus were even more receptive to Hitler's ideas.

Hitler's chance for success lay in his being able to stand apart from the plethora of warring factions on the right—to tower above them as the only leader, eventually gathering all of them under his umbrella. He also realized that he had to make peace with the government he was still planning to overthrow, since head-on opposition would clearly be a waste of time. One of his first steps, therefore, was to visit Heinrich Held, the new Bavarian Prime Minister. Held was a strict Catholic and a strong Bavarian federalist, and the Nazis had often attacked him in the past. Now, though, Hitler wanted only to present assurances of his loyalty to the government and his willingness to support the state in the struggle against Marxism. All he asked was to be given back his party and his newspaper, the *Völkischer Beobachter*, to help him in his fight. Held was not impressed with most of this nonsense, but he was convinced that Hitler was 'tame' enough for it to be safe to lift the ban on the NSDAP and their paper.

Hitler remained in semi-solitude for some weeks. Finally, on 27 February 1925, he made his return to public life at a party convention in the Bürgerbräukeller—the same hall from which he had launched the putsch. The large hall held 4000 people; by 1800 it was jammed with Nazis from all over the nation, and another 1000 had to be turned away. As he entered the hall his adherents—who had spent the last year battling with each other—broke into a frenzy of cheering, with people climbing on tables, waving beer mugs, and hugging each other. His speech

helm Frich, Rudolf Buttman of the German Nationalist Party—all gathered on the platform to ostentatiously shake hands and make up. Conspicuous by their absence were Ernst Röhm, Gregor Strasser and Alfred Rosenberg, who had refused to attend.

Having established absolute control over the party, Hitler immediately set about reorganizing the approximately 700 members who remained to suit his own tactical aims. The process turned out to be long, tedious and fraught with obstacles. One of the first was a ban on

Left:
Hitler studies his notes before an internal party meeting. On the extreme left sits Rudolf Hess who acted as Hitler's private secretary.

Below:
Hitler and his entourage in the Bavarian Alps in 1927. On the left is Gregor Strasser who was responsible for building up party numbers in the 1920s. He believed the party program should be more radical and this brought him into open conflict with the party leaders on many occasions.

that evening, which lasted two hours, built up to a dramatic climax:

> If anyone comes and wants to put conditions to me, then I tell him: 'My friend, wait awhile until you hear the conditions I will put to you.' I am not out to woo the masses. After a year you shall judge, my party comrades. . . . Until then, however, I and I alone shall lead the movement and no one sets conditions for me as long as I personally assume all responsibility.

He offered no compromises, asked for no support; acceptance of him as sole leader or withdrawal were the only two choices offered. When at the end of his speech the crowd burst into even louder cheers, his success was confirmed. Suddenly Max Amann leaped up and shouted 'The quarrelling must stop! Everyone for Hitler!' The erstwhile enemies—Julius Streicher, Herman Esser, Gottfried Feder, Wil-

public speaking placed on him by Bavaria and later by other German states, which deprived him of a major political weapon. In 1923 such a setback would have thrown him completely off balance, but the older, more mature Hitler took advantage of the opportunity to concentrate on rebuilding the party.

Much of his time was spent in one closed meeting after another, meeting members and consolidating his position. Esser and Streicher followed the same tactics with other local organizations in Bavaria.

Control of the North German party was turned over to Gregor Strasser, with whom Hitler had finally managed to come to terms. Strasser was a tireless and efficient organizer, who, having given his word, was absolutely loyal; but the traditional North German distrust of the flamboyant Southerners made many North German members wary of the Munich group. Strasser, his brother Otto, and the young business manager of the North Rhineland group, Joseph Goebbels, differed with Munich headquarters on almost every important point: more socialist in their orientation, they could easily envisage a union between Nazis and Communists; Goebbels openly questioned Hitler's view of the Jews as the universal enemy; and far from seeing the USSR as an area for conquest and future expansion, the North German group viewed it as a fellow oppressed nation deserving respect and co-operation. There were strong objections to the vulgarity and brashness of Esser and Streicher. No one thought of attacking Hitler personally, but rather saw him as being surrounded by bad advisers who were leading him to ruin. However, as the split grew wider and the North and West German parties grew stronger, the situation inevitably became a challenge to his authority.

Captain Röhm posed yet another problem. All the time Hitler was in prison Röhm had been building up a new organization of stormtroopers called the Frontbann (Front-Liners), which he saw as his own private auxiliary army that would help Germany avoid the restrictions of the Versailles Treaty. On 16 April he went so far as to present Hitler with a memorandum to the effect that the SA should be considered part of the Frontbann; it would thus be independent of the NSDAP and under Röhm's complete authority. But Hitler had learned his lesson well, and would never again depend on an organization he did not completely control. Incensed, he charged Röhm with betraying their friendship, and demanded that the Frontbann immediately swear allegiance to him personally. Röhm answered by tendering his resignation from the SA, hoping, no doubt, that such an extreme threat would force the Führer to rethink his position. A month later, after waiting in vain for a reply, he wrote: 'I take this opportunity, in memory of the great and difficult days we have been through together, to thank you for your comradeship and to ask you not to exclude me from your personal friendship.' Again there was no reply; the next day he sent a formal announcement of resignation from all his offices to the Nationalist newspapers. The Völkischer Beobachter printed the notice without comment. Hitler was finally free to establish the SA on his own terms, and Röhm was left with neither army nor party.

During the summer of 1925, Hitler spent most of his time in Berchtesgaden, where he had rented a summer home. For some months he rarely left his rural retreat except to attend the Munich opera or visit friends—the Hanfstängls, the Bruckmanns, or the Essers. Most of his time was spent finishing the first volume of Mein Kampf, which was published in July 1925.

By the beginning of 1926 it was no longer possible for him to ignore the growing opposition in the north. As his first step in dealing with the problem Hitler called a meeting of all party leaders in Bamberg for 14 February. The outnumbered delegation from the north was made to feel even more insecure at the sight of Streicher's display banners and huge posters announcing giant demonstrations in the area. Hitler's opening speech lasted five hours. Too clever to openly attack either Strasser or Goebbels, he caught the northerners completely off guard by taking the meeting (and the party) out of politics and into the religious mystique of The Leader: he was the Führer, the nucleus, the infallible, immutable personification of the idea. There would be no more discussion, no more splinter groups—accept him wholly or leave the party. After some hesitating, unconvincing responses, Strasser and his followers left the meeting—cowed, if not completely convinced.

Hitler followed up his victory at the Bamberg meeting with a direct, personal campaign to win over Strasser and Goebbels. Strasser was the first to relent, despite his reservations; in early March he sent letters to his followers recalling his own party program in favor of Hitler's.

The approach worked equally well with Goebbels, though it took a bit longer. He was a small man—just over five feet tall and weighing only about 100 pounds—and a bout of infantile paralysis had left him with a frail appearance and a club foot. Nevertheless, he was an excellent writer and a highly effective public speaker, with a magnificent baritone voice and a self-assured manner that always commanded attention. An academician (he received a PhD in literature from the University of Heidelberg in 1921) with strong mystical and romantic leanings, politically he was a folkish socialist who believed that the only thing separating the National Socialists from the Communists was the concept of internationalism. He hoped to convince Hitler of his theory when next the two met; instead, he found himself completely won

over to the Führer's side. He left Munich in April in a state bordering on ecstasy: '. . . I love him . . . I bow to the greater man, the political genius.'

Within a few months Hitler had established himself firmly in control of the NSDAP. At a general membership meeting in Munich at the end of May all democratic procedures were finally and firmly discarded; Hitler was given the power to select or dismiss any *Gauleiter* (district leader); the original 25-point party platform was declared inviolable; and the local Munich organization was made the hub of the entire party.

Hitler celebrated by holding the Second Party Rally in Weimar at the beginning of July, 1926. The site was chosen because Thuringia was one of the few German states where he was allowed to address public meetings. The Nazis had not yet developed the brilliant theatrical

Above:
The Nazi party headquarters, the Brown House, in Munich. The Brown House was acquired in 1929 and was situated on the Briennerstrasse, Munich.

Adolf Hitler im Gasthaus Märker anläßlich seines ersten Besuchs der Hattinger Ortsgruppe, einer der ältesten des Reichsgebiets

Above:
This postcard was made shortly after Josef Goebbels (on Hitler's left) had been made Gauleiter of Berlin. Goebbels had joined the party as a member of the Strasser faction but had abandoned it in 1926.

effects that marked later gatherings, but Goebbels, as he watched Hitler review a column of some 4000 stormtroopers with his arm upraised in the Fascist salute, saw before him the dawning of the Third Reich and the awakening of Germany.

By the end of 1926 there were approximately 50,000 party members tightly organized in a vertical framework. Germany was divided into districts (*gaue*) corresponding roughly to the Reichstag electoral districts; there were another seven gaue for Austria, Danzig, the Saar, and the Sudetenland. Each gau was headed by a Gauleiter appointed by Hitler and divided into circles (*Kreise*) led by a *Kreisleiter*. The next unit down was the local group (*Ortsgruppe*) which could, if necessary, be divided into street cells.

The Political Organization was divided into three groups: (1) an elaborate Propaganda Division; (2) PO-I, which was designed to attack and undermine the government and which contained the party's departments of foreign affairs, labor unions and the Reich Press Office; and (3) PO-II, a quasi-state containing the departments of agriculture, justice, economy, interior, labor, race and culture, and engineering. The Hitler Youth—which was established in 1925 to bring together young people, break their ties with Communist organizations, and indoctrinate them in the Nazi fight for Power—took in boys aged 15–18, and had its own departments for culture, schools, 'defense sports,' etc. Younger boys joined the *Deutsches Jungvolk*; girls were enrolled in the *Bund Deutscher Mädel*; and women joined the *N. S. Frauenschaften*. The Nazi Kulturbund existed for intellectuals and artists, while separate organizations were formed for teachers, doctors, lawyers, students, and civil servants. After the death of Horst Wessel, early in 1930, his song became the party anthem; and throughout the

Above:
Hitler greets SA men at a 1927 rally.

Right:
Hitler, accompanied by Julius Schaub leaves the Brown House in Munich to attend a meeting. During this period in Nazi Party history the leaders concentrated on recruiting members.

Below:
A 1927 Party rally.

year various memorial days were held to promote a feeling of solidarity.

The SA remained the most important organization within the party. Its leader, after Röhm's resignation, was Franz Pfeffer von Salomon, a born organizer, chosen by Hitler to mold the SA into a well-disciplined unit for propaganda and intimidation. As Hitler envisaged it, it was neither a secret society, an auxiliary army, nor a bodyguard; every effort was made to give it a special character—including mystical indoctrination rituals and carefully choreographed public appearances. The problems with the organization were never completely eliminated, however. The old front-line soldiers found it difficult to walk the thin line required of them, and the German tradition that gave the military a special place with respect to the civilian authorities encouraged their contemptuous attitude toward the PO. To make matters more uncomfortable, Hitler soon found Pfeffer as intractable as Röhm had been; Pfeffer, son of a Prussian privy councilor, had little respect for the man he called 'that flabby Austrian.'

In 'Red' Berlin the Nazi party was opposed on the streets by overwhelming numbers of Communists and Social Democrats. It was small, badly organized and relatively unknown until October 1926 when Hitler appointed Goebbels the new Gauleiter for the capital. Goebbels immediately set out to sell National Socialism, using every trick he knew and some he made up for the occasion. A genius in the art of emotional manipulation and propaganda, he would practice movements and rehearse speeches in front of a mirror by the hour. He was a brilliant improviser with a number of styles. Otto Strasser recalls him asking before a meeting, 'What record should I use—the national, the social, or the sentimental? Of course I have them all in my suitcase.' To attract attention to the party he

began to stage a series of street brawls with the Communists, which served a triple purpose. They gave the men of the SA the chance for a good fight—and more important, had them fighting together; they attracted the attention of both the press and the citizens of Berlin; and after they had been broken up by the police and the participants arrested, they helped promote a feeling of martyrdom and comradeship in adversity.

By May 1927 the government of Berlin had had enough. The NSDAP was banned in the city and Goebbels was forced to rely on innocent-sounding cover groups with names like 'The Beautiful Acorn' or 'Hikers of 1927.' When the police placed a ban on Nazi speeches throughout Prussia, Goebbels began a weekly paper called *Der Angriff* (The Assault) which turned out to be directed as much against the Strasser brothers' leftist movement as it was against rival political parties. At about the same time, the injunction against Hitler's public appearances was lifted in Saxony and Bavaria.

By the time the Third Party Rally was called in August 1927 Hitler had become much more professional in his approach. He had been studying the use of body movements in public speaking with Erik Jan Hanussen, one of the most famous seers and astrologers in Europe and a master of the use of gesture to emphasize words and control audiences. Though regularly received in some of the best homes in Germany, he still lived a spare, monastic life in his modest room on Thierschstrasse. In his public appearances, however, he was changing his image from folkish revolutionary fanatic to calm, reasonable man seeking only what was best for the Fatherland. His choice of the ancient city of

Nuremburg as the site of the third rally and the subsequent dramatic staging of the event showed his greatly improved sense of theater. Almost 20,000 members crowded into the city, many arriving on special trains with bands, flags and pennants. The Hitler Youth marched for the first time, along with some 8500 stormtroopers; the first elements of the elaborate ritual that was to develop in later years were clearly to be seen.

The years 1927–28 were not good for the Nazis; the tensions upon which the party thrived were relaxing as large American loans stimulated the expansion and modernization of the economy. Productivity rose dramatically; the number of unemployed was drastically reduced; while national income and the standard of living showed comparable increases. Fewer and fewer Germans wanted to listen to the gloomy predictions of Hitler and Goebbels.

This new, more optimistic mood was demonstrated in the presidential elections of May 1928. Though Goebbels won a Reichstag seat in Berlin, overall the Nazis only got 810,000 votes,

Above:
An official portrait of the Party Leader in 1927.

Above left:
Hess, Hitler and Streicher join a Nazi Party rally on 20 August 1927, in Nuremberg.

Left:
Hitler at the same rally obviously enjoying the occasion. By 1927 the Party had 72,000 paid-up members.

51

Below:
The founding of another
Nazi group in Thuringia
in 1929. In 1929 the Nazi
Party began to make an
impressive showing in
local elections in
Thuringia. In December
the Nazis got 11 percent
of votes cast in the
provincial elections.

giving them just 12 seats out of 491. (Among the other new members of the Reichstag were Hermann Göring—who had returned from Sweden to take up residence again in Germany, Gregor Strasser, Gottfried Feder, and Frick.) Though the NSDAP was in a much better position than in 1924-25, it was still a small-time party in relation to national politics. But during the next year of waiting, in the face of amused contempt and indifference from most of the German people, Hitler never lost faith in his belief that sooner or later the tide would turn in his favor. More important, he was able to keep that same faith alive in his followers.

Once the elections were over Hitler returned to Berchtesgaden where he rented a villa for 100 marks (about $25) a month from the widow of a wealthy industrialist. He had fallen in love with the place, called Haus Wachenfeld, the moment he saw it—a simple country house surrounded by a wooden veranda, with a pitched roof that had heavy rocks on the shingles to prevent their being blown off in high winds. He immediately called his half-sister Angela Raubal in Vienna and convinced her to come and keep house for him. She arrived with her

two daughters, Friedl and Angela Marie. Angela, usually called Geli, was 20—a charming, vivacious blonde who soon captivated Hitler. Although it is not at all certain that the ensuing affair was ever consummated, all his associates from that period agree that Hitler was deeply in love with his niece, who was 19 years his junior.

Hitler's opportunity to make the final breakthrough into national politics came in 1929. Stresemann's policy of 'fulfillment' had gained Germany entrance to the League of Nations. He was one of the chief architects of the Locarno Pact of 1925, which brought peace to Western Europe for the first time in a generation, and had negotiated the Treaty of Berlin, which included a settlement with Soviet Russia. Now he crowned his career by negotiating the Young Plan—which reduced the Allies' reparations claims—and by convincing the French to withdraw completely from the occupied Rhineland in September 1929, five years ahead of schedule. In October he died. Between that time and March 1930 the right wing in Germany united in an effort to defeat the legislation embodying the Young Plan, which had to be passed by the Reichstag.

For the fight Hitler—despite howls of anguish from his left wing—joined up with Alfred Hugenberg, a wealthy industrialist who owned a large network of newspapers and news agencies and also headed the German Nationalist Party. Their subsequent campaign to defeat the Young Plan legislation failed, but, as he intended, Hitler came out a winner. With a publicity campaign, paid for by Hugenberg's right wing alliance but conducted by the Nazis, Hitler proved himself the most purposeful figure on the right and by March was a familiar figure on the national scene. It was obvious not only to the business world, but to the public at large, that whatever small success had been achieved in the campaign against the Young Plan was due entirely to Hitler's efforts. Hitler underlined the fact by promptly breaking with Hugenberg and blaming the Nationalist's 'half-hearted support' for the failure.

He had attracted the attention of Hugenberg's backers in heavy industry and big business, and the money he began to receive enabled him to put the party on a new footing. The party headquarters was moved to an old mansion on Briennerstrasse, which Hitler had remodeled and renamed the Brown House. He changed his personal lodgings as well, to a new, opulent nine-room apartment at 16 Prinzregentenstrasse, a fashionable upper-middle-class street in Munich. Frau Reichert came along from Thierschstrasse to keep house, and Geli had her own room in the apartment. The two began to be seen together in the city; the gossip this caused bothered Hitler a little, but he probably also enjoyed the aura of freedom and drama that his grand passion entailed. The relationship was still ambiguous and contradictory; Hitler was beginning to act more like a suitor, but he was also the stern uncle who severely restricted his niece's social life—which made the vivacious girl increasingly unhappy.

From October 1929 on, the Nazis made steady gains in regional elections in Baden, Luebeck and Thuringia where, in January 1930, Frick became the first National Socialist to hold office when he became the Thuringian Minister of the Interior. In the summer of 1929 there had been some 120,000 people enrolled as members of the NSDAP; by March 1930 that number had risen to 210,000. This success was the direct result of unrelenting hard work in the form of a series of propaganda operations' which represented a whole new concept in the art of campaigning. A single district would be chosen and overnight every city, town, and remote village would be bombarded with posters, banners, and leaflets. The Party's top speakers would arrive, often addressing hundreds of meetings in the course of a week, while the SA would stage 'recruiting nights' which included athletic and musical events, plays, lectures and whatever else their resources would allow.

No country was more vulnerable than Germany to the effects of the Great Depression, which began in the United States in 1929 and spread around the world in 1930-31. German economic recovery had been based almost entirely on foreign loans; when these were no longer available, and the time for repayment arrived, the shaky financial structure could not stand the strain. As world trade, Germany's other economic mainstay, contracted, the country could not export enough to pay for the raw materials and food it so desperately needed. Between 1929 and 1932 production was almost halved; thousands of small businesses went bankrupt; millions of people were thrown out of work.

The psychological effects of the depression were much greater in Germany than in the United States or the United Kingdom, even though the economic and social consequences were no less far-reaching. In Germany, coming on top of war, defeat and inflation, this last in a seemingly never-ending series of disasters was the last straw. The mood of the German people turned to one of utter discouragement and hopelessness, which was punctuated by periods

Above:
Hitler arrives at the party congress in Nuremberg, 1929.

of wild hope and a longing for something completely different. Astrology, numerology and clairvoyants flourished, as people sought anything that would restore meaning and order to their lives.

In the Reichstag, the coalition of parties that had governed the Republic since 1919 began to fall apart as each group of supporters—farmers, landowners, unionists, industrialists—lobbied for their own relief at the expense of everyone else. In July 1930 the new Chancellor, Dr Heinrich Brüning, dissolved the Reichstag and fixed new elections for September. By doing so this well-meaning man unknowingly signed the death warrant of German democracy.

Hitler knew little about economics and cared less, but he could read the mood of the people and see his opportunity. The sudden economic and social collapse justified all the Nazi diatribes

against parliamentary government; Hitler's dire prophesies had been fulfilled. Instinctively he understood Germany's needs and moved in to offer to meet them. The periods of apathy which had occasionally overtaken him in previous years disappeared—he was ready for the fray.

In the whirlwind campaign that followed, the Nazis used every propaganda trick they could think of to attract attention and win votes. The Nazi press blanketed the country with special campaign editions. Every city and village was plastered with posters; there were torchlight parades; Goebbels organized over 6000 meetings and Hitler delivered at least twenty major speeches in six weeks. The campaign was designed to appeal to a wide range of voters—unlike the Communists, whose appeal was limited to the working class. Hitler could

Strasser, spokesman for the left wing of the NSDAP. Otto's views, which were often directly contrary to Hitler's, appeared in the three National Socialist newspapers for which he was the leading editorial writer. The problem had not been serious as long as the NSDAP remained an obscure splinter party. But as the Nazis gained prominence it became more important to take a definite stand and present a united front. The breaking point was reached when Otto supported a metal workers' strike in Saxony, despite threats from Hitler, who was being pressured on the other side by Fritz Thyssen, head of the United Steel Works. On 21 May 1930 the two men met at the Hotel Sanssouci in Berlin along with Max Amann, Rudolf Hess and Otto's brother, Gregor Strasser. The heated debate that followed lasted through two meetings and over seven hours—accomplishing nothing except to expose the deep-seated differences that existed between them. Even an offer of a job as party propaganda chief left Otto unmoved.

Otto realized at the time that he and his fellow socialists could not stay in the NSDAP, especially since Hitler said he had decided to emulate Mussolini and work to gain the support of industrial leaders. He also saw that Hitler had no intention of ever tying himself down to a concrete program, since he could exercise control much more effectively if the only solid plank in the party platform was the Führer principle. For the time being, he did nothing.

For his part, Hitler also let the matter drop temporarily—until the end of June, when Otto published a pamphlet titled *Cushioned Ministerial Seats or Revolution* in which he accused Hitler of betraying the socialist cause. Hitler immediately sent Goebbels instructions for expelling Otto Strasser from the party. 'As long as I lead the National Socialist Party,' he wrote, 'it will not be a debating club for rootless men of letters or chaotic parlor Bolsheviks, but will remain ... a disciplined organization created not for doctrinaire foolishness or political boy scouts, but dedicated to fight for a future Germany in which class distinctions have been smashed.' By the beginning of July Goebbels had succeeded in forcing Otto to resign from the NSDAP with his followers—all 24 of them. Even his brother Gregor rejected him, calling his fight against the party 'pure madness.' His departure marked the end of all dispute over principles within the Nazi party, at least for the time being.

Another break in the campaign came when Hitler had to step in and end a mutiny in the ranks of the Berlin SA. Pfeffer had recently resigned and the men were becoming increasingly dissatisfied. They considered themselves more than just glorified bodyguards, and were tired of being injured and arrested in battles with the police and the Communists while the civilian leaders in Munich lived in luxury and comfort.

talk to the workers in Communist terms, and in fact the two parties even shared the same slogan, 'Freedom, Work and Bread!' He also offered the middle classes hope and self respect; the farmers relief; and students and intellectuals a brave, idealistic new world. The Nazis' actual program was sketchy, which caused many of their opponents to underestimate them; the Social Democrats, for example, concentrated on defeating the Communists. The Nazis' noise and energy made up for the lack of a comprehensive, specific program. Over and over again Hitler denounced the Reds, Marxism, the money barons and especially the 'system' that had lowered agricultural prices, skyrocketed unemployment and wiped out the savings of the middle class.

In the middle of all the furious campaigning, Hitler also found time to deal with Otto

Goebbels finally had to ask for help from Hitler and from Himmler's SS (the *Schutzstaffel* or guard detachment—a small select group of blackshirted young men, sworn to act as Hitler's personal guardians and to protect him with their lives). A few days later one SA troop raided the party's Berlin district headquarters on Hedemannstrasse which was guarded by an SS detachment, and it took a personal visit from the Führer and the promise that he would personally take command of the SA to quell the riot.

Even Hitler, who had secretly dreamed of winning a hundred Reichstag seats, was surprised when the final election results came in: the Nazis had won 6,371,000 votes—more than 18 percent of the total cast—which gave them 107 seats and made them the second largest party in parliament. The Communists were the only other party to increase their percentage of the total vote (from 10.6 to 13.1 percent), and the four center parties were reduced to only 72 seats.

If the Nazis were surprised at their victory, their opponents were shocked. They obviously had gravely miscalculated the mood of the pub-

Below:
A big meeting of the Nazi Party members at the Bürgerbräukeller, Munich in 1929. This building had been the scene of the Beer Hall Putsch in 1923.

lic, and there was much talk of the 'bitterness vote.' Foreign opinion, on the whole, was not that unfavorable. Only the French expressed major misgivings; in America the news was taken calmly, and several editors were of the opinion that it was the logical result of the harsh peace treaty and Germany's subsequent treatment at the hands of the victors. In England Lord Rothermere—for the first time but certainly not for the last—wrote that Hitler posed no threat; on the contrary, he was building a bulwark against Bolshevism and the Soviet campaign to destroy European civilization.

Putzi Hanfstängl, who had been in disgrace for the past year because of his outspokenness, was recalled to become the party's foreign press secretary. A few days later he accompanied Hitler to Leipzig where three young officers were standing trial for disseminating Nazi propaganda in the Army—where the NSDAP had been banned since 1927. Hitler appeared as witness for the defense, but did little to directly further their case. Instead, he used the witness box as a national platform to make the rather paradoxical announcement that he would come to power peacefully through the ballot box and that he would fight against the Treaty of Versailles even if he had to use illegal means to do so. By the time he was finished he had managed to reassure ordinary citizens, the revolutionaries within his own party and most important, the Army that each of their widely disparate desires would be fulfilled.

On 13 October the new Reichstag session began. The 107 Nazi deputies marched in wearing brown shirts, shouting, and answering the roll call with a raucous 'Present, Heil Hitler!' The other members sat, appalled by the sight of what one described as a 'noisy, shouting, uni-

Above:
Hitler (third row to the left) attends the inauguration of the rebuilding of the Barlow Palace on Briennerstrasse in Munich. The Barlow Palace was converted into Nazi Party headquarters in 1930; and was renamed the Brown House.

formed gang . . . with the faces of criminals and degenerates.' Outside the usual battles between the SA and the Communists continued, but with a new element, introduced by Goebbels: hundreds of stormtroopers in civilian clothes were smashing the windows of Jewish businesses. (Later Hitler claimed that this destruction had been undertaken by looters and Communist sympathizers, while the *Völkischer Beobachter* announced that in the Third Reich Jewish shop windows would be better protected than under the Marxist police.)

After the election people flocked to join the NSDAP, attracted—as always—by the smell of success; in the next two-and-a-half months party membership increased from almost 100,000 to 380,000. Neither Hitler not Goebbels thought much of the new recruits, or 'Septemberlings,' as Goebbels contemptuously dubbed them. They remembered too well the

Above:
Wilhelm Frick became the leader of the National Socialists in the Reichstag in 1932. He was Minister of the Interior in Hitler's Cabinet, a post he retained until 1943.

licity arrived Hitler's nephew, William Patrick Hitler, and his appearance was not an occasion for rejoicing. William Patrick was the son of Hitler's brother, Alois, Jr, and an Irish girl named Brigid Elizabeth Dowling; the two had been married in Dublin where Alois was working as a waiter, and he had subsequently deserted them in England. When mother and son read about Hitler's success they decided to capitalize on it by giving an interview to the press; the result was an immediate summons to Munich where a furious Hitler demanded they return and tell the British papers that they were really no relations at all. The two would continue to be an embarrassment for several years, intermittently making rather clumsy attempts to get money in return for their silence about the Führer's family background—a subject about which he was inordinately sensitive. Eventually, however, they emigrated to America, and William Patrick served in the US Navy during World War II. Soon after their first visit to Munich an article appeared in the New York *American* under the name of Alois Hitler Jr; it was a fanciful account of Hitler's (and Paula's) grim struggle against poverty and near-starvation in Vienna, and Hitler's later career as a house painter in Munich.

Politically, the SA continued to be a problem. Despite his promise, Hitler had never taken command of the organization, and at the beginning of 1931 the stormtroopers were still leaderless. Even recalling Röhm from South America and giving him a fairly free hand in organizing the more than 60,000 men failed to resolve their deep-rooted complaints. They still felt intensely loyal to Hitler himself, but the inequities in the party and his constant series of conflicting orders were upsetting to say the least.

The men were unhappy when, at the end of February 1931, Hitler forbade any more street fighting with the Communists and the Jews. The next month, when he agreed to abide by a government decree that all political rallies had to have advance police approval, open revolt broke out in the Berlin detachment, led by Captain Walter Stennes. It took the SS only 24 hours to quell the revolt proper, but it needed another visit from Hitler himself to bring real unity again to the SA. Stennes was relieved of his command and an SS man appointed in his place.

During the years 1931–32 five men—in addition to Hitler—controlled the fortunes of the NSDAP—Goebbels, Göring, Frick, Röhm and Strasser.

Dr Goebbels (as he was invariably called) was Propaganda Director and Gauleiter of Berlin. His biting tongue did not make him popular with the other lieutenants or the rank and file, and in his cleverness he was apt to overreach himself (there were rumors that he was at least

Above:
Josef Goebbels, Gauleiter of the Nazi Party in 'Red' Berlin addresses a gathering of the SA.

hordes of 'inflation recruits' in 1923 who had deserted the party at the first hint of trouble, and neither wanted the party to become 'weighed down with the corpses of a ruined bourgeoisie.' But many who joined the Nazis in the months immediately following the election were motivated by reasons other than the simple desire to be on the winning side. Albert Speer, for example, signed up early in 1931 partly because he had heard Hitler speak and had been attracted by him, but also because he saw there was no more middle ground between the Communists and the National Socialists and felt that he had to make a choice between them. His mother joined the party at about the same time after seeing a SA parade in Heidelberg; 'the sight of discipline in a time of chaos, the impression of energy in a time of universal hopelessness . . . won her over.'

But the victory brought some unpleasant consequences too. With the international pub-

partly behind the attempted SA revolt). But Hitler knew he could count on his absolute loyalty, while his energy and ability to come up with a multitude of ideas at a moment's notice made him very useful—as did his remarkable skill as a propagandist and rabble-rousing orator.

Göring, who had been cured of his drug addiction while he was living in Sweden, was ensconced in a luxurious apartment in Berlin, which he used as a home base while cultivating his wide range of acquaintances. He soon became Hitler's contact man, with general orders to make contact and confer with other groups and parties. In 1932 Hitler chose him to be President of the Reichstag, and from then on the President's House became the center for many of the plots and intrigues against the very body he ostensibly served.

Frick, a typical civil servant—dry and humor-

less—had been one of Hitler's protectors in the police department during the early 1920s. He was loyal, efficient, and useful in working with other government officials; in 1932 he became the Nazi party leader in the Reichstag.

Röhm's importance lay as much in his contacts with the Army as in his abilities as an organizer and leader of the SA. But attacks on his alleged homosexuality and favoritism were becoming increasingly embarrassing, and eventually threatened to turn into a party-wide issue.

Genial Gregor Strasser was the most popular leader in the party after Hitler, and if he had had more ambition he would have posed a serious threat to the Führer's authority. He and Goebbels had been bitter enemies ever since the latter deserted the left in 1926—a situation that quite suited Hitler, who frequently operated on the 'divide and conquer' principle when it came to his staff. As head of the Political Organiz-

ation, Strasser had great influence among the local leaders and branches.

There were others too, who would later gain great power in the Third Reich: Rudolf Hess, the Führer's private secretary; Martin Bormann, also a secretary; Heinrich Himmler, the ex-poultry farmer, who was gradually building up the SS; Max Amann, the party's publisher; Hans Frank, head of the legal division; Walther Darré, the Argentina-born agricultural expert; and Baldur von Schirach, leader of the Hitler Youth.

Hitler spent the first part of 1931 courting several powerful interest groups—the Army, the Church and big business. For example, early in the year he ordered the SA to stop their street fighting in return for the admission of party members to the Frontier Guard, and he even had Röhm announce that if Hitler became Chancellor the SA would become 'superfluous' and would be disbanded. He convinced General

Above:
From left to right: Hitler, Wilhelm Brückner, Dr Frick, Ernst Saukel and Konstantin Hierl watch the march past of the SA in Weimar, 1931.

Top:
Hitler and his staff visit Braunschweig in February 1931.

Above left:
Hitler and Viktor Lutze, one of the reliable SA leaders.

Groener, the Minister of Defense, that 'Pretty-boy Adolf [was] dripping with loyalty.'

Göring was sent to Rome to talk to leaders of the Catholic Church, who so far had been markedly unfriendly to the Nazis. Meanwhile, in his own speeches and interviews Hitler successfully projected an image of a mature, responsible, supporter of the state.

Using his own friends, as well as contacts made through Göring and financial journalist Walther Funk, Hitler made a serious attempt to win over the captains of heavy industry, most of whom had so far avoided him.

In the Reichstag, however, the Nazis used their power to complete the destruction of that already faltering institution. They utilized every means open to them, from arguing against any attempt at stabilization to unruly shouting and catcalls that harassed their opponents, in order to paralyze the working of the legislative body and reduce its prestige. In February 1931 they withdrew altogether, forsaking the closed forum of the Reichstag for public meetings where they had a far better chance to project a clear image and win followers.

The summer of 1931 saw the prelude to one of the greatest tragedies of Hitler's life. Geli Raubal, who was still living in the apartment on the Prinzregentenstrasse, was finding her uncle's tyranny increasingly oppressive. She was in an impossible position. Her uncle loved her desperately, was fiercely jealous, and was determined to keep her with him at any cost. But at the same time he was too repressed and too cautious to have a real affair with her, though he did not lack for female admirers away from home (especially, by this time, Eva Braun).

During the summer Geli was secretly engaged to Hitler's chauffer, Emil Maurice, and the two became lovers. Maurice claims that Hitler actually encouraged the alliance–but when the chauffer finally told him that the engagement was a fact Hitler flew into a rage and Maurice was fired on the spot.

By September Geli was in love again, this time with a young artist from Austria–and again Hitler forced her to break off the affair. In the middle of the month Geli announced that she was returning to Vienna, and set off for Berchtesgaden to visit her mother. When she arrived she found a message from Hitler asking her to return to Munich. She did so, only to find Hitler preparing to leave the city himself for a conference in Hamburg. He forbade her to leave the city while he was gone, which led–not unnaturally–to a blazing row which continued until the morning when he departed.

As Hitler and Hoffmann drove off toward Nuremburg in Hitler's Mercedes with the new chauffer, Julius Schreck, at the wheel, Hitler confessed to an uneasy feeling, which Hoffmann did his best to dispel. Meanwhile, Geli had found a note from Eva Braun in one of Hitler's

jacket pockets and was–if possible–even more angry and depressed. She locked herself in her room, leaving orders that she was not to be disturbed.

That night both Frau Reichert and her daughter were awakened by a dull sound they could not identify, but they ignored it and went back to sleep. The next day, though, when Geli still had not appeared, they became worried and called Max Amann and Franz Schwartz. The two men found a locksmith; when they entered the room they found Geli on the floor, shot through the heart, a 6.34-caliber Walther pistol by her side.

Hitler and Hoffmann had spent the night at the Deutscher Hof hotel in Nuremburg and were continuing on toward Hamburg when a car from the hotel caught up with them. Hess was on the line from Munich. Back they rushed to the hotel; through the open door of the telephone booth Hoffmann could hear Hitler cry 'Oh God, how awful! Hess, answer me–yes or no–is she still alive?'

By the time they had raced back to Munich, Geli's body had been removed from the apartment. Hitler fell into a deep depression and was unable to face the subsequent press coverage of the event, which mainly consisted of scurrilous innuendos. He fled to Adolf Müller's country home where he spent three days pacing up and down in his room, refusing to eat.

Finally they received word that Geli had been buried in the Central Cemetery in Vienna and Hitler–though he was risking arrest to do so–paid a visit to her grave. Later, at the apartment of Alfred Frauenfeld (the young Nazi Gauleiter of Vienna) he ate a good breakfast and began at last to talk–not about his niece's suicide, but about his (and Germany's) political future. On the way back to Munich he told Hoffmann, 'So, now let the struggle begin–the struggle which must and shall be crowned with success.'

A few days later he spoke to the Gauleiters' Conference in Hamburg with all his old power and brilliance. Once again, as at Pasewalk Hospital and Landsberg Prison, he had bounced back from deep depression to find a new sense of purpose and renewed energy. In fact from that day on he never ate meat. 'It is like eating a corpse,' he once remarked to Göring.

The Gauleiters' Conference, attended by the major SA leaders and Gauleiters, marked the successful conclusion of the party's re-organization; Hitler was left free to concentrate on national politics–at least for the time being. The period between autumn 1931 and 30 January 1933 thus saw a complicated series of political moves and countermoves that would end in his legal appointment as Chancellor. What Goebbels called the 'chess game for power' had begun.

Since the virtual disintegration of the legis-

lature in 1930 Brüning (and later his successor, Franz von Papen) was forced to govern by presidential decree. This mode of government necessarily placed most of the political power in the hands of a very small group of men surrounding Reich President Hindenburg: the Chancellor himself; Otto Meissner, head of the Presidential Chancery; General Wilhelm Groener, the Minister of Defense; and Groener's liaison man, General Kurt von Schleicher.

Schleicher, who had become close to President Hindenburg through a friendship with his son Oskar, was the *eminence grise* of the Republic— a cynical, wary, adept politician who preferred spinning webs of intrigue in the background to overt political activity. Convinced (along with others in the Cabinet) that parliamentary democracy was dead in Ger-

that in his opinion Hitler was an odd fellow who would never make a suitable Chancellor; the best he could hope for was to become Postmaster General.

But the erstwhile Bavarian corporal was used to being underestimated and for the next few months he remained quiet, devoting himself to building up his base of mass support and trying to get more money from the industrial establishment. He was aided in his efforts by continuing developments in Germany, where the depressed economy and constant political infighting had brought the country back to the brink of civil war. In contrast to Hitler's vitality, the

many, he set about establishing a strong presidential government. Hitler, with his mass following and efficient organization, could be an important prop to the government, Schleicher thought, if he could be tamed and his revolutionary ardor cooled.

For his part, Hitler was anxious to be drawn into the ring of power. A year after his great victory in 1930 he was no closer to gaining office than he had been before. Having already ruled out revolution as a viable means of attaining real power (though he was not averse to using the SA as a threat), and with so many political parties vying for position, his chances of ever getting a clear electoral majority were slim. Even another attempt at combining forces with Hugenberg and the Nationalists did not give him the votes he needed. So he turned to a third alternative and began a complicated series of negotiations with the President and his advisers—to convince them to take him into partnership and give him power directly.

His first contact with the power structure came on 10 October 1931, in the form of a meeting with President Hindenburg which had been organized by Schleicher. It was not a success. Facing the Old Gentleman—a majestic 6 foot 5 inches figure with a booming voice and impressive bearing, Hitler found himself nervous and ill at ease, despite moral support from Göring whom he had recalled from Sweden and the bedside of his dying wife to accompany him. He made the mistake of talking too much in an effort to impress the President and ended up by boring him. Later Hindenburg told Schleicher

aloof Brüning could offer little to the millions of Germans suffering from hunger, cold, lack of work and an all-pervading hopelessness. As a result, the NSDAP rapidly grew stronger; by the end of 1931 the membership had risen from 389,000 to more than 800,000.

On 27 January 1932 Hitler visited Dusseldorf, capital of Germany's steel industry, where Fritz Thyssen had arranged for him to address a meeting of the Industry Club. Most of the West German industrialists present had never met him, and did not like what they had heard. Hitler, dressed in a dark pin-stripe suit, was there specifically to break down their objections. His two-and-a-half-hour speech was delivered in a correct, rational manner, and made a great impression on the audience, who were soon at least partly convinced that he was in fact their defense against Communism and the trade unions, as well as their ally in the perpetuation of private enterprise. Still, in terms of money delivered, their support was not, nor was it to become for some time, as great as many historians have claimed. In fact, up to January 1933, total donations from industry probably only added up to about six million marks—this to a party with an annual budget of 70 to 90 million.

Left:
The elaborately staged marches and parades were designed to impress. The SA marches through Braunschweig square.

and alienating the radicals in his own party, or he could insist on an election and oppose Hindenburg himself. Gregor Strasser argued that the Nazis had nothing to gain from a hopeless attempt to defeat the gray-haired national idol at the polls, while a defeat could have disastrous effects on the party. Röhm and Goebbels, on the other hand, were convinced that it would be a mistake for Hitler to seem as if he was avoiding an opportunity to go to the nation, especially when by so doing he would be supporting the same man he had been bitterly attacking for months. Finally, after much vacillation, Hitler announced that he would not support the amendment.

Hindenburg, angry at the right-wing's opposition, announced his candidacy in mid-February. But Hitler did not make up his mind to run until 26 February, only two weeks before the election. His first step was to obtain German citizenship, which he accomplished in short order with help from the Nazi Ministry of the Interior in Braunschweig. On 27 February he made his formal announcement and, characteristically, flung himself headlong into the battle, all earlier doubts forgotten.

He immediately embarked on a tireless

Hindenburg's term of office as President of the Reich was due to expire in spring 1932 and the old soldier—who was 84, ill and tired—was looking forward to retirement. But Brüning, who wanted to buy time until the economy improved, prevailed upon him to agree to remain if his tenure could be extended another two years without an election. To do so would require a constitutional amendment; for this he needed the support of the Reichstag leadership, which put the Nazis in a key position. Early in January 1932, therefore, Brüning invited Hitler to Berlin where he promised that in return for Nazi support of the amendment, he would himself resign when the reparations issue was settled.

Below:
Hitler with members of the Reichsführer School, which trained SA leaders in 1932.

Hitler, faced with a difficult choice, withdrew to the Kaiserhof Hotel on Wilhelmstrasse to consider his options: he could either support the 'system,' consolidating Brüning's position

Left:
A faked picture (see the original page 53) which shows Hitler with Alfred Hugenberg. This was concocted in connection with the launching of the 'Harzburger Front,' a right-wing National Opposition grouping, founded in October 1931. Hitler had been reluctant to join and eventually parted company in the February 1932 elections.

speaking schedule, backbone of an inventive campaign developed, of course, by Goebbels. Bright red Nazi posters glared from every wall; movies of Hitler's and Goebbel's speeches were shown at night in public squares throughout the Reich; and Nazi speakers addressed thousands of meetings, large and small.

Hindenburg, on the other hand, ran a disorganized campaign, with his followers spending more time trying to refute the rumors that the Nazis were spreading than in attacking their policies. Hindenburg himself put forth very little effort; he made only one public appearance, three days before the election, and relied on the magic of his name and reputation to see him through.

As the day of the election, 13 March, wore on, it became obvious that Hindenburg was pulling ahead and many in Hitler's camp, including Goebbels, moved from confidence to depression. When all the votes were counted Hindenburg had won by more than seven million, but was still 350,000 short of an absolute majority. There would have to be a run-off between the leaders.

Without a break, Hitler prepared to start all over again. Goebbels soon recovered his nerve, and together the two led the uphill struggle. The contest was marked by more imaginative campaigning such as the 'Hitler over Germany' flight, when Hitler covered more than 20 towns throughout the country, from the Baltic to Bavaria, by plane.

In the second election Hindenburg gathered a comfortable 53 percent of the total vote (about 19,250,000), while by their energetic efforts the Nazis pushed their own share of the electorate up to about 13,500,000. They gained about 2,000,000 votes the second time around, compared with Hindenburg's gain of about 700,000 While the *Daily Telegraph* in London predicted the end of Adolf Hitler, the NSDAP propaganda machine turned without pause to upcoming

Below:
A slogan on a canal siding reads 'With Hitler against the armament mania of the World.'

state elections in Prussia, Bavaria, Anhalt, Württemburg and Hamburg. Again, their strenuous campaigning increased their vote in the various elections, but failed to gain them a majority in any of them.

Before Hitler could decide on his next move Brüning struck a blow for the government, issuing a decree that dissolved the SA, the SS, and their affiliate organizations. Though Röhm contemplated resisting the order (the SA alone was four times the size of the regular army), Hitler decided to obey it; 400,000 men took off their uniforms and disappeared from view. The organization, however, continued to function.

Brüning's action brought a storm of protest and abuse from the entire right wing and gave Schleicher the chance he had been waiting for. The general considered Brüning too weak to control the Nazis in the kind of government he wanted to establish—a right wing coalition that would include the National Socialists but not give them any real power. The army, he was sure, could easily control Hitler and his followers who were, in his opinion, 'only little children who had to be led by the hand.'

To this end, he met with Hitler and made a deal: if the Nazis would promise to support a new rightist government, he would see to it that the ban on the SA was lifted. Next he

turned his attention to Groener, the Minister of Defense, who had originally proposed the ban; with the backing of the Nazis in the Reichstag, he soon forced Groener's resignation.

He then began working to replace Brüning with his own man—Franz von Papen, a wealthy Prussian aristocrat and former member of the General Staff. It was not a difficult undertaking; the dour Brüning was not popular with either the people or—since he had served his purpose in the election—with Hindenburg. To lull Brüning's suspicions Hitler left Berlin at the beginning of May to devote himself to campaigning in the provincial elections in Oldenburg and Mecklenburg.

At the end of the month Schleicher's efforts bore fruit: Hindenburg asked Brüning to resign and appointed Papen in his place. Hitler was summoned to Berlin for another interview with the President, and agreed to support the new government. The change in leadership was immediately and extraordinarily unpopular, except with Hindenburg, who found the ex-cavalry officer the most compatible Chancellor he had ever had. In the Reichstag the Catholic Center Party, furious at Brüning's abrupt dismissal, withdrew their support; Hugenberg, angry at not being consulted beforehand, withdrew the support of the Nationalists; the Com-

munists and Social Democrats were, of course, in complete opposition. That left just the Nazis, who had given only vague promises of neutrality in return for the government's promise to dissolve the Reichstag and lift the ban on the SA and SS.

Only Hindenburg's personal authority and appeals to patriotism made it possible for Papen to form a cabinet at all, which was therefore composed entirely of men of his own sort—seven noblemen, two company directors and a general. The new Minister of Justice was Franz Gürtner, one of Hitler's staunchest protectors during the 1920s in Munich. The hostile popular reaction to the 'cabinet of barons' and the indifference with which that hostility was received demonstrated the absence of any remnants of democracy in the Republic—and also showed the extent to which the aristocratic ruling class had ignored the changing political realities of the twentieth century.

Papen fulfilled the first of his obligations on 4 June by dissolving the Reichstag and calling for a new election on 31 July, but postponed lifting the ban on the SA for almost two weeks. Hitler, who was naturally anxious to dissociate the Nazis from the unpopular government, was forced to restrain himself—but after 16 June, virtual civil war erupted in the streets. In many cases, the army had to step in to stop the furious street battles; between the date the ban was lifted and 20 July there were 500 clashes in Prussia alone, resulting in 99 dead and 1125 wounded.

On 20 July Papen stretched the powers of the Presidential decree to the limit, by issuing an emergency order deposing Prussian Prime Minister, Braun, and Minister of the Interior, Severing, on the grounds that they could not control the Communists in Prussia. By this grand gesture of authoritarianism he hoped not only to placate the Nazis, but also to improve his own prestige and strengthen the position of his own party. What happened, of course, was that democracy and constitutional government were further discredited in the public mind, while extremism seemed the only means of achieving decisive action—helping both the Nazis and the Communists.

The by now well-seasoned and efficient Nazi electioneering machine was rolled out once more for the July election; far from being tired after all the campaigns of the past five months, the workers were, if possible, even more energetic and determined. As a result of their efforts, 31 July saw an overwhelming victory for the NSDAP, which won 230 seats with 13,745,000 votes. Though they were still without a clear majority (they had 37 percent of the total vote), the Nazis were far and away the most powerful party in the Reichstag. The Social Democrats were reduced to 133 seats and the Communists increased their representation

Bottom:
Hitler leaves, following his first interview with Hindenburg, the President of the Republic. The interview, which took place on 13 August 1932, was supposed to put Hitler in his place and although the reports on the meeting damaged Hitler's reputation their effect was not long-lasting.

by 12, to 89 members. The other middle-class parties, with the sole exception of the Catholic Center Party, were overwhelmed.

It is interesting to note that anti-Semitism was not an issue in any of the 1932 campaigns. If Hitler did not hide his hatred of Jews, neither did he dwell on it, and most voters seemed willing to ignore it as long as it was kept under control. Many Germans, too, objected—however mildly — to the apparent Jewish monopoly of the legal, retail clothing and entertainment fields. For their part, many Jews were inclined to discount Hitler's anti-Semi-

tism and even to overlook their friends' involvement with the NSDAP. They were so well integrated into the German economy and—except for a few exclusive clubs and hotels—into German society that they failed to recognize the depth and extent of Hitler's obsession and the degree to which he would obtain public acquiescence to his policies. For many it would prove to be a fatal miscalculation.

On 2 August Hitler met with other party leaders at Tegernsee, near Munich. Flushed with victory, the Führer was inclined to demand all or nothing. He rejected the notion of a

Right:
Hitler attends a Nazi Youth rally in Potsdam on 2 October 1932. The review began at 1100 hours and continued until 1800 hours.

Far right:
From left to right: Kurt von Ulrich, Edmund Heines, Heinrich Himmler, General Ritter von Epp, Ernst Röhm and Wolf Heinrich von Helldorf in 1932.

coalition with the Center Party, which would have given him a majority in parliament, because it would mean that he had to share power with a group he did not control.

On 5 August he met with Schleicher and presented his demands: the Chancellorship for himself and Nazi appointments to the Ministries of the Interior, Justice, Agriculture and Air Transport. He also insisted on forming a Ministry of Popular Enlightenment and Propaganda, to be headed by Goebbels, as well as on the appointment of Nazis as Prussian Prime Minister and Minister of the Interior. Schleicher was encouraging; Hitler left the meeting certain that he had attained power at last, and returned to Berchtesgaden to await the General's call.

But the call did not come. Papen was not anxious to resign his post: he argued that Hitler's failure to win an absolute majority, along with the continued division of the Reichstag, justified the continuance of the Presidential Cabinet system. Hindenburg agreed. He was loath to see his congenial Chancellor replaced by a Bohemian corporal, and was also angry that Hitler had broken his promise to support the current government. Both Hindenburg and Papan, along with Schleicher, felt that the Nazis' popularity had peaked and they soon would begin losing votes; they could therefore hold out for a deal on their own terms, not Hitler's. The government was also alarmed by the SA who, in jubilation over their victory, were threatening to get out of hand. Outbreaks of violence flared up throughout the country, especially in East Prussia and Silesia, where on 9 August a Communist named Pietrzuch was dragged from his bed and kicked to death in front of his mother. This sort of behavior could not help but make people ask themselves whether such a group was fit to have power.

By 11 August Hitler, tired of waiting, returned to Berlin. When he met again with Schleicher and Papen–at noon on 13 August– he was still in an all-or-nothing mood; when Schleicher offered him only the Vice-Chancellorship and the Prussian Ministry of the Interior he lost his temper and began raging uncontrollably about attacking Marxists in the streets and of letting the SA loose on the city. Even Papen's promise that he would eventually resign in Hitler's favor failed to calm him down. Finally he stormed out, still furious, and retired to Goebbels' apartment to nurse his frustration and disappointment.

At three that afternoon Papen's secretary called, summoning him to a meeting with the President. Though inclined at first to refuse, he finally agreed to go and found himself, still angry and shaken, facing the old soldier. Hindenburg's manner was cold and formal. He wanted to tell Hitler that while he would not appoint him to any really responsible post, he would make one

more appeal to his patriotism and ask him to support Papen's government. When Hitler categorically refused Hindenburg ended the interview with a humiliating lecture, from field marshal to corporal, on how he was shirking his duty to the Fatherland.

The snub did nothing to improve Hitler's temper, but he did retain enough presence of mind before retiring to Berchtesgaden to call off the SA–who were clamoring for action–and send them on a two-week leave.

At the opening session of the Reichstag and for several days thereafter, the Nazi deputies surprised everyone with their good behavior, as they sat silently listening to their opponents' speeches and docilely voting in the election of parliamentary officers. Their co-operation was rewarded on 30 August when, with Catholic Center Party support, Göring was elected President of the Reichstag. It was a worrying development for Schleicher and Papen–between them the two parties commanded an absolute majority in the legislature.

On 12 September Göring took the chair as the Reichstag convened for its first working session. The Communists almost immediately

Below:
Hitler attends an election meeting held in the Hotel Kaiserdorf in Berlin during the July elections 1932.

Below:
Hitler attends an election meeting held in the Hotel Kaiserdorf in Berlin during the July elections 1932.

moved for a vote of no confidence in the Papen government; when no one objected, shouting broke out in the hall, and Papen rushed out to get Hindenburg's signature on a document of dissolution which he had already drawn up. A few minutes later he returned with the order and tried to get Göring's attention. When he failed to do so he jumped up, waving the bit of paper; Göring, smiling, looked in another direction. White with anger, Papen stalked up and slapped the document down on the desk. Göring still ignored him and ordered the vote to proceed. As Papen and his ministers marched out, the Reichstag voted 513–32 against the government.

worn out and jaded. Money, after all the previous battles, was in very short supply; more support was withdrawn by the business community after the Nazis came out in support of a transport strike in Berlin.

In the middle of the sluggish campaign Hitler's personal life received another jolt. As political tensions mounted Eva Braun had become increasingly despondent over his lack of attention—especially when newspaper pictures depicted him at party functions surrounded by other women. On 1 November she made the first of two suicide attempts, shooting herself in the neck. Luckily she was discovered in time, and from then on became Hitler's constant companion during his leisure hours. Hoffmann insists that Hitler was motivated more by fear of scandal than by affection; it is hard to believe, however, that he was not flattered by her action or that he did not rather enjoy the feeling of responsibility her dependence gave him. Her blind, unthinking loyalty was just the quality he valued in his most trusted lieutenants, and her willingness to accept whatever treatment he cared to mete out made her the perfect mistress for an aspiring, self-centered political leader.

The results of the election were all Papen had hoped for: the Nazis lost two million votes, reducing their percentage of the total from 37.3 to 33.1 and their number of deputies to 196. The Nationalists, who had backed the government, gained a million votes and 15 seats for a total of 52, while the Communists came out with 11 more deputies than they had had previously—both, in other words, making significant gains at the Nazis' expense.

Papen was jubilant at the Nazi defeat and convinced that the NSDAP's appeal was on the wane; now, if Hitler wanted power, he would have to deal with the government on its terms,

Papen, of course, claimed that the vote had no validity, since the Reichstag had been dissolved before it was taken, while Göring perversely ruled that a Chancellor who had already been voted out of office could not dissolve anything. But all that was by the way. Everyone really knew that new national elections had to be held. In the meantime Papen had been made to look foolish; public confidence in the Reichstag had been undermined still further; it had been again demonstrated that most Germans opposed Hindenburg's presidential government; and the Nazis were shown to be willing to join even the Communists, if necessary, to achieve its downfall.

The new election was set for 6 November—the fifth major electoral contest since March of that year. For the Nazis it would be the most difficult yet. The people were tired of political campaigns and candidates' speeches, and even the most indefatigable party workers were

Above:
Hitler campaigning during the November elections in 1932. Hitler loved to be photographed with children. On his left is his bodyguard Sepp Dietrich and on his right is Magda Goebbels.

Right:
Eva Braun, Hitler's official girlfriend. In November 1932, when she was 21, she tried to kill herself probably because she wanted to receive more of Hitler's attention.

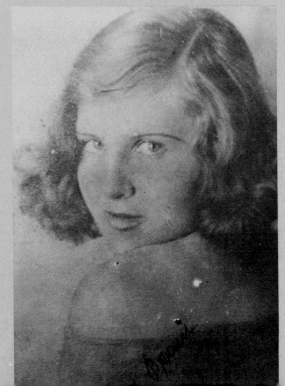

not his own. Though still badly outnumbered in the Reichstag, he confidently approached Hitler for support—only to be told in no uncertain terms that the Nazi leader had learned his lesson three months before; there was no way he would let himself in for a repetition of the events of 13 August. An official letter on 13 November brought a response that was little better—after three days Hitler replied by setting so many conditions on his co-operation that there was obviously no hope of coming to an understanding.

Lack of support did not bother Papen in the least; he was quite willing to establish a virtual dictatorship and rule by force. But Schleicher had other ideas. He was annoyed by Papen's unexpected demonstrations of independence and his influence over the President, and saw the Chancellor's personal vendetta with Hitler as a roadblock to any sort of national government. Noting the increased Communist vote and the recent Nazi-Communist co-operation, Schleicher saw the prospect of a civil war with both Nazis and Communists on the same side as a very real one. He decided Papen's usefulness had come to an end.

Under great pressure from Schleicher and the Cabinet Papen resigned, certain that the deadlock could not be resolved. He was correct. In a meeting on 19 November Hindenburg offered Hitler two choices: the Chancellorship if he could establish a working majority through a coalition in the Reichstag; or the Vice-Chancellorship under Papen in another Presidential cabinet. It sounded very nice, but they were really non-choices. Hitler could not get a working majority in the legislature, nor would he play second fiddle to Papen; after a long correspondence between Hitler and Hindenburg's State Secretary, Meissner, the President did what he had wanted to do all along. On 1 December he reappointed Papen as Reich Chancellor. As Papen and Schleicher left that meeting, Schleicher turned to the Chancellor and repeated the famous remark made to Luther as he was departing for the Diet of Worms: 'Little monk, little monk, you have chosen a difficult path.'

The very next day the slippery general showed Papen just how difficult that path would be: at 0900 Schleicher informed a Cabinet meeting that any attempt to form a government would certainly result in civil war—and that the army could not ensure law and order. Finding himself suddenly deprived of army support, Papen hurried to Hindenburg, hoping that the President would fire Schleicher as Minister of Defense. Instead, the stout old man, tears running down his cheeks, told him, 'You will not think much of me if I change my mind. But I am too old to accept the responsibility for a civil war . . . I must withdraw the task with which I charged you last night.'

Above:
Hitler and Göring arrive at the Tempelhof Airport in Berlin following a whistlestop tour of Germany during the fifth and last election campaign of 1932.

Schleicher took office on 2 December and was finally forced to come out from behind the scenes and publicly accept responsibility for his policies. He did so at the worst possible moment, when his own credit with Hindenburg was used up, when virtually no one in government trusted him, when the depression was at its height, and the Weimar Republic on the wane. Goebbels wrote in his diary, 'Schleicher is named Chancellor. He won't last long.'

One of the new Chancellor's first acts was to offer to make Gregor Strasser Vice-Chancellor and Prime Minister of Prussia; if the Nazis would not join his government, then he would try to split the party by luring away their number-two man. For his part, Strasser's personal loyalty to Hitler never wavered. But at the same time he felt that under the undue influence of Goebbels and Göring, whom he despised, the party had reached a dead end. The money was gone, the more radical members

were defecting to the Communists, and on top of it all the Nazi vote in the provincial elections on 3 December in Thuringia had been cut by 40 percent. He was sure that the only way to keep the party intact was to abandon Hitler's all-or-nothing policy and come to terms with the government.

On 5 December the party leaders met in a stormy session at the Kaiserhof in Berlin. Strasser, backed by Frick (leader of the Nazi deputies in the Reichstag), begged Hitler to take the Vice-Chancellorship for himself and at least 'tolerate' the government. Göring and Goebbels, however, strenuously opposed him, and Hitler eventually came down on their side. In addition to agreeing with their arguments, he had already been informed about Strasser's meetings with Schleicher, and felt betrayed.

Two days later Hitler and Strasser met again at the Kaiserhof and this time quarreled bitterly. Hitler openly accused Strasser of treason—a charge Strasser strongly denied before he stormed out, too furious to speak further. The next morning, 8 December, he wrote to the Führer resigning all his party offices, but asking all other party officials to stay at their posts. Then he waited by the telephone for a call from the Kaiserhof; he had left the door open for a reconciliation by not giving up his seat in the Reichstag or revoking his party membership. When no call came, however, he packed his bags, spent the afternoon drinking beer with a friend, and caught the night train to Munich.

As Goebbels describes it, the letter fell on the Kaiserhof 'like a bombshell.' There was a real danger that the party would fall apart. The leaders' mood was not lightened by a telephone call at two that morning from Robert Ley, the Gauleiter in Cologne, who reported increasing unrest at the local level. Finally Hitler decided to

make up with Strasser after all—but the man was nowhere to be found. He had stopped in Munich just long enough to pick up his family, and had taken them for a vacation in Italy.

Strasser's abrupt departure gave Hitler the opportunity he needed. He himself took over the Political Organization, which had been under Strasser's control. Ley was installed as his chief of staff, and Hess was made chief of a political secretariat to counterbalance the power of other leaders. To complete the decentralization, the former subdivisions of agriculture and education were made into independent departments led by Darré and Goebbels respectively.

Next, Hitler called all party leaders to Berlin where Strasser's old allies were required to take a public oath of loyalty. He had not completely solved the problem; the dissatisfaction and complaining continued and the money situation grew desperate (SA men were even sent onto the streets with canisters, asking pedestrians to give a little something 'for the wicked Nazis'). But he had held the party together against all odds and would continue to do so, still supported by his overwhelming conviction that this latest problem was only a prelude to victory.

Schleicher soon found the business of governing more difficult than he had expected. He had a good program, but could not implement it. His overtures to labor were met with suspicion from the Social Democrats and alienated big business. In a similar manner he managed to antagonize practically every party in the country. But despite all the evidence he remained optimistic, thinking that his opponents were in no position to combine against him. He had not reckoned with Franz von Papen.

On 4 January 1933 Papen arranged a meeting with Hitler through the good offices of Baron Kurt von Schröder, a Cologne banker and active Nazi supporter. The meeting was held in Schröder's home under what were supposed to be conditions of strictest secrecy. After some jockeying for position the two came to an agreement on principle. Hitler would head the government, while several Papen men would be made ministers on condition that they agreed to co-operate in removing Social Democrats, Communists and Jews from leading positions in the nation. Hitler also learned that Schleicher had not been granted the power to dissolve the Reichstag—a valuable piece of information, since it meant that the Nazis and Communists could combine to defeat him whenever they wanted. Further, Schröder agreed to mobilize industrialists and bankers to help the NSDAP solve their financial problems; within a few weeks the party was solvent again.

Schleicher had lost none of his talent for spying and intrigue; next morning the Berlin papers carried news of the 'secret' meeting on their front pages, and Papen received a summons from the President to come and explain himself. But Hindenburg, far from being angry, listened to Papen's plans for softening Hitler up and ended by giving him authority to continue the negotiations; he was still too fond of his 'young friend' to believe him capable of deception. He even told his aide Otto von Meissner not to mention Papen's orders outside the office—in effect, the President had joined the plot against his own Chancellor. Schleicher, who of course found out about the conversation, made matters worse by overreacting and declaring war on the large landowners—of whom Hindenburg was one. His proposals to reduce agricultural shelters and threats to expose the scandal of the *Osthilfe* (Eastern Relief) loans (which had lined the pockets of hundreds of the oldest Junker families) made him enemies not only among the landowners, but among many in the military establishment as well.

Hitler, meanwhile, was throwing everything he had into the provincial elections in the tiny state of Lippe, staging lavish demonstrations and using all his best speakers. He himself spoke eighteen times. The election offered him an opportunity to improve his bargaining power

with Papen. From the very beginning of the campaign, he kept repeating that Lippe was a decisive test. After he had said it often enough, people began to believe it: not only his own party members, not only the voters in Lippe itself, but the country at large and even most government leaders waited to see how 100,000 voters were going to decide the fate of some 68 million people.

When the votes from the 15 January election were counted, the Nazis had received 39.5 percent of the total. While it was their first gain since the previous July, it was not as great a percentage as they had received at that time. In fact, the democratic parties together gained more than the Nazis; in terms of the effort that had been put into the campaign the success was not that outstanding. Hitler, however, touted the results as proof that the party had regained its irresistible impetus and his view was accepted almost without exception.

The Lippe elections gave Hitler enough confidence to finally make the break with Strasser, who had returned from his vacation in Italy and had recently been negotiating again with Schleicher. Strasser was no more prepared for a showdown, however, than he had been in

Below:
In the foreground from left to right: Gregor Strasser, Hitler and Dr Frick. This is the picture of the last meeting which Strasser took part in. He resigned from the positions he held in the party on 8 December 1932. Strasser had been at odds with Hitler's leadership of the party since the mid-1920s and the break finally came because Strasser had tried to split the party and join the Schliecher government.

December; although he could have gathered at least some support from within the party he gave up without a fight, resigned his seat in the Reichstag, and drove back to Munich.

The greatest remaining obstacle to Hitler's Chancellorship was Oskar von Hindenburg, the President's son. Papen suggested he at least meet Hitler, and at length a confidential meeting was arranged at the luxurious home belonging to Joachim von Ribbentrop – Papen's friend and an ardent Nazi supporter. Elaborate precautions were taken to ensure secrecy. Oskar and State Secretary Meissner made an appearance at the opera and slipped out after the intermission to throw Schleicher's spies off the track, while Papen, Hitler, Göring and Frick all arrived separately. Soon after everyone had gathered Hitler drew Oskar off into a separate room. When the two returned after about an hour Oskar had pledged allegiance to the Führer. No one knows what was said during that meeting, but from subsequent events it seems likely that Hitler used a combination of flattery, threats and bribes to obtain his co-operation. After supper the members of the party went their separate ways as furtively as they had come. But Schleicher's ubiquitous spy network had not let him down. First thing next morning Meissner had a telephone call from the Chancellor: 'How did you enjoy last night's supper of peas and bacon?'

Schleicher knew that he must act quickly if he was not to be overthrown by the forces combining against him. He tried to get Hindenburg to agree to dissolve the Reichstag and rule by decree. Hindenburg refused, and when word of the plan leaked out – as it was bound to – Schleicher was more unpopular than ever. Then, when he attempted to redeem himself with the Social Democrats and the Communists, he alienated Hugenberg and the Nationalists, who promptly went over to the Papen-Hitler camp.

Hitler returned to Berlin on 27 January, but by that time the web of intrigue was so complicated and counterproductive that he became frustrated and decided to leave again. He did, however, finally agree to let Ribbentrop talk to Papen one more time, and somehow Ribbentrop managed to convince Papen that making Hitler Chancellor was absolutely the only way out of an untenable situation; right up to that point Papen had been hoping to arrange for Hitler to become Vice-Chancellor in his government.

On the morning of the 28th Papen saw Hindenburg and argued that a government under Hitler was the only solution. Although the old man disliked 'that Bohemian corporal' as much as ever, the additional pressure from his son made him more receptive to the idea. Schleicher arrived sometime later, having admitted that since he could neither form a majority in the Reichstag nor get permission to dissolve it, he was finished. The resignation he bitterly offered was accepted without further ado.

At noon that same day the President sent Papen to talk to Hitler about forming a government—but only on the condition that Papen be Vice-Chancellor and that General Werner von Blomberg be named Minister of Defense. On Sunday, 29 January, Hitler agreed—with the new stipulation that a general election be held as soon as possible and that an

enabling act be passed giving him more power than any Kaiser had ever held. By early afternoon Papen was back with Hindenburg, calming the Old Gentleman's fears about a new election by repeating Hitler's promise that they would be the *last* elections. Neither Hindenburg nor Papen quite grasped the implication of that promise.

That afternoon and evening rumors of a military coup (spread by Schleicher) raced through the capital, causing a considerable amount of panic and confusion. They came to nothing, however, and early the next morning the leaders of what would become the new government met at Papen's house, next door to Hindenburg's residence. At the last minute the whole carefully fabricated structure nearly fell apart when Hugenberg balked at the idea of an election. A bitter argument broke out and con-

tinued as the group crossed the snow-covered garden and entered the anteroom of the President's office. Even Hitler's powers of persuasion failed to dent Hugenberg's obstinate front. Finally Meissner appeared, watch in hand, and informed them that they were fifteen minutes late for their appointment; the President would not wait much longer. Respect for Hindenburg succeeded where argument had failed. Hugenberg reluctantly agreed to support the government and the men entered the President's chambers.

The swearing-in ceremony was conducted hastily and with little formality. Hindenburg was still angry at being kept waiting. A few minutes after he had entered, on 30 January 1933, the former Vienna tramp, a corporal from World War I and revolutionary fanatic walked out of Hindenburg's office as Chancellor of Germany.

Above:
The making of a legend: Hitler visits the grave of Horst Wessel on 22 January 1933. Wessel was an SA youth leader in Berlin who wrote *Die Fahne Hoch*. He was killed by the pimp of the woman he had had an affair with. His story was made into a film *Hans Westmar* but the sordid details of his death were left out.

IV Internal Germany 1933-39

Right:
Hitler and his new Cabinet pose in the Reichs Chancellor Palace in Wilhelmstrasse at 1830 on 30 January 1933. Sitting: Göring, Hitler and von Papen. Standing: Schwerin-Krosigk (immediately behind Göring), Frick, Blomberg and Hugenberg.

Right:
The torch-lit parade before the Brandenburg Gate on 30 January 1933.

Far right:
The Marshal and the Corporal, Hitler and Hindenburg pay their respects at the Tannenberg Memorial. Hindenburg, the World War I hero, despised the Bohemian corporal.

The evening of 30 January was a tour de force for Goebbels who managed, almost on the spur of the moment, to organize a night of intoxicating pageantry. As darkness began to fall every SS and SA stormtrooper for miles around—25,000 men—gathered at the Tiergarten; carrying torches and singing, they marched down Wilhelmstrasse for hours while crowds cheered the disciplined columns on their way, almost hypnotized by the steady beat of drums and the flare of torches in the clear, cold air.

Liberals may have been dismayed and foreign observers filled with foreboding at Hitler's ascension to the Chancellorship; the average German citizen, who felt that anything had to be better than the chaos of the previous year, was conscious only of being caught up in the uncanny excitement and happiness of a new beginning. Before he went to bed Goebbels expressed that mood in his diary: 'It is almost like a dream . . . a fairy tale . . . the new Reich has been born.'

Papen was happy too, but for other reasons. As he saw it, he had succeeded where Schleicher had failed. He had made Hitler a puppet Chancellor with a cabinet in which the Nazis were outnumbered eight to three by experienced conservatives. He thought he had Hitler firmly boxed in; with his own special relationship with Hindenburg and supporters in key positions in the cabinet, he predicted that 'within two months we will have pushed Hitler so far into a corner that he'll squeak.'

But Hitler, as Papen and his followers would have realized had they been able to see beyond their own complacent prejudices, had no intention of allowing himself to be boxed in anywhere, by anyone. He had risen to his present position because his opponents (63 per-

cent of the electorate) had been unable to combine against him; he would continue to succeed for the same reason. His ruthless, singleminded pursuit of a clearly defined goal gave him an immense advantage over the opposition, who had no real values or goals beyond a vague desire to restore some sort of authoritarian government.

To obtain a working majority in the Reichstag, the new National Socialist/Nationalist government had to bring the Catholic Center Party into their coalition. On the day after his appointment, therefore, Hitler met with Monsignor Kaas—ostensibly to discuss the partnership. But the Führer was careful to see that the negotiations would break down before they were ever really begun; he was then able to return to his colleagues and report that, since no agreement could be reached, the only course left open was to dissolve parliament and hold

new elections. On Papen's advice Hindenburg signed a dissolution order and set new elections for 5 March. Hugenberg, the only one who had clearly seen Hitler's trap, reluctantly agreed to go along after receiving many solemn promises of loyalty from the new Chancellor.

While Goebbels prepared for the elections, which he intended to make a 'masterpiece of propaganda,' Hitler took the first step toward making his peace with the other powerful interest groups in Germany. Four days after he became Chancellor he met with leaders of the armed forces at a dinner arranged by the new Minister of Defense, General von Blomberg. After dinner he told his listeners what they wanted to hear: rearmament was of primary importance to the New Germany, to be followed by conquest in the East. The Army would

Top:
Part of the celebration of the 'Day of Potsdam' was a night at the opera. From left to right: Göring, Blomberg, Hitler, Hindenburg, Papen and Admiral Räder.

Above:
Dr Hjalmar Schacht was appointed President of the Reichsbank by Hitler in 1933 and Minister of Economics in 1935. He is generally considered to have been the architect of Germany's economic recovery.

remain the sole bearer of arms in the country, and their structure would not be tampered with; they were not to worry any more about unrest at home, but should turn all their energies to the main objective—training for the defense of the Fatherland. Some of the generals felt nervous at his talk of aggression; others felt he was trying to bribe them. But though reactions to his speech were mixed, he did manage to win several new adherents and to reassure several others. Most were inclined to accept him out of respect for Hindenburg.

On 20 February he turned his attention to a second interest group. Göring invited some 20 to 25 representatives of industry—including Krupp von Bohlen, Bosch and Schnitzler of I G Farben, and Vögler of the United Steel works—to a party at the Reichstag President's Palace. Again, Hitler told the assembly exactly what they wanted to hear: he would eliminate Marxism and begin rebuilding the Army (rearmament being of special interest, especially to firms like I G Farben and United Steel). Goebbels, who rose next, stressed the need for 'financial sacrifices,' justified on the grounds that 'the election on 5 March will surely be the last one for the next ten years.' The enthusiasm generated among the businessmen by the prospect of no elections, the end of democracy, and the beginning of rearmament was so great that Dr Schacht collected 3,000,000 marks before the end of the evening.

Meanwhile, Hitler began a systematic campaign to paralyze the other political parties. Using the emergency powers of the Constitution, and backed by Papen and his colleagues in the cabinet, he issued a decree controlling political meetings and restricting the press—for the 'protection of the people.'

Anyone foolish enough to believe that the jovial Göring had been relegated to an unimportant post as Prussian Minister of the

Interior was soon disillusioned. Moving with consummate energy and ruthlessness he completely ignored Papen (the Prime Minister of Prussia and his titular superior) and began a purge of the entire Prussian administration. Hundreds of republican officials were removed and replaced by Nazis, many of them SS or SA leaders; the police were ordered to avoid showing hostility to the SS and SA at all costs, but to show no mercy to 'enemies of the state'; he began building up the *Geheime Staatspolizei* (Secret State Police, or *Gestapo*) at an accelerated pace. On 22 February an auxiliary volunteer police force of 50,000 men was established. Since about 40,000 of them came from the ranks of the SA and the SS, the effect was to give free rein to the Nazi terrorist gangs. Lest it seem that events in one state are of minor importance, it should be remembered that the administration of Prussia controlled two-thirds of Germany. Göring's role during 1933–34 was one of the major reasons for Hitler's success.

The major Nazi effort during the pre-election period was directed against the Communists. They had called for a general strike and demonstration when Hitler was appointed; Göring had responded by banning all Communist meetings in Prussia, and a state of subdued civil war began in the form of innumerable street battles between the Reds and the SA (and police). On 24 February police raided Karl Liebknecht Haus, the Communist headquarters in Berlin; next day the official press and radio releases reported uncovering 'tons of treasonable material' including plans for a Communist revolution–which, however, were never published.

On 27 February the Nazi campaign to discredit the Communists received a boost from what now seems to have probably been an unexpected source. On that evening a 24-year-old Dutchman named Marinus van der Lubbe, a member of a splinter Communist organization, bought four packages of firelighters and broke into the Reichstag. At 2130 a student on his way home heard breaking glass and saw a figure inside the building; by the time the fire brigade arrived, just before ten, the Session Chamber was in flames. Hanfstängl, who had an apartment across the street, was sick in bed. When he saw the fire he telephoned Goebbel's apartment, where a party for Hitler was in progress–but Goebbels thought the story was a rather bad joke, and would not even mention it to the Führer. Later, however, he had second thoughts, made a few phone calls, and finally informed Hitler, who slapped his thigh in glee and exclaimed, 'Now I have them!' Clambering into a car, the two raced at top speed to the Reichstag, where they found a puffing, excited Göring already shouting about a 'Communist crime against the government.'

The Communists vehemently denied any

connection with the fire, and no one will ever really know whether van der Lubbe was a dupe of the Nazis or if he was acting on his own; Herr Fritz Tobias' exhaustive investigation in 1955, which was published in *Der Spiegel* in 1959, tends to support the latter view.

Whoever started the Reichstag fire, Hitler certainly was the beneficiary. Some 4000 arrests were made that night, including not only Communists, but many others (mainly Social Democrats) whom the Nazis also disliked. The specter of Communist revolution was very real to ordinary people, who were thrown into a panic by the supposed threat. The very next day, 28 February, Hitler and Papen persuaded a still-stunned Hindenburg to sign a decree titled 'For the Protection of the People and the State,' suspending all constitutional individual and civil liberties–freedom of speech, freedom of the press, the right to privacy, freedom of assemblage and the inviolability of private property. It also gave the central government power to assume complete control of state governments when necessary, and made a number of crimes including 'serious disturbances of the peace' punishable by death.

Though Hitler could now do virtually as he pleased, he was clever enough to avoid an outright ban on the Communist Party, so that the working-class vote would continue to be split between the Communists and the Social Democrats. The National Socialist election campaign was the biggest propaganda effort yet, and this time it was backed by all the resources of the state. At mass rallies, at torchlight parades, on radio, and in the newspapers, the German people were alternately lured by promises of the utopian Germany to come and threatened with horror stories of imminent revolution; meanwhile, Hitler refused to discuss, or even outline a substantive program.

On 5 March Germany, with almost 90 percent of the electorate voting, still refused to grant the majority Hitler so badly wanted. While the National Socialists led the voting with 17,277,180 votes, it still came to only 44 percent of the total. The Social Democrats maintained their position as the second largest party with 7,181,629 votes; the Communists obtained 4,848,058—a loss of only 1,000,000—and the Center Party actually increased their total from 4,230,600 to 4,424,900. The Nationalist Party of Papen and Hugenberg gained only 180,000 for a total of 3,136,800—or 8 percent.

Hitler controlled 288 Nazi seats in the new Reichstag; with the 52 Nationalist seats he had a majority of sixteen. He could carry on affairs of state with Nationalist help, but he was short of the two-thirds majority he would need to amend the constitution and establish a legal dictatorship.

Immediately after the election, which the National Socialists chose to tout as a great victory, the SA took to the streets. All over Germany they besieged governments and forced resignations—in Hamburg, Bremen, Lübeck, the Free Cities, Hesse, Baden, Württemberg, Saxony and eventually, on 9 March, even in Bavaria. Hitler was pleased at first, but was not as happy when the orgy of violence showed no sign of abating. It was not that he had any objections to violence as a tool, but he did not approve of undisciplined and directionless applications.

Der Reichstag brennt!

On 13 March Hindenburg signed a document creating the Ministry for the People's Enlightenment and Propaganda, to be run by Josef Goebbels. The new Minister's first job was to organize the opening of the first Reichstag of the Third Reich. With his usual acumen, he chose the Potsdam Garrison Church for the ceremony—a site which contained the tomb of Frederick the Great and was rich in the Prussian military tradition to which Hitler considered himself heir. Together he and Hitler planned every detail of the script, from the gun salutes and the order of the marching columns, to the child with a handful of flowers standing beside the road.

The ceremony, on 21 March, was brief and dignified. Hindenburg, an imposing figure dressed in the field-gray uniform of a Prussian Field Marshal, opened the proceedings, which ended when the old man placed wreaths on the tombs of Frederick the Great and Frederick Wilhelm I. Throughout Hitler maintained a respectful, slightly ill-at-ease posture that convinced all present—the military men, the Junkers, the monarchists—that he was now completely subservient to Hindenburg and the Prussian aristocracy. That conviction, as they

Below:
Hitler's speech in the Potsdam Garrison Church, given on 21 March 1933.

would discover only two days later, could not have been further from the truth.

The atmosphere in the Kroll Opera House, temporary home of the Reichstag, was quite different on 23 March. Black-shirted SS units had cordoned off the building, while inside SA troops lined the corridors. A huge swastika flag hung behind the seats of the President and presiding officers of the legislature.

At 1405 Göring opened the session and almost immediately turned the chair over to Hitler, who stepped forward dressed in a simple Brownshirt uniform. His speech was a model of restraint and modesty: the Enabling Act he was requesting (titled the 'Law for Alleviating the Distress of People and Reich') sounded like an extreme measure, but he promised that it would be used only when absolutely necessary and that it certainly would not infringe on the rights of parliament, the President, the various states, or the church.

This Enabling Act, which was to become the fundamental law upholding the National Socialist regime, was short (only five paragraphs) and deceptively simple. In brief, it removed all legislative power from the Reichstag and transferred it to Hitler and his cabinet for a four-year

period. Included in the transfer were control of the national budget and the power to approve treaties with foreign states. Further, all laws enacted by the cabinet were to be drafted by the Chancellor, and—perhaps more important—could vary from the constitution. Since its passage required a constitutional amendment, a two-thirds majority was necessary; but that problem had been easily solved.

The number of deputies in the Reichstag had been reduced enough to give Hitler the majority he needed; all 81 Communist representatives and 26 of the Social Democrats were gone—some to end up in the concentration camps which had been established as early as 8 March. Only Otto Wels, Chairman of the Social Democratic Party, had enough courage to speak out against the bill. His speech sparked off a violent reply from Hitler, reminiscent of his Munich beer hall days in its vigor and crudity. Wels' action was too little, far too late—but at least he did something. One after another the other deputies rose to speak in favor of the legislation—including Monsignor Kaas of the Center Party, who managed at the very last minute to persuade himself to support the bill.

The final vote was 441 to 94 in favor of the Enabling Act; the Social Democrats were the only ones who refused to jump on the bandwagon. As the result was announced the Nazis rushed to the front of the room and began singing the 'Horst Wessel' song—over the grave, as it were, of parliamentary democracy in Germany.

In less than three months Hitler had managed to outwit all his opponents, and as the *Völkischer Beobachter* commented, 'For four years Hitler will be able to do anything he wants.' Even Hindenburg began to warm toward him, tending to ignore the persecutions that affected many of his own supporters; if Hitler was stopping that 'wretched, undisciplined party nonsense,' more power to him. All the old President wanted now was some peace and quiet. Happily he sent a message to the cabinet via Meissner: due to the passage of the Enabling Act his presence was no longer required and he was taking a much-needed rest.

Within two weeks every state government was under the central control of the Reich, with Nazis in all the important positions. For the first time in its history, Germany was a truly unified country. Hitler then set about consolidating all power within the country. The unions were disposed of with little difficulty, despite their huge membership and independent power base. Union leaders hoped to come to terms with the new government, even while at the local level the SA was raiding their branch offices. It looked as if there was some basis for those hopes when the Nazis declared May Day a national holiday—something for which the unions had been agitating for years. To mark

Below:
The 1933 Nuremberg rally. From left to right: Göring, Bodenschatz, Frick, Hitler and Hess.

the occasion, Goebbels prepared a stupendous celebration with torchlight parades and demonstrations, marching bands, and fireworks; labor leaders were flown to Berlin from all over the country to attend the show. The next day, however, union offices throughout the Reich were raided by the police; many officials were arrested, beaten up, and/or sent to concentration camps. Before the month was out a new law had abolished collective bargaining.

Next, Hitler turned his attention to the systematic elimination of all the other political parties—a task that was so easily accomplished that even he was surprised. 'One would never have thought so miserable a collapse possible,' he declared later. The Communist Party had been suppressed almost totally following the Reichstag fire. On 10 May police seized the Social Democrats' buildings, newspapers and property. The party tried to appease the Nazis by voting in the Reichstag to approve his foreign policy on 19 May, but to no avail; a month later Frick dissolved the Social Democratic Party altogether, announcing that it was 'subversive and inimical to the state.'

The Nazis' former partners in government, the German Nationalists, were next to go: on

21 June the police took over their offices, and on the 29th the party 'voluntarily' disbanded itself. During the next week Stresemann's People's Party, the Catholic Center Party, the Democrats – all the middle-class parties in fact – disappeared from the political scene. On 14 July a new law commemorated the occasion: 'The National Socialist German Workers' Party constitutes the only political party in Germany. Whoever attempts to form a new political party will be punished.'

Violence had been part of the German street scene for many months (indeed, years) before 1933, but with the Nazi accession to power, law and order virtually disappeared. Brown-shirted

SA gangs arrested, abused, and sometimes murdered whomever they pleased, often for no other reason than to satisfy private vendettas; in the big cities, anyone who incurred the dislike of the SA was liable to be kidnapped and taken to the local 'bunker' where he might be tortured or held for ransom. The normal authority of the police and judiciary were completely absent; Hitler was the law.

Anti-Semitism began to make its reappearance as early as March 1933, and when Jews all over the world sent up a cry of protest, Goebbels and Streicher urged the Führer to retaliate by staging an all-out program of intimidation and terror. This he was too canny to do, but a one-day boycott of Jewish shops and offices was ordered for 1 April. Posters on the windows urged Germans not to enter Jewish establishments, and SA men were stationed at the doors to reinforce the message. But the boycott did not have the desired effect. On the whole the German people appeared apathetic, amused, or slightly ashamed of the Nazis'

methods. Sales figures for most Jewish firms, especially outside the big cities, remained about the same, and Hindenburg was moved to issue a statement condemning any form of discrimination against Jewish veterans. The tactic was not repeated; the Nazis turned to quieter methods, using the legal system to force Jews out of business and society.

By midsummer 1933 Hitler was master of Germany. Papen's cabinet, which was to have isolated the Nazis, had sunk without trace; only Papen himself remained in an ambiguous position as Vice-Chancellor (Göring had replaced him as Prime Minister of Prussia). All the other members of the cabinet had been forced out to make room for Nazi ministers.

The people, for the most part, supported the government. A wave of idealism swept the Reich, even the intellectual community. Of course, during the first few weeks of the regime many famous writers and professors either left Germany or were hounded out of their positions. But many others remained and offered their services to the government—not entirely out of opportunism, but because they had been drawn in by the great flood of emotionalism. One of Hitler's fundamental insights was the knowledge that most people want to belong—and under National Socialism they were given ample opportunity to do so. Professional organizations, leagues, bureaus, chambers and social clubs proliferated at an amazing rate. While there was indeed some coercion to join, that does not explain away the phenomenon, which was attributable to the need for social participation.

Slogans, parades, and festivals—all organized by Goebbels' Propaganda Ministry—popularized the regime by giving people concrete images instead of abstract ideas to identify with. The political liberty they had enjoyed in the past appeared to the public to have profited them nothing; now they felt they were part of a great reform movement—their work became meaningful again, and though there was no great improvement in the economy until 1934, there at least seemed to be hope for the future.

In the foreign-policy arena Hitler was forced to take a conciliatory attitude at first and try to counter the bad press he was getting internationally (mainly because of SA excesses). He therefore left the diplomatic corps (whom he privately referred to as 'those Santa Clauses in the Wilhelmstrasse') virtually untouched for the time being (even including one Jew and one man who was married to a Jew) and publicly stressed his determination to continue the moderate Weimar policies.

On 17 May 1933 he made his famous 'Peace Speech' in which he stressed his devotion to reconciliation, making an excellent impression on the other powers. His scarcely veiled threats

Right:
Hitler ceremonially inaugurates the building of an autobahn in Frankfurt on 23 September 1933.

Below:
Hitler and other Nazi leaders attend the opening ceremony in the Luitpold Hall for the Nazi Rally at Nuremberg in 1933.

to withdraw from the Disarmament Conference and the League of Nations if Germany was not granted equal rights were worked in so well that they went practically unnoticed, and the overall impression he gave was of a reasonable, fair-minded man with whom it would be easy to deal. In the summer of 1933 the Four-Power Pact (signed by England, France, Germany and Italy) symbolized a moral acceptance of Germany as one of the great powers, even though it was never ratified. The Berlin Treaty with Soviet Russia was renewed, and in July an agreement was signed with the Vatican.

In August Hanfstängl persuaded Hitler to allow the release of *Fact against Ink*, a collection of anti-Hitler caricatures designed to show the differences between the real and the fictional Adolf Hitler. Though Goebbels was appalled at the very idea, it turned out to be a clever way to perpetuate Hitler's affable facade and to reinforce the notion—common in many foreign circles—that he was more a figure of fun than a menace.

At meetings of the Disarmament Conference in Geneva, which had been going on since 1932, the Führer argued persuasively that Germany would be happy to disarm—provided the other powers did too. If, on the other hand, they insisted on rearming at an ever-increasing rate, then it was patently unfair not to allow Germany to do the same. For some time France, despite the unpopularity of her position, was the only country to hold out against German rearmament and block negotiations. But eventually the constant comparison between Hitler's reasonable tone and the facts of life in an increasingly militaristic Germany brought the other countries round to France's view.

On 14 October Hitler, as a dramatic gesture, announced Germany's withdrawal from both the Disarmament Conference and the League of Nations. The other powers were stunned and embarrassed, but no one really minded that those two faltering institutions had been dealt yet another crippling blow. They had already been shown to be ineffectual on several occasions, and in many circles Hitler actually gained in popularity as the man who had enough courage to put an end to the waste of time and money.

Germany's withdrawal gave Hitler an excuse for one of the cleverest ploys in his consolidation of power. On 24 October in a major speech at the Berlin Sportpalast, he announced that there would be a plebiscite on 12 November to determine whether he had a mandate from the people. The Nazis' subsequent campaign, like their election campaigns before, featured demonstrations, emotional speeches at rallies and over the radio and hundreds of thousands of posters plastered on walls throughout

the country. The results were all that Hitler hoped for—even enemies of the government took the opportunity to express their resentment of the Treaty of Versailles, the League of Nations, and all the trials and tribulations of the last fifteen years. Some 95 percent of the voters approved the government's decision—and, through the clever wording of the issue, approved Hitler's domestic policies as well. Even despite an intimidation campaign by the SA before the plebiscite and blatant manipulation of the results (over 2100 of the 2200 prisoners in the concentration camp at Dachau, for example, voted in favor of the government), the outcome

was still a true reflection of the mood of the public.

Within a few weeks, on 1 December, Hitler was able to pass a new law proclaiming the unity of party and state, and Germany stood on the brink of totalitarianism. Freedom of the press, electronic media, literature and the fine arts had long since gone by the board. Those who had not succumbed to the fever of conformism and evangelistic zeal (which is not a peculiarly German disease, as many who lived through the McCarthy Era in America can attest) were subject to the threat of the ubiquitous SA and the growing number of concentration camps

Above:
A memorial ceremony held in the Unter den Linden in Berlin on 25 February 1934.

Left:
Hitler inspects the preliminary works for the Frankfurt autobahn in September 1933. Hitler's regime inaugurated public works to solve the unemployment problem. The unemployed were organized into the Reichs *Arbeitsdienst* and built an extensive new highway system, which is still in use.

(another non-German invention—the term derived from British establishments set up in South Africa during the Boer War).

The only institution that escaped being drawn under Nazi control right away was the Army—and for good reason. Its benevolent neutrality during the critical months immediately before and after Hitler's appointment as Chancellor had been a key factor in his success—just as its opposition had been instrumental in his failure in 1923. The Führer, therefore, went to great lengths to cultivate General Werner von Blomberg, the Minister of Defense, and other military leaders. As proof of his friendship the

needed those powerful interest groups. He also saw clearly that he had risen to his present status because of Germany's fear of revolution—and that his only chance for future success lay in being able to restore the confidence of the people and in avoiding even the appearance of a traditional revolutionary government. Thus, Nazi radicals who had taken over the powerful employers' associations were removed and replaced by the former leaders, Krupp von Bohlen and Fritz Thyssen. Dr Karl Schmitt, head of Germany's largest insurance company and an orthodox (if brilliant) businessman, replaced Hugenberg as Minister of Economics. The SA's

Above:
Hitler opens a huge International Car Show held in Berlin in 1934.

Army Law, passed in July, ended the civil courts' jurisdiction over the military, and confirmed the Army's unique position in the German state.

The SA, however, was becoming increasingly obstreperous. As the only real rank-and-file movement within the party, its members were becoming more and more upset by what they saw as Hitler's betrayal of the revolution: though he was moving against the left, he had largely ignored the right — big business, the Junker aristocracy and the Prussian generals.

Hitler, of course, was interested only in achieving total power, and realized that he

unauthorized 'protective custody' bunkers were broken up and the auxiliary police squads disbanded. Statements began to appear in the official Nazi press to the effect that the SA's job was finished.

All this infuriated the SA leadership, who felt cheated of the just rewards of victory—especially Ernst Röhm, who had never given up his dream of turning the SA into soldiers and taking over the army ('drowning the gray rock in the brown tide'). In short, Hitler faced the age-old problem of any revolutionary leader after the first phase of the revolution is complete: how to deal with the embarrassing legacy of the years of struggle—the Old Guard, whose fanaticism makes the take-over possible, but which then becomes inappropriate and downright dangerous to its continuing success.

Röhm, an old-fashioned, straightforward soldier, did not help his own cause by his clumsy maneuvering; he flaunted the SA's growing power in a series of parades and demonstrations and kept up a constant, bitter stream of criticism against the regime, both in public and in private.

For once Hitler abandoned his usual policy of letting his enemies fight out their own disagreements, and came down solidly on the side of the Army. The SA leaders were told in no uncertain terms that what Germany needed most was order and that any so-called 'second revolution' would be dealt with ruthlessly. At the same time he attempted for some months to pacify his old comrades. As part of the Law to Secure the Unity of Party and State passed on 1 December 1933, both Röhm and Hess were made members of the cabinet. At the beginning of 1934 the Führer wrote to Röhm, thanking him for services rendered to the National Socialist movement; in February another law granted pensions to members of the SA and other members of the Nazi party who had been injured during the political struggles.

But Hitler never lost sight of his main goal. Hindenburg was very ill and obviously could not live much longer. If Hitler could become President too (and, therefore, Supreme Commander of the armed forces) he would finally have total control—but not if an independent military organization still existed to challenge his authority. This made it necessary to arrive at a definite decision, when his natural inclination would probably have been to do nothing and let events take their natural course.

During the second week in April 1934, while taking part in naval maneuvers aboard the cruiser *Deutschland*, Hitler came to an agreement with Blomberg, Colonel General Freiherr von Fritsch (Commander in Chief of the Army), and Admiral Raeder (Commander in Chief of the Navy). He would suppress Röhm and the SA, and guarantee the regular military's position as the only armed force within Germany, in return for their continuing loyalty and support. Back in Berlin, he contacted the British and French governments with an offer to reduce the SA by two-thirds. When news of the offer leaked out, as it was bound to do, it widened the rift still further.

Röhm's enemies were rapidly combining against him. On 1 April Göring, who had been building up a special police force under his own command, appointed Heinrich Himmler (already head of both the Bavarian Police and the SS) as leader of the Prussian Gestapo. Himmler and Reinhold Heydrich immediately set about

Right:
Hitler attends a memorial for the composer Richard Wagner held in Leipzig on 6 March 1934. On Hitler's right sits Winifred Wagner and on Hitler's left Mayor Karl Gördeler. Gördeler became the unofficial ambassador of the resistance movement against Hitler and was involved in the July Plot in 1944 to kill Hitler.

Below:
Ernst Röhm was the leader of the SA, who was purged in the Night of the Long Knives, 30 June 1934.

mercy. Röhm's only friend was Goebbels, a fellow radical, who for a long time was the only link between the SA and the Führer—until mid-June when, true to form, he abandoned his radical principles and came down solidly on Hitler's side.

At the beginning of June the sky began to darken, and the storm warnings were clear to anyone who cared to read them. The SS and the SD (*Sicherheitsdienst*, the SS Security Police) were placed on alert and given orders to watch the SA more closely; a 'Reich List' was begun by Göring, Blomberg, Himmler and Heydrich, containing names of people to be arrested or shot when the time came.

On 4 June Hitler sent for Röhm and the two talked for nearly five hours. No one knows what passed between them, but they must have reached at least a superficial accord. On 7 June Hitler instructed the SA to go on leave for the month of July; Röhm made it known that he was going on sick leave and set off for Bad Wiessee with his coterie of young men. Hitler had agreed to meet him there along with the other SA leaders, on 30 June.

Rumors were flying in Berlin and the ominous tension mounted daily. Brüning and Scleicher were advised to leave the country. Brüning took the advice seriously and slipped over the Swiss border in disguise; Schleicher, however, merely took a short holiday and then

building up a police empire within the state. Röhm was the major obstacle in their path, since the SS was subordinate to the SA. Meanwhile, Hess, Bormann and others in Hitler's inner circle, jealous of Röhm's enormous power base, assiduously collected complaints and scandalous stories about the private lives of the members of his homosexual clique, and even began to spread rumors of treason. The army, too, did everything possible to stir up disagreement and promote ill will between Röhm and Hitler, hoping that Hitler would, by dismissing Röhm, effectively disarm himself and be at their

Above:
Hitler addresses the
crowd in the Lustgarten
on National Labor Day
in 1934.

returned to Berlin. Hitler, meanwhile, still had not decided definitely on a purge. Then, within a few days, events conspired to force his hand.

On 14 June he flew to Venice to meet Mussolini for the first time. The visit was a humiliating failure from the very beginning, when Hitler, in an old trench coat and blue serge suit, stepped off the plane to be greeted by Il Duce—resplendent in black shirt, gold braid and jackboots. From then on, things went from bad to worse: the two could not even communicate effectively (Hitler could not understand Mussolini's eccentric German, while Mussolini was thoroughly confused by Hitler's Austrian accent); and Mussolini became so bored at one point that he walked out in the middle of an official reception.

Hitler returned to Berlin in a bad temper; a few hours later his Vice-Chancellor, Papen, stood up at the University of Marburg to give a speech. It was not to be just an ordinary political speech; he had allowed himself to be pushed into the background but now, seeing the divisions within the National Socialist party, thought he had a chance to reassert his authority. His talk was a direct attack on Goebbels, the controlled press, the Nazi use of propaganda, and on the single-party system in general. Though Goebbels immediately confiscated every copy of the speech he could find and forbade its scheduled broadcast later that evening, Papen had forestalled him by already distributing advance copies to foreign correspondents in the capital. Hitler was furious. On 21 June he flew to Neudeck to see President Hindenburg, in order to find out what backing Papen had for his public insubordination. But before he even met with the President, Blomberg sternly informed him that unless the present state of tension in Germany ended quickly, the President would declare martial law. In his short interview with Hindenburg later, the message was confirmed; obviously, if the Nazi government was to survive, he had to keep his agreement with the army and quickly suppress the SA.

While the intrigues against Röhm gathered momentum in Berlin and the Führer was deluged by reports of supposed SA plots, Röhm himself remained in Bad Wiessee, blissfully unaware of any danger. He had even left his staff guards behind in Munich. Early in the morning

day; Göring's list had been expanded to include not only enemies of the government, but all those against whom the Nazi held grudges or who perhaps knew too much about things the Führer preferred suppressed. General von Schleicher and his wife were shot in their home that evening, and Gregor Strasser ended his life in a Gestapo jail cell. Papen was spared, but many of his associates—including his private secretary, his collaborator on the 17 June speech (Edgar Jung), and other members of his staff—were gunned down. Old enemies like

Above right:
Another major road is announced by Hitler in 1934.

of 30 June Hitler landed at Munich airport, and shortly before dawn a long column of cars was heading toward Bad Wiessee. Röhm and his associates were taken back to Munich and incarcerated in Stadelheim Prison; the SA leader was finally shot, in his cell, at 1800 the following day.

Meanwhile the death toll was mounting in the rest of the country, for Hitler had telephoned the code word (*Kolibri*—hummingbird) to Goebbels just before setting out to arrest Röhm. Some 150 SA leaders were shot by firing squads; among them was Karl Ernst, leader of the Berlin SA detachment, who had been dragged back as he was setting out on a honeymoon trip to Madeira. Ernst, who was none too bright, believed to the end that he was the victim of a rightist anti-Hitler putsch, and died with the words 'Heil Hitler' on his lips.

SA leaders were not the only ones to die that

Gustav von Kahr (who had suppressed the Beer Hall Putsch in 1923) disappeared; several other people were murdered by mistake. The final death count is not known since Göring made sure all documents relating to the purge were burned; Hitler claimed that only 77 were killed, while estimates at the Munich trial in 1957 went as high as more than 1000. Newspapers were forbidden to run obituaries for any of those who had been executed or who had 'committed suicide.'

The average citizen knew little of what was going on at the time; on Sunday, 1 July, while the executions were still in progress, Hitler was hosting a tea party in the Chancellery garden. In the afternoon Göring released a statement that, by a clever blend of truth and fiction, managed to suggest that a nasty job had been accomplished as cleanly as possible and that there was nothing more to worry about. In fact, most

Germans were pleased to see the brown-shirted roughnecks get their come-uppance. Hindenburg, though upset by the news of Schleicher's death, sent a congratulatory telegram to the Führer on Monday; on Tuesday Blomberg extended the army's congratulations to the cabinet and issued an order of the day expressing their satisfaction with the turn of events.

Finally, on 13 July Hitler came before the Reichstag to give his version of what had happened. He was slightly defensive at first, beginning with a lengthy recital of his achievements as Chancellor, moving on to Röhm's immorality and perfidy, and finally ending with a pledge to the army that they would remain the sole bearer of arms in Germany. When it was all over the Reichstag applauded vigorously and unanimously approved a bill legalizing the executions as 'emergency measures of the state.'

Left:
Leni Riefenstahl and Heinrich Himmler in the Luitpold Arena during the filming of *Triumph des Willens* in September 1934.

Right:
Hitler checks the SA and SS banners in the Luitpold Arena.

Below right:
Hitler inspects the ranks of the Hitler Youth in Nuremberg 1934. Some 60,000 youths were present in this spectacular ceremony.

Below:
The 1934 Nuremberg Rally showing Hitler standing in the center with Himmler and Lutze.

to fulfill their part of the bargain. Within three hours of the Old Gentleman's demise it was announced that Adolf Hitler had taken over the powers of President and Supreme Commander of the Armed Forces in addition to his duties as Chancellor, and that he would henceforth officially be known as Führer and Reich Chancellor. With Blomberg's prompting, all officers and men of the armed forces immediately swore a new oath of allegiance—not to 'nation and fatherland' but to Hitler personally.

Hindenburg's funeral, an elaborate pageant such as only Goebbels could devise, was the prelude to yet another plebiscite on 19 August. The results, though decisively in Hitler's favor, were not as overwhelming as he might have wished; 84.6 percent of the electorate voted yes, but in some regions almost a third of the population (mainly the socialists and Catholics)

The military was delighted with the outcome, assuming that the Nazis could no longer pose any threat to their own power and authority. Their attitude was not only incredibly short-sighted, but showed how drastically they had underestimated Hitler. On 26 July the SS was rewarded for its loyalty by being released from its subordination to the SA. Heinrich Himmler was made Reichsführer-SS, responsible only to Hitler. From the beginning he was allowed to retain one armed division; during the next ten years the SS would grow into a huge, many-tentacled organization penetrating every corner of German life and undermining not only the military, but every other institution more completely than the less-subtle Röhm could ever have dreamed of.

On 2 August Hindenburg finally died at the age of 87, and Hitler was able to call on the army

voted against the merging of the two offices. Some 4,500,000 voters in all voted no, while another 870,000 spoiled their ballots.

Nevertheless, he was able to project a confident attitude when he addressed the Sixth Nazi Party Congress in Nuremberg on 4 September, predicting: 'In the next 1000 years there will be no other revolution in Germany.' That spectacle, the largest of its kind so far, was directed by the young Albert Speer, who designed an impressive stage setting around a stone altar 1300 feet long, 80 feet high, and surrounded by thousands of swastika banners. Leni Riefenstahl, already a well-known actress and director, was commissioned to produce a film of the occasion. In spite of harassment from Goebbels (occasioned probably by jealousy), she and her sixteen cameramen shot the proceedings from every conceivable angle, using planes, cranes, trenches, rollerskates and tiny platforms atop flagpoles to get the angles she wanted. When she finished editing thousands of feet of film, *Triumph of the Will* was generally acknowledged, even by Goebbels, to be an extraordinary achievement. The film won many prizes and awards, and is still recognized as an important documentary—if not for its message, certainly for its artistry and innovative techniques.

The German people lost much of their personal freedom during the 1930s, but most did not mind all that much. Despite the purge of 30 June, and the constant threat of the Gestapo and their concentration camps, Nazi terrorism touched relatively few people. The vast majority, who were working again by the fall of 1936, felt only a new hope, confidence in the future and a revitalized faith in themselves and their country.

Most of Hitler's popularity in the early years of his regime rested on Germany's economic recovery, which seemed all but miraculous to a people who had struggled through the miseries of postwar inflation and the Great Depression. Between 1932 and 1937 the national income doubled, production totals doubled, and unemployment was reduced from 6,000,000 to less than 1,000,000.

Hitler was not at all concerned with economics, and most of the National Socialist policies were the result of the economic wizardry of Dr Schacht, former president of the Reichsbank, who replaced Dr Karl Schmitt as Minister of Economics. Schacht's first effort centered around creating jobs for the unemployed, largely through an expanded public works program and the granting of tax reliefs to encourage private enterprise.

But as in America, what really ended the Depression and set the country on the road to real economic recovery was the shift to a war economy (known in Germany as *Wehrwirtschaft*). Dr Schacht was made Plenipotentiary for War Economy in May 1935, but he had begun taking the necessary steps to prepare Germany for war as early as 1934. Though he had almost no liquid capital or financial reserves, his skill in manipulating currency and negotiating profitable trade agreements with other countries created credit almost out of thin air. Funds for rearmament came from the government printing press in the early days, supplemented by money confiscated from 'enemies of the state' or from blocked foreign accounts. Schacht also invented 'Mefo' bills—certificates created by the Reichsbank and guaranteed by the state, which were used to pay armaments manufacturers. Since they were not 'real' money they appeared in no accounting records or budgets, and thus concealed the extent of German rearmament.

In 1936 Schacht was forced out of his position and Göring, who knew little about business, was installed as administrator of Hitler's Four-Year Plan, which was devised to convert Germany to a total war economy. The Führer felt that time was running out, and he wanted to make Germany self-sufficient, to protect

Above:
Hitler gives the National Labor Day speech to millions of radio listeners in 1935.

Left:
Hitler congratulates General Karl Litzmann on the occasion of his 85th birthday in January 1935.

Like every other segment of society the German working class, probably the most skilled and industrious in Western Europe, found their lives completely changed under National Socialism–both for better and for worse.

The Labor Front, which supposedly replaced unions, controlled not only wage earners, but employers and members of the various professions as well. Nazi-appointed labor trustees set all wages, which were deliberately kept low (sometimes even against the wishes of employers) by order of the government. The 'workbook' introduced in February 1935 was a record of each individual's skills and employment; without it no worker could legally change jobs. In June 1938 the government went a step further with labor conscription: workers were assigned to their jobs by the state and could neither quit nor be fired without official permission.

But though German workers were perhaps the most cynical about the aims and purposes of the Nazis, they did not despise their lot either. There were some advantages to working in the National Socialist state. For example, Dr Robert Ley, head of the Labor Front, devised an organization called *Kraft durch Freude* (Strength Through Joy) to provide entertainment for their leisure hours. Extraordinarily inexpensive vacations–cruises, skiing holidays, etc–were available for members, as were discount tickets to concerts, theaters, operas–making culture available to the working classes, in keeping with the spirit of the new socialist

against the possibility of a wartime blockade. Dividends were restricted to six percent, strict price and wage controls were imposed, and imports were reduced to a minimum. Small businesses were rapidly phased out; larger ones found themselves buried in red tape. But though many businessmen became disillusioned (including Fritz Thyssen, who left Germany when war broke out), for the most part they were philosophical about the difficulties and pleased about the advantages they were enjoying. Profits soared and there were no more strikes or uncomfortable wage demands.

Right:
A Hitler Youth parade on National Labor Day in 1935. Hitler's *Gleichschaltung* **included the takeover of all youth groups by the Hitler Youth, which was led by the half-American Baldur von Schirach (front row on Rudolf Hess' right). Membership was made compulsory and it was the perfect weapon for indoctrinating German youth in Nazi doctrine.**

democracy. *Kraft durch Freude* even had its own 90-piece orchestra which toured the country (especially the more remote areas), and, of course, the organization controled a huge sports program.

In the late 1930s an attempt was made to design a car that would sell for under $400, so that—as in America—every German working man would have the opportunity to own his own automobile. It was Hitler's idea, and the Führer even took a hand in the design, though most of the work was done under the supervision of an Austrian, Dr Ferdinand Porsche. The result of their labors was the Volkswagen, or 'People's Car.' A huge factory was built at Fallersleben and thousands of workers made advance payments on their new cars. Unfortunately, not one ever came off the production line during the Third Reich; as soon as the war began the factory was converted to the production of items of greater military importance.

The major achievement was the fact that the workers had jobs again and knew they would keep them. They simply did not mind losing their political and personal freedom if at the same time they were also deprived of the 'freedom to starve.' Under the Nazis, as well, there was a real feeling of equality, cameraderie and social mobility that made everyone a worker for the welfare of the community—a welcome change from the divisiveness that had marked German life and politics since the end of World War I.

Farmers, too, were reasonably satisfied under the Nazi regime. The Nazi Minister of Food and Agriculture, Walther Darré, was an outstanding agriculturalist who reorganized the entire farm and marketing structure. He accomplished the reorganization with two basic laws. The Hereditary Farm Law of September 1933 decreed that farms could not be sold, divided, mortgaged or foreclosed upon; this protected the German farmer against losing his property, but also meant that he could not sell his farm even if he wanted to. The Reich Food Estate, also established in September 1933, put every aspect of farm production under government control. Darré's first objective, to stabilize prices at a reasonable rate; was very successful. His second, to make the Reich self-sufficient in food, never quite materialized.

During the early years of the Nazi regime, Germany—in direct contrast to Soviet Russia—was open to anyone who wanted to visit; indeed, the thriving tourist business brought in badly needed foreign currency in addition to showing the world that the Nazis had nothing to hide. Most German citizens could travel freely throughout the world, and apparently no one worried about their being contaminated by visiting democratic countries. Foreign observers poured into Germany. The reports they brought back, of trains that ran on

Above:
Hitler inspects the Volkswagen factory in May 1938. One of the *Kraft durch Freude* campaigns was for a hire purchase scheme to enable every German family to own a car. Many subscribed to the scheme but when the war broke out the money was impounded for the war and no Volkswagens were produced for the domestic market.

Right above:
Leni Riefenstahl lines up a shot during the filming of *Olympia*, a documentary on the 1936 Olympic Games. Her film was stunning to look at and was given its premiere in 1938 but because of the Nazi overtones it has not been shown extensively in Western Europe and the United States.

Right:
Berlin's Olympic Stadium during the Games in 1936. Hitler wished the Games to be a showpiece for German and Aryan sporting ability. When Jesse Owens, an American black athlete, ran away with the sprint gold medals it was a slap in Hitler's face.

time, of a healthy, happy people, of an administration based on law and order, were as true and as valid as those of the exiles who told of Nazi persecution and terror—again illustrating the dual nature of the National Socialist state.

In August 1936 the Olympic Games, which were held in Berlin, gave Hitler a golden opportunity to impress the foreign community; visitors did come away with a picture of a friendly and industrious though somewhat overbureaucratic nation. Thanks to the excellent organization of the games themselves, the pomp and pageantry and the lavish parties given by Goebbels, Ribbentrop and Göring, the bad press Germany had been receiving of late was countered. It was the first occasion that the Olympic Games were consciously used for political gain, and the experiment must be considered a great success. Again, Leni Riefenstahl was on hand, resisting Goebbels' interference, to produce a two-part documentary of the event. Again she produced a magnificent documentary; many of the techniques she devised are still used in sports' filming today.

All Germany was on its best behavior for the games, and part of that preparation involved quietly taking down signs that read 'Jews Not Welcome,' 'Jews Enter at their Own Risk,' etc. Token Jews (notably, fencer Helene Mayer and hockey star Rudi Ball) were allowed to compete in German teams and the organizer of the Olympic Village, Captain Wolfgang Fürstner, was also Jewish. (As the games ended Captain Fürstner, seeing only too clearly what the future held in store but unable to face a life outside the German Army, went home and shot himself.)

By the time of the games so many Jews had been either legally or forcibly deprived of employment that about half the Jewish population was out of work. They were often deprived of the necessities as well; lodging was difficult to find, and in some towns a Jew could not even buy milk or medicine.

The worsening situation was the result of a series of decrees issued since the Nazis came into power, the most notable being the laws passed during the spring and summer of 1933, which removed all Jews from the civil service professions (along with everyone else who had ever shown any left-wing tendencies) and reduced the number of Jews at institutions of higher learning, and the so-called Nuremberg Laws of September 1935. The first of these deprived all Jews of German citizenship while the second, The Law for the Protection of German Blood and Honor, forbade both marriage and extramarital relations between Jews and Aryans and annulled existing marriages. The law forbade Jews to employ female Aryan servants under the age of 45.

These were but the first steps toward Hitler's goal: extermination of the Jewish race in Europe—and when Hitler used the word 'extermination' he did so deliberately and meant it literally. His anti-Semitism—one of the most consistent themes in his entire life—colored his every idea, and Jews came to be associated in his mind with everything he hated. Democracy, capitalism, freedom of the press, Christianity, the class war, prostitution—all were devices used by Jews to subvert other peoples.

Persecution of the Christian Church was slower and more subtle. In July 1933 Hitler had signed an agreement with the Vatican guaranteeing religious freedom for Catholics and the right of the Church to govern its own affairs. Ten days later he signed a sterilization law that was directly contrary to the Church's wishes. Within the next few years thousands of Catholic priests and nuns were arrested, Catholic publications were suppressed, and the Gestapo even refused to recognize the sanctity of the confessional. By spring of 1937 Pope Pius XI issued an encyclical condemning the Nazi government.

The Protestant churches split into three groups. At one extreme were the ardent Nazis led by Ludwig Müller, who formed the German Christian group; on the other hand, the Confessional Church led by Reverend Martin Niemöller opposed all Nazification of churches; and in the middle were the majority of Protestant church-goers, who sat on the fence as long as possible and eventually sided with Hitler by default. By 1937 most resistance to Nazification within the Protestant churches was at an end, with a majority of clergymen taking a personal oath of allegiance to Hitler.

After the passage of the Enabling Act, law in Germany was what Hitler said it was. Judges whose devotion to National Socialist principles

was suspect were arbitrarily removed (as were all Jews, of course). Those who remained were instructed in no uncertain terms that the days of decisions based on an objective interpretation of the law were over. Instead, they should ask themselves at every point, 'What would the Führer do in my place?' The right to try cases of treason (which by this time covered a wide range of activities) was transferred from the Supreme Court to a People's Court (*Volksgerichtshof*) consisting of two professional judges and five other officials drawn from the ranks of party leaders, the SS and the armed forces. The Special Court (*Sondergericht*) handled ordinary political crimes; there was no jury, and the three judges had to be trusted party members. Even the defense lawyers had to be approved by the party. If a judge passed too light a sentence, the defendant still had to face the possibility that Hess would arbitrarily decide to have him committed to a concentration camp anyway, or would order the Gestapo to arrange an 'accident.' For the Gestapo was completely above the law, and the courts were forbidden to interfere in any way with their policies or actions. 'Protective custody' became the blanket term covering arrest or incarceration.

After the Röhm purge, control of the concentration camps was given to the SS, specifically the tough, elite Death's Head divisions (*Totenkopfverbände*). Theodore Eiche was put in charge of administering some 50 camps containing 20,000 to 30,000 political prisoners; he closed many of the smaller ones and improved and expanded the larger establishments.

The intelligence unit for the Gestapo was the SD, or Security Service, run by Reinhard 'Hangman' Heydrich. Though the SD employed only about 3000 full-time agents, its part-time informers eventually numbered about 100,000 ordinary people who assiduously reported neigh-

Above:
Shortly after Hitler came to power anti-Semitism was given official sanction. A boycott of Jewish shops was started in 1933 and in the picture a Jewish shop has a sign warning Germans not to buy Jewish goods.

Above right:
Hitler greets the Papal Nuncio. Hitler's policy toward the Catholic Church was to try to maintain official relations while persecuting local priests and nuns.

bors, business associates and even relatives for harboring anti-Nazi sentiments. In June 1936 police forces in all the states were combined into the German Police Force, with Heinrich Himmler as Chief of German Police. From that point on, Germany was truly a police state.

Under Dr Goebbels the Reich Chamber of Culture labored mightily to gather all areas of cultural life into a unified organization that would serve the propaganda purposes of the new regime. Hundreds of thousands of books were burned and many more confiscated from libraries and private homes; the authors included not only Germans like Thomas Mann, Stefan Zweig, Erich Maria Remarque and Albert Einstein, but also many foreigners, among them Jack London, Upton Sinclair, Sigmund Freud, Emile Zola, Marcel Proust and HG Wells. Soon every book or play manuscript had to be approved by the government before it was published.

Music in the Third Reich remained excellent, as did much in the theater. The fine arts, on the other hand, came to grief, mainly because of Hitler's hatred of all modern art and his determination to replace it with a new 'Germanic' art—a term that was synonymous with neoclassical work that was badly executed and tasteless. One of his first acts was to disband the Bauhaus—an innovative group formed after World War I by Walther Gropius that included architects, graphic designers and painters like Paul Klee and Piet Mondrian.

Newspapers, of course, were told what to publish, how to write both news articles and editorials, even what headlines to use. As might be expected, the press soon became inane and monotonous—as did the output of the motion picture industry. But when the quality of the movies declined, even the hitherto submissive German population rebelled: William Shirer, a correspondent in Berlin during the 1930s, tells

Below:
An anti-Semitic poster.

DU SOLLST DIE VÖLKER DER ERDE FRESSEN

us that the few 'B' films from Hollywood that were screened were usually jammed, while theaters showing Nazi films were deserted. Hitler's favorite actress was Greta Garbo, and one of his favorite films was *Lives of a Bengal Lancer*, which was made required viewing for the SS since the Führer was fond of the story depicting a handful of Englishmen ruling an entire continent. Radio programs were equally bad, but as time went on the radio, under Goebbels' direction, became the Nazis' most important propaganda weapon.

Hitler may have been contemptuous of the professors he knew in his youth and of academia in general, but he fully realized the importance of training young people early for service to the new state. In February 1933 all public schools were put under control of the Reich Ministry of Education. Textbooks were rewritten and courses changed; many teachers were fired or left their jobs voluntarily, while those who remained began to teach 'German' physics, chemistry, mathematics, etc. Standards (and enrollments) in the universities dropped drastically—a result that was to have a disastrous effect on Germany's fortunes when war finally came.

The education of younger children ultimately became the province of the Hitler Youth, led by Baldur von Schirach, rather than of the school system. Prior to 1933 the Hitler Youth had been but one of many organizations in the country, which had a large, vital youth movement. Though its enrollment began to rise during the

Above:
Baldur von Schirach,
The Hitler Youth leader.

early years of the Reich, its real growth came after December 1937, when all non-Nazi youth movements were banned and Schirach was made directly responsible to Hitler. The Hitler Youth was a vast, paramilitary organization, on the surface much like the Boy Scouts. Boys entered the movement at age six; when they were ten they moved up into the *Jungvolk* after passing various tests in athletics, camping and history; at fourteen they entered the Hitler Youth and were given daggers engraved with the words 'Blood and Honor'; when they were eighteen they graduated into the Labor Service and then into the army.

Girls followed a similar path: from age ten to fourteen they were *Jungmädel*; between fourteen and eighteen they were members of the *Bund Deutscher Mädel* (or BDM); and at eighteen they completed their *Land Jahr* (land year)—a year's service usually spent on a farm. Throughout their years in the movement the pressure was on women to become the healthy mothers of healthy children. Since the emphasis was on motherhood and Nazism as opposed to marriage, moral problems soon arose—or at least they were considered so by parents who were not quite such fanatical Nazis.

The Hitler Youth soon replaced both home and school as the dominant factor in the rearing of German children. That their minds were deliberately and very efficiently being twisted, no one can deny. But that was often less obvious, especially to outsiders, than the fact that they were a group of young men and women with

Above:
Eva Braun enjoys the sun in the Obersalzburg. She was kept in the background and rarely made an appearance in Berlin.

strong, healthy bodies and a feeling of fellowship that broke through all class and economic barriers—in distinct contrast to young people in other European countries.

But what of Hitler during this period? What sort of man had he become? What kind of private life did he have? Physically he was middle-aged (he turned 50 in 1938); an undistinguished figure with a face that was coarse and unimpressive in repose, except for his eyes. What we rarely see in photographs, however, was the extraordinary mobility of that face, which could express a whole range of moods—delight, haughtiness, cynicism, rage—in a matter of moments.

In truth, he had no 'private life' as it is commonly understood; he apparently put too much energy into public affairs to have much left over for his off-duty hours. Even at his retreat at the Obersalzburg, which he enlarged during 1935 and 1936, he was surrounded by secretaries, chauffers and adjutants rather than friends. Days at the Berghof were long and rather dull; evenings were, if anything, even worse. After supper the company would gather in the living room for two or three hours of movies, when the Führer's favorites—usually insipid social comedies—were shown over and over again. Then everyone would assemble in huge chairs in front of the fireplace. There was no conversation—either Hitler lectured, or he sat staring off into space while the others remained silent, either out of respect or boredom. Finally, at about two or three in the morning, he

would send Eva Braun to bed and a little later would depart himself. The smokers would surreptitiously light up their forbidden cigarettes and there would be a few moments of hectic, forced gaiety before the group staggered off to bed themselves. Life in Berlin was much the same, only more stultifying because of the increased formality in the capital. His working methods were chaotic and idiosyncratic. He seldom read a file before making an important decision, would avoid making any decision at all for as long as possible in the hopes that the problem would clear itself up, and was singularly erratic about choosing which visitors he would see and which he would ignore for days on end.

Joachim Fest has aptly dubbed Adolf Hitler an 'unperson'—the mask never slipped to show feelings of any sort, and as a result the man we see in the historical accounts is a cardboard cut-out rather than a real human being. Hitler was always playing a part, so afraid of showing spontaneous emotion that he would put his hand in front of his face when he laughed. His whole life was a series of disguises; even his famous rages, when he would scream abuse and drum his fists on a table or wall, with his face red and swollen with anger, were often an act—the next moment he could be equally sincere and charming, as if nothing had happened. His extraordinary personal magnetism has never been adequately analyzed; his eyes have often been described as having some sort of hypnotic power, and in fact Albert Speer states categori-

Right:
Heinrich Hoffmann
takes a photograph of
Hitler surrounded by
the various Nazi
Ministers of State and
Gauleitern. Front row
left to right: Josef
Bürkel, Josef Goebbels,
Wilhelm Kube, Rudolf
Jordan, Rudolf Hess,
Adolf Hitler, Robert
Ley, Erich Koch, Josef
Wagner, Gustav Simon,
Alfred Meyer and
Wilhelm Frick.

Left:
Hitler reads a local
paper in his retreat in
the Obersalzburg
known as the Berghof.

cally that Hitler was able to mesmerize his associates. Several military leaders have stated that they hesitated to visit headquarters during the war for fear of losing their judgment and becoming convinced to follow a course they knew was unwise.

Hitler's obsession with theatricals was reflected in his musical taste, which admitted only the most grandiose and often silly effects, but is especially evident in the monumental spectacles staged by the Nazi party. The Olympic Games of 1936 are a good example; the party rallies, which became more and more magnificent, are another. In addition, a series of other festivals throughout the year commemorated past events such as the Munich putsch or glorified Nazi martyrs. Most of these affairs were held at night, when the spotlights, bonfires and smoking torches superimposed against the black sky lent drama and a hint of fear to the occasion.

The Führer had a mania for size, speed and numbers: his Mercedes could out-run any car on the road; he owned the largest, one-piece marble table top in the world, etc. His architec-

Above right:
Hitler receives Oswald
Mosley (left), leader of
the British Blackshirts.
Mosley, his wife Diana
Mitford and his sister-in-
law Unity Mitford
stayed with Hitler on
several occasions before
the war. Unity became
infatuated with Hitler
and attempted suicide
when war broke out in
1939.

Right:
Hitler and Goebbels in
1938. Goebbels was one
of the few who remained
completely loyal to
Hitler until the end.

tural plans, avidly developed with his young associate Albert Speer, also relied more on size than on basic design; years later Speer would remark on the striking similarity between the plans they drew up in the 1930s and a Cecil B DeMille movie set. All the schemes for rebuilding the major German cities show gigantic blocks of buildings along vast avenues, with hardly a blade of grass to be seen.

After the reoccupation of the Rhineland in 1936 Hitler became more interested in foreign policy at the expense of party and domestic affairs. He also began to withdraw from many of his old comrades (probably because some of them did not stand in proper awe of the Führer) and to build a wall between himself and his companions. That circle of companions was changing, too, though he was still at ease only with members of the Old Guard—Göring, Goebbels, Ley, Hess, his chauffers and adjutants, Max Amann or Hoffmann. Martin Bormann was fast becoming his indispensable right-hand man, largely because of his assiduous toadying to the Führer's wishes in even the smallest matters. Albert Speer and Joachim von Ribbentrop were two of the few upper-middle-class, bourgeois followers he really came to trust.

Other old friends were dropping out of the picture. Some, like Julius Streicher, were simply too disreputable to be allowed to hold office. Others had shown themselves to be unequal to the task and had been shoved into the background, like Hermann Esser and Alfred Rosenberg. Putzi Hanfstängl found himself increasingly out in the cold, mainly because he insisted on saying what he thought, whether or not it suited Hitler; the already tense situation

autumn 1936, the situation became so tense that she gave up her post as housekeeper and left the Obersalzburg to marry a professor in Dresden, leaving Eva sole mistress of Haus Wachenfeld.

During the 1930s Hitler appears as an almost mythical figure, towering above the other world leaders before a backdrop of adulation and energetic industry. He had many admirers, not only in Europe but in America and England, and groups similar to the National Socialists formed everywhere (including the British Union of Fascists under Oswald Mosley, the *Action Française* led by Charles Maurras, the German-American Bund, and even Chiang Kai-shek's Blue Shirt movement in China).

This was the period when Hitler's fortunes were at their height, when he seemingly could do nothing wrong. As soon as he had solidified his domestic power base he turned its administration over to his lieutenants and directed most of his energy to foreign affairs—with the same apparently effortless manner, the same infallible sense of timing and the same astonishing degree of success.

was exacerbated when his wife Helene divorced him in 1936. Hanfstängl's personal devotion to Hitler never diminished, but he told his fifteen-year-old son Egon that his enemies in the party were bound to try to liquidate him sooner or later. Though unwilling as yet to desert the Führer, the two made contingency plans: any message beginning with the word 'perhaps' would be the signal for Egon to quietly board the next train to Switzerland without a word to anyone, even his mother.

Within six months that plan had to be put into effect. Hanfstängl, on a mission for the Führer to Spain, was informed that he was to parachute over the Red lines between Madrid and Barcelona—a death sentence. The sympathetic pilot suddenly detected 'engine trouble.' After they had landed at a small airfield Hanfstängl pretended to call Berlin for instructions and then reported that his orders from Hitler were to return to Germany immediately. Once home he quickly took a train to Zurich, where he sent the emergency message to Egon. The boy packed a few things and caught a Zurich-bound train, hiding in a toilet for several hours until he was safely across the border and reunited with his father.

During the same period Hitler's relationship with Eva Braun improved somewhat, especially after her second suicide attempt in the autumn of 1935; he became slightly more attentive, first renting her an apartment, then buying her a little house not far from his own Munich apartment. As the liaison with Eva prospered, his relations with his half-sister Angela deteriorated; Angela had little use for *die bloede kuh* (the stupid cow) and never missed a chance to snub her or sabotage the union. Finally, in

V Preparations for War

Hitler's primary foreign policy goal in 1933 was to overthrow the Treaty of Versailles. Since this goal threatened the security of almost every European nation, how did he manage to achieve it so easily in the mid-1930s?

One reason is that many of his ideas and policies, though carried to extremes, found some reflection in the general European mood of the time. Communism, for example, was seen as a potent menace; many people felt that the Nazi assaults on freedom and democracy were the German people's business—they were not as important to outsiders as was Germany's position as a bulwark against Soviet Russia. In many intellectual circles, furthermore, democracy was seen as anachronistic and impotent, while authoritarianism had a growing popular appeal. Anti-Semitism in other countries—Poland, France, England, Hungary, Rumania and the Baltic States—was as strong or stronger than in Germany. Hitler was even able to use many principles from the Versailles Treaty itself—self-determination of peoples, equality, honor—as arguments to support Germany's case.

Most important of these factors was that foreign statesmen, almost to a man, exhibited the same short-sighted overconfidence in their ability to control and limit Hitler as had his erstwhile colleagues in Germany. In fact, Hitler himself called the diplomats of England and France 'my Hugenbergers.'

During his first two years in power Hitler had few options as to how he conducted his foreign affairs; until his secret rearmament had made Germany strong enough to remove any threat of punitive action by the Allied powers, his country was highly vulnerable to armed intervention.

Thus during 1934 all three services were ordered to begin rebuilding as quickly and as

Meanwhile, Hitler's major preoccupation was an alliance with England—an idea which had appealed to him since 1923. His overtures were met coolly at first, and received a serious setback in July 1934 when, after months of agitation, Austrian Nazis murdered Chancellor Engelbert Dolfuss. Their attempted coup was badly organized; Dr Kurt von Schuschnigg took over and restored the government. But the murder sparked off strong protests from both England and France, while Mussolini, furious at what he considered a breach of faith, massed

Above:
Anthony Eden, Minister for League Affairs, and Sir John Simon, British Foreign Minister, discuss the German rearmament in March 1935 with Hitler, Baron von Neurath, German Foreign Minister, and von Ribbentrop, Hitler's Foreign Affairs adviser. These talks were eventually to lead to the signing of an Anglo-German Naval Pact in June.

secretly as possible. The army was to aim at bringing its numbers up to 300,000 by the beginning of October; the Navy began construction of *Scharnhorst* and *Gneisenau*, two 26,000-ton battlecruisers; Göring, as Minister of Civil Aviation started designing war planes and training pilots (as members of the League for Air Sports). The great German arms manufacturers were busy too. Researchers at IG Farben began to develop synthetic oil, gasoline and rubber, while Krupp already had completed designs for tank armaments and turrets as well as for several of the most important field guns that Germany would use during the war.

Italian troops on the Austro-Italian border. Hitler quickly drew back and denied all knowledge of the affair, even returning the conspirators—who had fled to Germany—back to Austria to stand trial.

At the end of 1934 he approached Britain with an offer to negotiate a naval agreement (which would also, incidently, give Germany parity with Britain in the air); but for the time being his efforts yielded few results. In January 1935 his stock in the international community rose when the Saar region voted overwhelmingly for reunion with Germany; Hitler's remarks after the plebiscite, to the effect that

Germany had no further claims on France, added to the atmosphere of goodwill and co-operation.

Britain and France continued to press, as they had been doing since the previous summer, for an extension of the Locarno Pact, to include mutual assistance pacts with Eastern and Central Europe. They also proposed to strengthen the existing treaty by including an agreement relating to unprovoked aggression from the air. In return, they hinted that they would be willing to withdraw their objections to German rearmament.

However Hitler was not anxious to make commitments in the East, and also preferred the idea of a bold, unilateral repudiation of Versailles to the prospect of long negotiations in which he would have to make concessions to the other powers. So he hedged, setting a tentative meeting with the British Foreign Secretary, Sir John Simon, for 7 March in Berlin. On the 4th, however, the British Government published a White Paper condemning German rearmament; Hitler seized the opportunity to postpone the talks, making the feeble excuse that he was ill. On 9 March he tested the Allies' determination by formally announcing what everyone had known all along—that Germany had a military air force. As expected, France reacted by extending her own term of military service, while in England Simon merely announced that he and Anthony Eden, then Keeper of the Privy Seal, still hoped to go to Berlin. The French reaction, in turn, served as the ostensible reason for Hitler's next pronouncement on Saturday, 16 March: reluctantly, and only in response to the warlike threats of his neighbors, he had issued a decree reinstating universal military service and establishing a peacetime army of 36 divisions—about 550,000 men. On the next day, 17 March, Goebbels organized a parade that reflected the joy and celebration that was felt throughout the country. Germany's honor had been restored; the Versailles Treaty was dead and Germany lived again.

The other powers made their obligatory noises of condemnation: Britain sent a formal note of protest; the League of Nations set up a committee to deal with any future actions; and a three-power conference in Stresa on 11 April, arranged by France and Italy, petered out with a routine protest through lack of any real British support.

On 21 May Hitler made another eloquent 'peace speech' to the Reichstag, wherein he expressed his own horror of war, disclaimed any thought of wanting to conquer other peoples, renounced all claim to Alsace-Lorraine, guaranteed the safety of both Poland and Austria, and finally—especially for Britain—offered to limit the new German navy to 35 percent of the British naval forces. At the same time Hitler made economic preparations for war.

Above:
Hitler and Mussolini in 1934. Hitler was very much an unknown quantity for all foreign leaders. His first foreign visit was in June 1933 when he visited Mussolini in Venice who treated him like an inexperienced diplomatist.

Britain rose to the bait with incredible speed and Ribbentrop, who had become Hitler's special envoy, went to London right away to begin talks on an agreement. As he made abundantly clear in the first meeting, he was not there to negotiate; 35 percent was not a proposal, it represented the Führer's final decision. Once he had conquered his initial anger, however, Simon not only agreed to 35 percent, but also conceded parity in submarines. The Anglo-German Naval Treaty was signed on 18 June 1935—on the 20th anniversary of the day a combined British/Prussian force had defeated France at Waterloo.

Though public reaction to the treaty in Britain was almost universally favorable the British, in their eagerness to secure a private advantage and assure their continued domination of the high seas, had demolished once and for all the existing political relationships in Europe. The solidarity of the Allies was irrevocably sabotaged by Britain's unilateral action, which was taken greatly amiss by the other naval powers, France and Italy. The Russians were equally upset (although that did not prevent them signing a new trade treaty with Germany).

This disintegration of the relations between the Allies was clearly demonstrated in their reaction to Mussolini's invasion of Ethiopia on 2 October. Far from continuing her policy of appeasement, Great Britain angrily demanded the imposition of sanctions against Italy and ostentatiously reinforced her Mediterranean fleet. France, who saw Germany as a far greater threat to European security and who was unwilling to lose another member of the anti-German alliance for the sake of the rather dubious ally who had recently come to terms with Hitler, objected, angering Britain even more. It would only have taken the closing of the Suez Canal or an oil embargo to deny Mussolini his 'place in the sun.' But of course Britain was not willing to go that far, and backing down only served to further diminish what little prestige the Allies and the League of Nations retained – as well as strengthening Hitler's faith in the ultimate success of his plan for an Anglo-German alliance.

For his part, Hitler publicly refused to help Haile Selassie, at the same time sending supplies to both Ethiopia and Italy. No matter what happened, he was a winner: if Mussolini became too heavily involved in Africa he would be in no position to worry about Austria; if Italy won it would force a split with England and France, and thus Mussolini would be ready for an alliance with Germany.

Mussolini's adventure in Ethiopia gave Hitler the confidence to take his next step: renunciation of the Locarno Pact and occupation of the Rhineland – the demilitarized zone that included not only the cities of Cologne, Dusseldorf and Bonn east of the Rhine, but all German territory to the west as well. If England and France had been willing to let Italy's invasion go by without any substantive protest, he reasoned, surely they would do the same in this case. His chances looked even better since Edward VIII, who made no secret of his sympathy with many of Germany's aims, had ascended the throne in England in January following the death of George V.

Hitler's excuse, he soon determined, would be the ratification of a long-proposed Franco-Soviet mutual assistance pact. In February the German Ambassador to Italy, Ulrich von Hassell, was instructed to obtain Mussolini's views on the treaty; the reply indicated that though help from Italy might not be forthcoming, Il Duce would at least remain neutral in any dispute over the Locarno Treaty.

On 27 February France ratified the treaty, which had been drawn up the year before. On 2 March Blomberg formally ordered all three services to prepare to transfer units into the demilitarized Rhineland, according to plans laid with great secrecy during the winter of 1935–36. Operation Winter Exercise had begun. The occupation was set for Saturday 7 March.

The German generals were worried; if it wished, the French army could destroy the small German force without really trying. In his own mind Blomberg had already decided to withdraw his troops if France showed the slightest sign of resistance. Hitler too was anxious. Over and over he asked himself what France would do. 'I knew what I would do if I'd been the French,' he later told Hoffmann. 'I

Above:
Hitler attends the memorial service held in Berlin on the occasion of Marshal Pilsudski's death in May 1935. Hitler was engaged in delicate negotiations with Poland at the time and sent Göring to attend the funeral service. The Non-Aggression Pact between Germany and Poland had been concluded in January 1934.

should have struck, and I would not have allowed a single German soldier to cross the Rhine.'

At 1130 on 7 March 1936 the first German soldiers moved across Hohenzollern Bridge, under the eyes of a hand-picked group of reporters and a crowd of cheering German patriots. Foreign Minister Neurath had already informed the ambassadors of Britain, France and Italy of Germany's renunciation of the Locarno Treaty. By noon Hitler was addressing a delirious Reichstag at the Kroll Opera House. Germany was no longer bound by the Locarno Treaty, he announced, and had re-established absolute sovereignty over the demilitarized zone. On the other hand, he claimed, 'We have no territorial demands to make in Europe. . . . Germany will never break the peace!'

Above:
Hitler attends Army maneuvers in the summer of 1935. With him were Blomberg (on his right) and Generals Beck and Bock (on his left). Hitler had to make sure that the Army would follow his orders as he prepared for his next move, the occupation of the Rhineland.

Despite his fears that the French would march, he managed to keep his nerve and preserve an aura of confidence. The French Foreign Minister flew to London to ask for Britain's support in a countermove, but was refused. The British government believed, according to Anthony Eden (the Foreign Secretary), that there was no reason to suppose that Germany's action threatened hostilities. Without British support France dared do nothing more than to mass thirteen divisions along the Maginot Line. Hitler's colossal bluff had succeeded—and Britain and France had lost their last chance to halt Germany without risking a serious war. Events had followed what had become the usual pattern: loud cries of protest followed by anxious consultations and finally a series of conferences and calls for calmness and reason, at the end of which any opposition to Germany that remained had lost all its momentum.

At home Hitler was able to use the Rhineland to solidify his popularity even further; in a plebiscite called for 29 March, 98.8 percent voted in his favor. The incident also established his power over the generals, for he had stood firm when they wavered—and he had been right! France's failure to defend the Rhineland also had important consequences for her eastern

allies—Russia, Poland, Czechoslovakia, Rumania and Yugoslavia suddenly realized that the French would not be much help in a crisis. In Austria Dr Schuschnigg 'knew that in order to save Austrian independence I had to embark on a course of appeasement.'

On 11 July 1936 after lengthy negotiations between Schuschnigg and Papen (the German Minister in Austria) the Austro-German Agreement was signed in Vienna. The published clauses of the treaty did much to improve relations between Germany and Italy: Germany recognized Austrian sovereignty and promised not to interfere in her internal affairs, in return for Schuschnigg's agreement to consider Austria a 'German state' in matters of foreign policy. In the secret clauses of the treaty, however, Schuschnigg agreed to a relaxation of the press war between the two countries, amnesty for Nazi political prisoners in Austria, details concerning treatment of Austrian Nazi refugees in Germany, and—most important—he agreed to give 'respectable' members of the Austrian National Socialist Party, like the Viennese lawyer Dr Arthur Seyss-Inquart, positions of political responsibility. For the next eighteen months Germany would use the agreement to force more and more concessions from the Aus-

trian government; but for the time being everything was amicable on the surface at least, while Mussolini interpreted the successful conclusion of the agreement as a personal triumph.

For sometime feelings of mutual respect and liking had been developing between the two Fascist dictators, despite their unpropitious first meeting in Venice. Though outwardly very different, the two shared many traits: an insatiable thirst for power, a love of theatrical displays, even the memory of a humble background and subsequent rise to leadership. Hitler admired Mussolini's style and political acumen and, as we have already seen, was not averse to imitating him. For his part, Mussolini—although he could see the disadvantages of having Hitler as an ally—was impressed with the Führer's repeated defiance of the Allies and League of Nations. He was also concerned lest the energetic German would pre-empt his position as 'elder Fascist' in Europe.

During that July two other factors contributed to a rapprochement between Germany and Italy. On 4 July the League of Nations tacitly capitulated and withdrew its sanctions from Italy. On the 17th civil war broke out in Spain, and Hitler lost no time in reaping every possible benefit from the situation. On 25 July two Nazi

Above:
German generals attend the 1935 Nuremberg Rally. From left to right General Blomberg, Minister of War, Göring, General Fritsch, Commander in Chief of the German Army. Fritsch was opposed to foreign policy which might lead to war because he did not think Germany was ready for war.

Left:
Hitler outlines his foreign policy to the Reichstag, in the Kroll Opera House.

speech on 1 November 1936, when he spoke of the two countries becoming an 'axis around which all those European states which are animated by a desire for collaboration and peace may work together.'

Meanwhile, Hitler was still pursuing his dream of an alliance with England. In August 1936 he had appointed Ribbentrop as German Ambassador to the Court of St James. The new minister was an unattractive figure—lazy, arrogant, humorless and generally inept—but his slavish loyalty was a great recommendation, as was his success in negotiating the Anglo-German Naval Treaty. For months Germany continued to press for further agreements, puzzled by the lack of response from Britain—whose distrust of Hitler outweighed even their fear of the Communist menace. Hitler was of two minds: on one hand he hesitated to alienate Britain and lose his chance for an alliance; on the other, he saw Britain's value as an ally as negligible and believed that the country was no longer a world power.

Ribbentrop was busy in other areas at the same time; on 25 November he flew from London to Berlin to sign the Anti-Comintern Pact with Japan, which he had negotiated behind

leaders from Morocco and Spain arrived at Bayreuth, where Hitler was attending the annual Wagner festival, carrying a personal note from General Franco. Without even consulting Göring and Blomberg, Hitler decided to lend active support to the Spanish Fascists, and directives to that effect were issued immediately. Several formations of Junker-52s were dispatched immediately, to help Franco ferry troops across the Mediterranean and establish a beachhead in Spain. For the next three years Hitler sent advisers, technicians, military supplies and even the famous Condor Air Legion to Franco's assistance. But Germany never sent enough men or materiel to significantly affect the conduct of the war. In fact, it was to Hitler's advantage to keep the conflict going as long as possible, since the confusion it caused in European politics worked to his advantage. Mussolini sent almost 70,000 men, which satisfied his pride by making him the dominant Fascist force in Spain. Italy was thus prevented from making up the quarrel with the Allies—which could easily have been done after the withdrawal of sanctions. On the other hand, the common cause in Spain strengthened the ties between Italy and Germany. In October Count Galeazzo Ciano, Mussolini's son-in-law and Foreign Minister, visited the German Foreign Minister, Konstantin von Neurath, at Berchtesgaden. There the two signed the secret October Protocol, outlining a joint policy for foreign affairs—a document which was to become one of the cornerstones of the Rome-Berlin Axis. The latter term was first used by Mussolini in a

the back of the Foreign Office. The treaty purported to be a general agreement to oppose the Communist 'world conspiracy,' but it also contained a secret clause in which both parties agreed to sign no political treaties with the Soviet Union and to come to the other's assistance in case either was the victim of an unprovoked attack or threat of attack. Hitler saw the October Protocol and the Anti-Comintern Pact as the bases of a military alliance between the three have-not nations.

On 30 January 1937 Hitler looked back at the successes of his first four years in office with an understandable degree of satisfaction. Germans

Above:
Hitler gave General Franco much active aid during the Spanish Civil War. This investment of effort never paid off and Franco did not try to pay off his debt to Hitler during World War II.

whose self-respect had been all but destroyed by defeat and humiliation could feel pride again in the fact that Germany was once again a respected member of the world community; his rearmament program, his Rhineland bluff, his single-handed destruction of the Versailles Treaty, and above all his confident leadership—as contrasted with the weakness and vacillation of the other countries in Europe—greatly increased his own prestige and that of Germany. At home his achievements were even more obvious. Only a few years before Germany had been divided into many bickering factions, quarreling over who would get the lion's share of a very small pie; the people were all but destroyed by their desperate struggle for survival in a world of insane inflation and astronomical unemployment. Now the factories were humming, social inequities were being corrected and the German public—released from its long sojourn in the Slough of Despond—was discovering a new confidence in itself and in its nation's destiny as a great world power. But though most of the foreign observers who flocked to Germany to study its amazing rebirth and even many Germans themselves were unable to admit it, all the activity, the new sense of militant national purpose and identity could have but one end—aggressive war. Among those in power, however, there was never any doubt about Hitler's ultimate objectives.

Hitler spent most of 1937 consolidating his alliances, nurturing Germany's growing might and preparing, always preparing, for war.

When Germany had occupied the Rhineland and thus moved up the Belgian border, King Leopold had withdrawn his little country from the Locarno Pact and announced that henceforth Belgium would be strictly neutral. Another breach in the Western Powers' system of alliances was caused by Hitler's assiduous courting of Poland, which resulted in loosening that country's ties with France. The signing of the non-aggression pact in 1934 had been followed by many visits back and forth by Polish and Nazi leaders. In 1936 the Poles, worried by increasing Nazi influence in predominantly German Danzig and spurred by Hitler's reoccupation of the Rhineland, had made an attempt to renew their bonds with France. Hitler immediately went to great lengths to reassure them of his honest intentions; Göring was sent to Warsaw early in 1937 to convince the Polish Foreign Minister, Colonel Josef Beck, that Germany saw a strong, independent Poland as being in her own best interests. To strengthen these reassurances a minorities treaty was negotiated and finally signed in Berlin on 5 November 1937. The treaty, and Hitler's subsequent reiteration of his friendly intentions, ensured Poland's neutrality in the East—a condition that was of vital importance to Hitler's plans for Czechoslovakia, just as Mussolini's benevolence was the key to his ambitions in Austria.

The friendship between Germany and Italy was still growing, despite lingering suspicions on both sides; in January 1937 Ciano had signed an agreement with England regarding their mutual interests in the Mediterranean, and

Above:
Galeazzo Ciano, Mussolini's son-in-law and Italian Foreign Minister (center) with Göring on his right and Baron von Neurath, German Foreign Minister, on his left in the Italian Embassy in Berlin in October 1936. During his visit the terms of German-Italian co-operation were laid down.

Austria continued to be a touchy issue. But the advantages of partnership with Germany seemed increasingly attractive to Il Duce, and on 23 September he set out for Munich along with 100 followers. When he arrived two days later he was met by Hitler, holding out his arms in welcome before a cheering crowd. The two leaders had just enough time for a one-hour chat at Hitler's apartment on Prinzregentenplatz before Mussolini was whisked off on a round of ceremonies and spectacles, including a parade of SS stormtroopers that made an indelible impression on him. Army maneuvers in Mecklenburg and a visit to Krupp factories in Essen were other highlights of the tour, which reached its finale in Berlin on 28 September.

Almost a million spectators lined the streets and enthusiastically cheered Mussolini's progress from the railroad station to the town center. Next day 800,000 people gathered in the Olympic Stadium to hear him speak. Before his oration was over, however, a torrential thunderstorm broke; the Italian dictator was left to make his way back to Berlin alone, in an open car, without a rain coat. But even this failed to dampen his spirits. He had come to Berlin feeling some disdain for the German Chancellor—he left captivated by Hitler's charm and by the demonstrations of Germany's military might and industrial power. The attraction between the two men was sincere. Even when Hitler became disillusioned with

Right:
Polish Foreign Minister Colonel Jozef Beck visits Hitler in Berlin in January 1938. This visit was undertaken to solidify Polish-German relations following the treaty in November 1937 settling the German minorities in Poland question.

Right:
Mussolini visits Germany in September 1937. This visit impressed Mussolini with Germany's industrial and military might.

Below:
The start of Mussolini's official visit in 1937: the two dictators meet in Munich.

Italy's conduct of the war, he would not lose his regard for Mussolini, nor would he betray him. For the Italian, it was the beginning of a friendship that would cloud his judgment and lead him to take the first steps on the road to disaster and a gibbet in the Piazzale Loreto in Milan.

Finally, Hitler felt strong enough to make his next big move. On 5 November he held a secret meeting in the Chancellery. Present were his adjutant, Colonel Hossbach (who took minutes of the meeting); the War Minister, Field Marshal von Blomberg; the Commanders in Chief of the Army, Navy and Air Force—Colonel General Werner von Fritsch, Admiral Raeder and Göring; and Germany's Foreign Minister, Neurath. It was no ordinary top-level conference. Hitler began by making the case that Germany's future could only be assured by the

acquisition of additional *Lebensraum* (living space), which could only be found in Europe at the risk of war—since the attacker always comes up against a protector. The country's problem could only be solved by force, and the only questions to be asked were 'When' and 'How.' The first step must be to secure the southern and eastern flanks by taking control of Austria and Czechoslovakia. These grandiose plans were opposed by Blomberg and Fritsch, who did not discount England and France as easily as the Führer did, and who were also frankly worried about the Army's ability to carry out these contests. Neurath was also worried, and Raeder was dismayed by the prospect of war, since the Navy at that time had no battleships in service.

Much has been made of this meeting, but it is unlikely that it was a real commitment to go to war; Hitler was too much of an opportunist to burn his bridges in such a manner. Probably the reason he gave to Göring was the real one: he wanted to put pressure on Blomberg and Fritsch, who had been opposing the accelerated rearmament; the flood of conscripts and materiel was becoming more than the small regular army could handle effectively. However, the meeting also demonstrated a change of mood marking the end of the cautious moves of Hitler's first period and the beginning of the second phase, when he felt able to run more risks and put more pressure on other nations.

The conference also marked the beginning of the mutual disillusionment between Hitler and

Above:
General Werner von Fritsch meets General Ludwig Beck during Army maneuvers in the Teutoburger Forest in the summer of 1937. Fritsch was removed from his position of Commander in Chief of the Army in January 1938 after being framed by the SS. Beck, the Army Chief of Staff, was forced to resign in August 1938 when the generals' revolt against Hitler's war plans fizzled out. He was later involved in the July 1944 Bomb Plot.

Right:
General von Fritsch, General von Blomberg and Hitler. Blomberg was forced out of office in January 1938 as was Fritsch, his obvious successor.

his generals. Angered by their opposition, he lost any trace of respect he might have retained for the old military ruling class. Their inhibited, cautious responses infuriated him; his own ideal general would be like 'a butcher's dog who has to be held tightly by the collar lest he attack everyone in sight.' The generals realized belatedly that Hitler really meant all he had been saying for years. Their contempt for the former corporal had blinded them to the perils of their own situation until it was far too late to change it.

Soon, however, the Führer found an opportunity to reorganize the High Command to better suit his own purposes. It all began innocently enough with Blomberg's decision to remarry; a step he was determined to take even though the lady in question, Erna Grühn, had a somewhat disreputable past. Realizing that the socially conscious Officer Corps would be shocked, Blomberg went to Göring for advice, who strongly urged him to follow the dictates of his heart. The lovers were married quietly on 12 January 1938 with Hitler and Göring as the principal witnesses. Only a few days later, however, a police dossier turned up, revealing that Blomberg's new wife had a police record as a prostitute and had once been convicted of modeling for obscene photographs. When Blomberg returned from a brief honeymoon twelve days later, Göring coldly informed him that he would have to resign his commission.

The next question was who to appoint as the new Minister of War and Commander in Chief of the Armed Forces. (Hitler, as President, was Supreme Commander of the Armed Forces, or Wehrmacht.) Since Fritsch was Commander in Chief of the Army, or *Reichswehr*—which was part of the Wehrmacht—he was the obvious man for the job. But Hitler was disinclined to raise the status of the man who had opposed his views on 5 November. In addition, Fritsch's appointment was strenuously opposed by Göring, who wanted the job for himself, and by Himmler, who resented the general's attempts to limit the influence of the SS within the army. These two managed to produce yet another dossier, this time revealing that Fritsch had been guilty of homosexual activities; though the charges it contained were obviously trumped up, it was enough to give Hitler an excuse to send Fritsch on indefinite leave.

Hitler's solution was announced to the cabinet during what was to be its last meeting, on 4 February. The post of War Minister was abolished, and Hitler himself would take over as Commander in Chief of the Wehrmacht. The work of the old War Ministry would be carried on by a separate High Command of the Armed Forces (*Oberkommando der Wehrmacht* or OKW), headed by his lackey, General Wilhelm Keitel. General Walther von Brauchitsch was named Commander in Chief of the Reichswehr.

At the same time Göring was given the rank of Field Marshal as a consolation prize. Sixteen senior generals were asked to retire, and 44 others were transferred to other commands. Neurath was replaced by Ribbentrop in the Foreign Ministry and three key ambassadors—Papen in Vienna, Hassell in Rome, and Dirksen in Tokyo—were simultaneously recalled. The Ministry of the Economy was divested of all its powers and placed under the insipid Walter Funk.

The bloodless purge had removed the last of the old-school conservatives; Hitler had all foreign, economic and military policy under his direct control. The last stage in the Nazi revolution was complete.

In Austria the Chancellor, Kurt von Schuschnigg, a decent, intelligent, if somewhat narrow-minded man, had become increasingly worried about his country's future. Ever since the signing of the Austro-German Agreement in July 1936 Austrian Nazis had been working to undermine his government, keeping up a constant pressure with terrorist tactics and massive demonstrations. He had also received clear indications that Mussolini was no longer as concerned with Austria's fate as he once had been. On 25 January 1938 police raids on Nazi headquarters in Vienna unearthed plans for an uprising that spring, in which both Schuschnigg and Papen were marked for assassination. Ten days later Papen received another surprise when he was informed of his recall to Germany. Immediately he hastened to Berchtesgaden, to see Hitler and try to reinstate himself.

He arrived armed with the proposal that Hitler and Schuschnigg meet face to face and discuss their problems—a prospect that intrigued Hitler so much that he forgot about firing Papen and sent him back to Vienna to arrange the meeting. Schuschnigg readily agreed to the idea, realizing that it might well be his last opportunity to reach some sort of arrangement with Germany. On 12 February he and an undersecretary in the Foreign Office, Guido Schmidt, arrived at the Obersalzburg.

Hitler and Schuschnigg had hardly settled into Hitler's study when the Führer launched into a furious diatribe against virtually all of Austria's policies. As Schuschnigg later recalled, the conversation during the next two hours was 'somewhat unilateral.' He tried to appease the angry Chancellor and yet stand his ground, while Hitler raved about Austria's 'treason' and his own determination to take over the country by force if his demands were not met. Schuschnigg had no idea what those demands were until mid-afternoon when Ribbentrop presented him with a two-page draft of an agreement that in effect bound him to turn the Austrian government over to the Nazis within a week: the ban on the Nazi Party was to be lifted; an amnesty for all imprisoned Nazis

was to be declared within three days; Dr Seyss-Inquart was to be made Minister of the Interior with control of the police; and Glaise-Horstenau, another Nazi sympathizer, was to be appointed Minister of War. There was to be an exchange of officers between the Austrian and German armies, and Austria would be assimilated into the German economic system.

Try as he might, Schuschnigg could not obtain any changes in the agreement, he was told it was Hitler's last word, and that he must either sign or take the consequences. When the beleaguered Austrian Chancellor saw Hitler again, he gave in and said that he was willing enough to sign the document—but that the constitution gave the President of the Republic sole power to accept and carry out the agreement. Hitler abruptly threw open the study door, curtly dismissed Schuschnigg, and called for General Keitel. It was pure bluff; when the general breathlessly arrived he was greeted with a grin, and when he asked for his orders was told, 'There are none. I just wanted to have you here.' Half an hour later Hitler again sent for the by now thoroughly intimidated Schuschnigg and announced that 'for the first time' in his life he had changed his mind. He would give Austria three more days before the agreement went into effect. Schuschnigg had no choice but to agree and sign the document.

Back in Vienna, the Chancellor had four days—until 15 February—to get President Wilhelm Miklas to agree to the alliance and another three—until 18 February—to take action. On the 13th General Jodl received orders via Keitel to fake military activity along the border; Miklas retreated before the threat of invasion and informed Papen on the 15th that he would honor the agreement. On the 16th the government announced the amnesty for Nazis and the appointment of Seyss-Inquart (soon to become the first of Hitler's puppet leaders) as Minister of Security.

From the beginning Seyss-Inquart made it clear that he took orders from Berlin, not Vienna. Schuschnigg still tried hard to hang on; he made a nationalistic speech to the Austrian Bundestag in an attempt to rally the opposition, and even turned to the workers for help. Even though the unions and the Social Democratic party had been suppressed by Dolfuss in 1934, they agreed to forget their past differences in the service of Austrian independence. But it was too late. Finally Schuschnigg decided to play his last card.

On 7 March he sent a message to Mussolini telling him that he was going to have to resort to a plebiscite; he hoped to destroy Hitler's strongest argument, that most Austrians favored Anschluss with Germany. Though Mussolini advised against it, Schuschnigg persisted, and the plebiscite was set for 13 March.

On the 9th, when the news reached Hitler, he

flew into another rage; to the surprise of his generals he decided to use military occupation if that was what was necessary to prevent the plebiscite. All that day, while Hitler composed an explanatory letter to Mussolini, the members of his military staff raced back and forth, trying to improvise an invasion plan from a theoretical study called Special Case Otto, drawn up years before to prevent Otto of Hapsburg from reclaiming his throne. At 0200 on 11 March Hitler issued Directive No 1 for Operation Otto; by the time he went to bed tanks and trucks were already rolling south toward the frontier.

In Vienna Schuschnigg was awakened at 0530 with the news that the Germans had closed the border at Salzburg. By 0615 he was on his way to his office; by 1000 he was closeted with Seyss-Inquart and Glaise-Horstenau. After a two-hour argument over Hitler's demand that the plebiscite be called off, in which they got nowhere, Schuschnigg went to President Miklas. After lunch he was able to tell Seyss-Inquart that the election would be canceled.

At 1445 Seyss-Inquart telephoned Göring with the news, and from that point on the Field Marshal took over conduct of the affair, displaying in the moment of crisis a cold-blooded calm that earned the undying admiration of the more highly strung Hitler. Within a few minutes he was back on the telephone with Germany's further demands: Schuschnigg had to resign and be replaced by Seyss-Inquart within two hours. As soon as he was officially Chancellor Seyss-Inquart had to send a telegram requesting armed German intervention to quell civil disorder in Austria.

Schuschnigg ordered his troops to the border and in desperation wired London for help. But the reply from the new Foreign Minister, Lord Halifax (the replacement for Anthony Eden, who had objected too strenuously to Prime Minister Chamberlain's appeasement of Mussolini), was—on Chamberlain's orders—that the British government could not guarantee Austria any protection. With no illusions left about getting help from Italy, Schuschnigg had no choice.

At 1600 he tendered his resignation to Miklas, who accepted it, but refused to appoint Seyss-Inquart Chancellor. While Miklas tried in vain to find someone else willing to take the job, Göring was keeping up the pressure. So were the Austrian Nazis, who by now filled the streets and were even occupying public buildings—with little opposition, since they controlled the police.

At 1950 Schuschnigg went on the radio to broadcast his resignation to the entire nation; he announced that the Austrian army was to retreat without resisting, and denied the rumors of civil war. A few minutes later, on learning that Schuschnigg still had not been re-

Above:
Hitler's reception in Vienna on 16 March 1938 was enthusiastic.

Above right:
Hitler addresses an enormous crowd from a ramp in front of the Hofburg Palace, in Vienna on 15 March 1938.

Right:
Hitler is received in Vienna on 9 April 1938 after he had campaigned throughout Austria for support for the plebiscite deciding on unity with Germany.

placed, Göring ordered Syess-Inquart to take over and form a government anyway—and to send that telegram!

At last Hitler signed Directive No 2, ordering German troops to cross the Austrian border at dawn. The time was 2045. Some three minutes later Göring was on the telephone again, sending a message to Seyss-Inquart: he did not have to actually send the telegram—all he had to do was indicate agreement, and the Germans would take care of the rest. Wilhelm Keppler, Hitler's agent in Vienna and Göring's go-between, was not able to obtain agreement and report back for almost an hour.

One of Hitler's greatest worries during this trying period had been the Italian reaction, but at 2225 that evening Philip of Hesse telephoned from Rome: he had just returned from speaking to Mussolini. Il Duce had been very friendly and had said that Austria was of no importance to him. Relieved and elated, Hitler almost stammered his thanks: 'Please tell him I will never

streets and along highways lined with cheering crowds. The first troops had crossed the border at eight that morning, and anything less like an invasion force would be hard to imagine: General Heinz Guderian's Second Panzer Division was using *Baedeker's Guide* to find their way and refueling at gas stations en route. Almost half the vehicles broke down along the way and the road between Salzburg and Vienna was soon littered with disabled tanks and trucks.

Hitler's reception in the town where he had gone to school was so enthusiastic that the Nazi leaders were amazed; the next morning he visited nearby Leonding so that he could place a wreath on his parent's grave; later he revisited places he had known as a child, and held a reception in his hotel for his old friends. Earlier in the day he had forwarded the draft of a new law for Austro-German reunification to Seyss-Inquart in Vienna, with orders to get it passed that day. It was, despite President Miklas's stubborn refusal to sign it.

forget him for this! ... never, never, never, no matter what happens!'

Czechoslovakia could have been another problem had the Czech government decided to come to Schuschnigg's assistance. Göring therefore took time off from his telephoning to drop in on an official reception, where he immediately drew aside the Czech Ambassador, Dr Mastny. He assured the minister that Czechoslovakia had nothing to fear from the 'family affair' between Germany and Austria; after a quick call to Prague, Mastny was able to promise Göring in turn that his country would not mobilize troops or try to interfere with events in Austria.

Completely isolated both at home and abroad, Miklas finally gave in just before midnight on 11 March. Seyss-Inquart was appointed Chancellor and the Nazi list of cabinet members was accepted.

One of Seyss-Inquart's first acts as Chancellor was to ask Keppler, the Führer's representative, to try and have the invasion order canceled. After much discussion in Berlin, Hitler was awakened at 0230 with the request. He refused to consider it, but the argument among the military leaders continued. General Keitel, head of OKW, took the brunt of the generals' entreaties to call off the operation; General von Viebahn worked himself into such a state that he finally locked himself into a room and threatened to shoot anyone who came in, while Keitel later described that night as having been 'sheer hell.'

By the afternoon of 12 March Seyss-Inquart and Himmler (who had already begun to put his SS and Gestapo machinery into operation) were in Linz preparing to meet Hitler. The Führer crossed the border at his birthplace, Braunau, and began a triumphal procession through

Hitler had not come to Austria considering Anschluss—the full incorporation of Austria into the Reich—but the enthusiastic reception had convinced him that it would be possible. He had also received good news from Rome in the form of a congratulatory telegram from Mussolini. The Italian leader's formal approval removed the last nagging worry from his mind. When he learned that evening that the law making Austria a province of the German Reich had been passed, tears ran down his cheeks as he said, 'Yes, a good political action saves blood.'

On Monday morning Hitler set out for Vienna, where crowds jammed the streets, shouting their approval. Another of his youthful dreams came true when he walked up the red carpet into the Hotel Imperial—the place that had seemed like an unattainable paradise to a cold, hungry young man down on his luck in the big city many years before. On Tuesday, after a speech to an enthusiastic crowd of 200,000, he reviewed a parade, and then flew back to Munich and Berlin for another triumphal reception.

By and large Hitler's welcome in Austria was genuine. Austria too had experienced many problems during the postwar period, and, to many people who felt that the country could no longer exist on its own, union with Germany

was the only course that would ensure a viable future. The desire to see the end of unemployment and a relaxation of the tension that had been growing for the last few years, combined with sentimental ties of language and history made Germany's task easier.

Most Austrians soon found themselves disappointed. Hess and Himmler were busy even before the Führer left Vienna, reorganizing the Austrian security system and drawing up lists of people to be arrested (the total would reach 76,000). Nazi stormtroopers, particularly the fanatical Austrian Legion, began a persecution of Jews that was so vicious that many who had welcomed the Anschluss were shocked and disgusted. Jews were dragged out and made to scrub Schuschnigg's propaganda slogans off walls with acid, clean the latrines in the SS barracks, sweep the streets and endure public humiliation. Thousands of refugees, including Sigmund Freud and Stefan Zweig, poured out of Austria.

On 18 March Hitler reported to the Reichstag on the great events in Austria and announced that on 10 April the population of the Greater Reich would go to the polls to approve the Anschluss, as well as to extend the Enabling Act another four years, so that he would have time to consolidate the country. It would be the

last election-plebiscite in Germany during the Nazi regime. He and other Nazi leaders spent the next weeks traveling around the country whipping up enthusiasm for the union. The last ten days were spent electioneering in Austria; his final campaign speech was made in Vienna on 9 April. The next day 99.73 percent of the voters in Austria and 99.03 percent in Germany voted in favor of union. Hitler had added seven million citizens to the population of the Reich and had also gained a good strategic position: Austria was the gateway to southeastern Europe, while Vienna was the center of the communication and trade system. In addition the country had resources of iron and steel that Germany desperately needed.

As usual, the other nations of Europe had done nothing to stop Hitler. Mussolini, making the best of a bad situation, had loudly proclaimed his support of the Axis. Poland repeated its assurances that it would do nothing. France and Russia were uneasy—France reaffirmed its support of Czechoslovakia while Russia proposed a four-power conference to discuss limiting further aggression—but neither made a substantive protest. In England Mr Chamberlain, still hoping for a settlement, refused to support the Russian and French proposals, which he claimed would aggravate the division of Europe into two blocks. The League of Nations did not even bother issuing a condemnation. Hitler was ready for his next step—into Czechoslovakia.

He wasted little time. On 28 March, two weeks after his annexation of Austria, the Führer met with Konrad Henlein, leader of the Sudeten Germans. Henlein would henceforth consider himself Hitler's agent; his orders were to press constantly for demands which would be rejected by the Czech government. This, Hitler hoped, would create tension in Czechoslovakia that could be exacerbated until he could appear to once again be forced by circumstances to intervene.

There were tactical reasons for an immediate move against Czechoslovakia, which occupied a position of immense strategic value in Central Europe; Hitler had recognized this as early as November 1937 in his talk to the generals, and a staff study called Case Green (a surprise attack on Czechoslovakia) had been in existence for some time. The Czech defenses along the German border compared to the Maginot Line in strength and were manned by first-class Czech troops, supplied by the famous Skoda armament works. The country was less than an hour by plane from Berlin and important German industrial centers; Hitler was not far wrong when he called it 'a dagger pointed at the heart of Germany.'

But aside from its strategic importance, there were psychological reasons why Hitler wanted to destroy Czechoslovakia. The republic was

Above:
Hitler 'blesses' an admirer during his visit to Austria following the Anschluss.

the creation of the hated Versailles Treaty—a small, multi-national state that had evolved into a democratic, prosperous and progressive country under the guidance first of Thomas Masaryk and then of Eduard Beneš. But it was never really able to solve the problem of its minorities: 1 million Hungarians, 3.25 million Sudeten Germans, 2.5 million Slovaks, all of whom felt that they were being oppressed by the Czech government. The rise of National Socialism in Germany increased the Sudeten Germans' discontent—which the Nazis took care to encourage.

The Czech government, fully aware of its dangerous position, had done its best to build up its defenses and to make alliances with France and Russia. But by 1938 no one wanted to pick a fight with Hitler and the network of alliances did not help the Czechs as their allies sought to avoid being drawn into a war.

tain that Mussolini would raise no objections if there was a move against Czechoslovakia.

Meanwhile, Britain and France had been putting increasing pressure on the Czechs to acceed to the Sudeten German demands while Chamberlain, in statements both on and off the record, made several attempts to reassure Germany. On 20 May Hitler was taken by surprise when the Czech government, reacting to rumors of German troop movements along the frontier, ordered a partial mobilization. The little country was taking the initiative against its larger neighbor and making a valiant attempt to make its reluctant allies stand by their word. Britain, France and Russia immediately repeated their support—a display of unanimity which left Hitler no option but to assure the Czechs that he had no belligerent aims and to self-righteously deny all reports of troop concentrations.

Hitler was not just furious at being opposed before his preparations were finished; he was deeply humiliated and the situation was made worse by the foreign press, who took great pleasure in underlining the way he had been forced to back down during the 'May Crisis.' For a week he shut himself up in the Berghof. On 28 May he suddenly appeared again in Berlin, and at a hastily assembled conference an-

Germany was not quite ready for invasion yet, so Henlein was sent home to keep the pot simmering, but with instructions not to let it boil over. On 21 April Hitler met with Keitel and instructed him to prepare detailed plans for overcoming the Czech defenses.

On 2 May the Führer and his entourage set out on a state visit to Italy, where Mussolini outdid himself in trying to match his own reception in Germany. Hitler was not pleased by the fact that protocol required Mussolini to stay in the background while he stayed with the Royal Family. The formality and arrogance of the court irritated him beyond endurance and he in turn offended the King with a series of small, studied discourtesies. On the plus side, he fell in love with Italy itself; years later he would extoll the magic of Florence and Rome, and the delights of Tuscany and Umbria. More important, he was able to dispell lingering Italian uneasiness over the Anschluss and to ascer-

Above:
Heinrich Himmler,
Hitler and Admiral
Raeder on an official visit
to Italy in May 1938.

Right:
Hitler returns to Munich
following his visit to
Italy, May 1938.

nounced that it was his 'unalterable decision to smash Czechoslovakia by military action in the near future.'

Throughout June, July and August Hitler was content to keep quiet and let the tension build up of its own accord. Henlein continued to demand more and more concessions, Britain and France continued to press the Czech government to agree, while Hitler quietly encouraged territorial demands from Hungary and Slovak nationalists, in addition to encouraging Poland and Rumania to stand firm against any Russian moves. He also continued his own military preparations, but here he ran into serious opposition from the Army High Command.

German military leaders were appalled at the prospect of an invasion, for they knew better than anyone else that they could not hope to win a general war. The Chief of the General Staff, General Beck, who had been pestering Brauchitsch for some time with memorandums criticizing Hitler's plans, sent another on 30 May. In fact, civilian opposition to Hitler's regime had been gathering for some time. In 1936 Karl Gördeler, the mayor of Leipzig, had broken with the Nazis over their anti-Semitism and their rearmament policy; in 1937 he went so far as travel to England, France and the United States to spread warnings of the dangers posed

Above:
Hitler and King Victor Emmanuel III in Rome on 8 May 1938. Hitler was not used to being in the company of royalty and did not enjoy that aspect of his visit.

by the National Socialists. Later he was joined by others, including Dr Schacht and Ulrich von Hassell, former ambassador to Italy—but without army support the group was powerless.

On 10 August, after Brauchitsch finally sent him one of Beck's memos, Hitler called a meeting of some of his younger officers at the Berghof, in an attempt to persuade them of the validity of his plan. Unexpectedly he was met with open opposition from General von Wietersheim, Chief of Staff for the Army of the West. Hitler's plan would leave Germany defenseless in that area, he claimed, and there was no way they could hold out against the French. Hitler, flying into one of his famous rages, refused to admit the possibility of defeat. In fact, from that time on, he refused to countenance any criticism or opposition from the army at all.

Beck, seeing that he was defeated, resigned as Chief of the Army General Staff. Though his resignation was not followed by a wave of

Right:
Hitler greets Chamberlain in the Hotel Dreesen in Bad Godesberg on 24 September 1938.

others, as he had hoped (in fact, news of his departure was kept secret until the end of October), it did help crystalize opposition to Hitler within the army, and several other officers decided to join the civilian conspiracy.

Beck's replacement was General Franz Halder—the first Bavarian and the first Catholic to hold such a position. Halder shared Beck's views, and became a key figure in the first serious plot to overthrow the Führer. Toward the end of August a specific plan evolved: to seize Hitler at the very moment an attack on Czechoslovakia was ordered; arraign him before the People's Court on charges of recklessly hurling Germany into war; and establish a military dictatorship which would eventually give way to a conservative democratic government. The entire plan was based on the premise that Britain and France were actually willing to fight over Czechoslovakia. But even though they sent emissaries to London and Moscow, the conspirators could not obtain sufficient

Above:
Hitler looks out at the Hotel Dreesen during the difficult negotiations with the British Prime Minister Chamberlain over Czechoslovakia's future.

evidence that there really was grave danger of war, and the plan was held off.

Up to September Hitler was extremely careful to make it seem that the only dispute was between the Sudeten Germans and the Czech government; all his own machinations to increase tension were kept in the background. On 5 September he nearly had the wind taken from his sails when Beneš announced that he would accept all the Sudeten Germans' demands. The embarrassed Sudeten Party had to find an excuse quickly to break off negotiations; not long after, Henlein departed for Germany. On 6 September the Party Rally in Nuremberg opened. Hitler's refusal to discuss any foreign policy matters led to a proliferation of rumors. Sir Nevile Henderson became convinced that he was quite mad, and refused even to discuss the possibility of Britain going to war against him, for fear of pushing him over the brink. The world waited with bated breath for Hitler's closing speech on the 12th, which was expected to decide whether there would be peace or war.

But meanwhile, events did not stand still. On 7 September London's *The Times* published its famous editorial, proposing that the Sudetenland be ceded to Germany. This helped confirm Hitler's opinion that Britain and France would not mobilize over Czechoslovakia. On the 9th he held another stormy conference with Keitel, Brauchitsch and Halder, when he tore the Army's invasion plan to shreds and castigated his generals for their timidity and general incompetence.

When the Führer finally took his place before the crowd gathered in the huge stadium on 12 September, he did not disappoint them; his speech was a violent, brutal attack on Czechoslovakia in general and on President Beneš in particular; at every pause the roar of 'Sieg Heil! Sieg Heil!' from thousands of throats shook the stadium. But for all his shouting, Hitler still refused to tie himself to specific demands or to issue specific threats.

For this reason the speech inspired relief among the Allied powers, but the denunciation of Beneš was the trigger for an uprising in the Sudetenland in which several people were killed. The Czechs kept calm, declared martial law, and eventually contained the uprising–but Britain and France panicked. Chamberlain sent a telegram post haste to Hitler offering to meet anywhere, anytime to discuss the Czech situation personally. The move was greeted with enthusiasm in England and Hitler was bemused and flattered, but in Italy Mussolini remarked to Count Ciano, 'There will be no war. But this is the liquidation of English prestige.'

On the morning of 15 September the 69-year-old Prime Minister boarded an airplane for the first time in his life and set off on the nearly seven-hour journey to Berchtesgaden. (Despite the flattery implicit in the prospect of an elder statesman coming to plead with him, Hitler did not feel it necessary to meet him at a more convenient location.) When the two were finally tête-à-tête in the Führer's study, Hitler embarked on a tedious monologue about the history of the current crisis, ending with a demand for annexation of the Sudetenland. Chamberlain, who had hardly been able to get a word in, finally lost his patience and responded angrily that if Hitler was determined to move against Czechoslovakia, he did not see why it had been necessary for him to make so long a journey. His trip was obviously a waste of time, and he might as well return to England at once.

Faced with this unexpected counterattack, Hitler became slightly more conciliatory: if Britain would agree to the principle of self-determination for the Sudeten Germans, then they could continue the discussion to see how to apply that principle in practice. Finally the two agreed to let matters rest while Chamberlain returned to talk things over with his cabinet. Hitler promised to take no military measures in the meantime. It was not a difficult promise to make–Case Green had established 30 September as X-Day for the march into Czechoslovakia!

In America President Roosevelt was worried, noting that Chamberlain's 'Peace at any Price' policy was merely postponing the inevitable. But Britain, despite some dissension within the government, remained firmly wedded to its appeasement policy. On 18 September French Premier Edouard Daladier and his Foreign Minister Georges Bonnet arrived in London for consultations. While Hitler continued his preparations for invasion–authorizing formation of the Sudeten German Free Corps, drawing up

detailed military plans, and negotiating with the Poles, Slovaks and Hungarians—the two Western Powers, without consulting Czechoslovakia, drew up their own plans for detaching the Sudetenland.

Their proposals were presented to the Czech government on the 19th and were angrily rejected, along with a few uncomfortable reminders about their treaty obligations. On 21 September, however, after Beneš vainly tried to find some support in other quarters, the Czechs capitulated and accepted the Anglo-French proposal. The Czech cabinet, feeling bitter and betrayed, resigned in a body.

No one was more surprised than Hitler by the news that even Prague had agreed to the plan. Now he was in a dilemma, since his real aim was still the military occupation and destruction of the Czech state. Chamberlain approached their second meeting, at the Hotel Dreesen in Bad Godesberg, in a happy mood—only to be abruptly jolted out of his

complacency by the news from Hitler that the situation had changed and that the proposed solution would no longer be sufficient.

In the bitter discussion that followed, Chamberlain, who was confused and vexed, never seemed to realize that Hitler was simply playing the traditional blackmailer's game: issuing new demands as soon as his original ones were met. Now he stated that before 1 October the Czechs must agree to evacuate the chief areas to be ceded and allow them to be occupied by German troops. Finally the conference reached a deadlock. Chamberlain returned to his own hotel on the other side of the Rhine and requested a written memo and a map from the Führer, outlining Germany's new demands.

The Godesberg Memorandum was flatly rejected by Britain, France and Czechoslovakia. The Czechs had already announced a general mobilization; now preparations for war began in England and France as well. Hitler, apparently enraged by this unexpected opposition, set 1400 on 28 September as the deadline for Czechoslovakia's acceptance of the memorandum. When Sir Horace Wilson, Chamberlain's confidential advisor, reminded him that an invasion by Germany would lead to armed British and French intervention, the Führer declared, 'The Germans are being treated like niggers! . . . If France and England decide to strike, let them. I don't care a penny!' That evening, 26 September, he delivered another speech in the Sportpalast, unleashing a furious verbal attack on Czechoslovakia, directed mainly at Beneš personally; William Shirer, who attended the meeting, noted in his diary later that Hitler 'seemed to have completely lost control of himself.'

On the 27th, however, Hitler's war fever had died down somewhat. He had ordered the Second Motorized Division to pass through Berlin on its way to the Czech border, hoping to whip up public enthusiasm for the coming conflict. But instead of the expected crowds gathering to cheer the soldiers on their way, people reacted in the opposite manner. They were not just indifferent; many turned their backs or disappeared into subways to avoid watching the troops.

This lack of public enthusiasm made a great impression on Hitler, as did the news of mobilization abroad. Late that evening he sent a definitely conciliatory letter to Chamberlain, who responded by suggesting an international conference to settle the matter. The Prime Minister had already obtained Mussolini's support for the idea and Hitler, with only a few hours to go before his deadline, agreed to meet—on condition that the conference be held immediately and that Mussolini himself attend it. Invitations were sent out to London and Paris (but not to Prague or Moscow); the conferees were to meet in Munich the next day, 29 September.

By his decision Hitler, unknowingly, had confounded the hopes of the conspirators within Germany. The events of 26 and 27 September had convinced them that the time to strike had come at last; Hitler was apparently set on war, and England and France were obviously determined to oppose him. All the plans were laid, and the men were in readiness, when news of the Munich conference fell like a bombshell. With its whole basis for action removed, the conspiracy – already overburdened by moral indecision about the oath of allegiance and conflict of interest – collapsed in confusion.

Early next morning Hitler traveled to Kufstein to meet Mussolini and co-ordinate their policy. Still undecided about whether to attend the conference in good faith or wreck it, he allowed himself to be quieted by Mussolini's assurances that if the conference failed to produce the results he wanted, Italy would stand behind him.

The Munich Conference began at 1245 on 29 September, in the new Führerhaus on Königsplatz. The hastily organized meeting began in muddle and confusion until Mussolini – amiable, completely at ease and the only one present who could speak to all the others in their own tongues – introduced some order by presenting his preliminary proposal for solving the Sudeten problem. In fact, the draft had been written the day before by Göring, Neurath and the German State Secretary, Ernst von Weizsäcker.

Sometime between 1400 and 1500 on 30 September, the Munich Agreement was signed: German troops were to occupy the Sudetenland between 1 and 10 October, with an international commission to oversee the operation. Hitler had won a great victory – he had obtained possession of Czechoslovakia's famous fortifications, improved his own strategic position enormously, acquired new industries, forced his enemy Beneš into exile – and most important, had won a personal victory, with the representatives of the great powers scurrying back and forth across Europe at his command. Still, he was unhappy. Not only did the argument upset his timetable and force him to move back his scheduled invasion, but it deprived him of his glory. As he was overheard to remark to an SS aide, 'That damned Chamberlain has spoiled my parade into Prague!'

During the months following the Munich Agreement, Hitler continued operations in several areas, all the while becoming more irritated by the appeasers, who were attempting to reason with him in what he saw as a patronizing manner.

On the diplomatic front, he concentrated his efforts on driving a wedge between Britain and France, cultivating the French by negotiating the renunciation of German claims to Alsace-Lorraine in return for the French adopting a hands-off policy in Czechoslovakia. He also went to some lengths to strengthen his alliance with Italy; he agreed to joint German–Italian arbitration of a frontier dispute between Hungary and Slovakia and finally, in January 1939, obtained Mussolini's agreement to a military alliance – which eventually would become the Pact of Steel.

Militarily, orders went out to the armed forces on 21 October to prepare for the defense of Germany, the military suppression of the rest of Czechoslovakia and occupation of the Memel region. On 24 November he added a postscript, ordering preparations for the occupation of Danzig; on 17 December he told the army to base their plans for Czechoslovakia on the assumption that they would encounter little or no resistance. In the meantime, he took care to see that the other countries surrounding Czechoslovakia and the minorities within the truncated Czech state received the utmost support in pressing their own claims against the beleagured government.

He also had to do something about the German people themselves, who were obviously not ready for war. A psychological campaign for mobilization began immediately after Munich, with major speeches by the Führer and orders to the newspapers to start taking a more aggressive tone. He thought he saw his chance to unite the country in November when a 17-year-old Jewish exile in Paris shot the third secretary of the German Legation, Ernst von Rath—who was, ironically, under investigation by the Gestapo at the time for his failure to demonstrate proper anti-Semitic feelings. On the night of 9–10 November a pogrom, well planned by Heydrich, was carried out all over Germany; it was later given the name *Kristallnacht* (Crystal Night), because of the enormous number of glass windows that were broken. But the orgy of killing, looting, arson and mass arrests did not have the desired effect. The mildly anti-Semitic, solidly bourgeois German population could only be alarmed by a renewal of disorder in the streets and the excesses of the SS; only in Vienna was the campaign a popular success. America and Great Britain reacted with a concerted outcry of horror and indignation; and Hitler, in turn, was furious that either should dare comment on his treatment of German Jews. Added to his smoldering resentment of Britain from the Munich Conference, his anger soon led him to see London as the headquarters of the international Jewish conspiracy, and Great Britain as the major check to his ambitions.

In March 1939 Hitler was ready to move. The deposed Slovak Premier, Monsignor Josef Tiso, was abruptly summoned to Berlin on the 13th, where he was subjected to a long, angry denunciation of the Czechs and then to exclamations of disappointment at the Slovaks' lack of enthusiasm for independence. Confronted with the news that failure to declare Slovak independence would result in German occupation of Bratislava, Tiso returned to the Slovak capital early next morning, and by noon on the 14th had persuaded the Slovak Parliament to accept the independence that was being forced upon it.

To dilute the effect of the news from Slovakia, the German press erupted on 13 March with front-page stories of wild excesses perpetrated upon the German residents of Bohemia and Moravia. There was little truth to the horror stories—which bore a distinct resemblance to those circulated in August 1938—despite the best efforts of the German minority to provoke some sort of real incident.

President Emil Hacha, in one last attempt to avert disaster, requested a personal interview with Hitler; after keeping him in suspense for some hours, the Führer finally agreed to see him. On the 14th the elderly President, accompanied by his daughter and his Foreign Minister, Frantisek Chvalkovsky, boarded a train for Berlin (his bad heart made flying impossible). On their arrival at 2240 the small Czech delegation was received with all the honors due a head of state, but the President was not allowed to see

Below:
Hitler visits the Schöber
Line during the
occupation of Sudeten
Czechoslovakia.

Hitler until after 0100 on 15 March. When he was finally admitted to the dictator's presence, all that the frail, tired old man could do was throw himself on Hitler's mercy and plead for the right of Czechoslovakians to lead their own lives.

Hitler's only reply was a catalog of the wrongs perpetrated by Masaryk and Beneš, and the announcement that at 0600 that very day (it was then nearly 0200) German troops would enter Czechoslovakia. The two Czech diplomats were then taken into another room for discussion – during which Göring described the bombing of Prague so graphically that Hacha fainted. Luckily for the Germans, who would have been in a very unpleasant situation if anything serious had happened to him, Hitler's personal physician, Dr Morell, was on hand to revive him. By the time Hitler received him again, shortly after 0400, Hacha had been able to talk to Prague and was ready to sign a communique to the effect that he had 'confidently placed the fate of the Czech people in the hands of the Führer.' Hitler burst into his secretaries' room and asked them to embrace him, crying 'This is the greatest day of my life! I shall go down in history as the greatest German!' (By this time Hitler and his colleagues had so perfected the art of intimidating foreign statesmen that the process was given a name: 'Hacha-izing').

That same evening Hitler entered Prague, announcing, 'Czechoslovakia has herewith ceased to exist.' On the 16th Tiso sent Hitler a telegram requesting that Germany take Slovakia under its protection. Hitler graciously consented and German troops moved in, while Ruthenia was left to Hungary. On the 18th he was in Vienna. By the time the British and French ambassadors had presented their obligatory protest notes in Berlin, the Protectorate of Bohemia and Moravia had already been established, Neurath had been installed as Protector and a treaty with Slovakia had been drafted and initialed. In Italy Mussolini, tired of hearing about his ally's actions after the event, was angry but his resentment was tempered by his desire to stick with a winner.

In retrospect Czechoslovakia appears to have been Hitler's first major mistake. In time the country might have fallen under Germany's influence; by breaking the Munich Agreement Hitler set off a violent reaction in both France and Britain that resulted in a complete change in both official and public opinion. The Western Powers felt that their good will had been abused; in their disillusionment their vision cleared and the statesmen finally began to realize what was the logical conclusion of Hitler's policies and excuses. Hitler appreciated the significance of his action, but he had not expected to provoke such a violent reaction; after all, he was only using the same arguments that had worked so well after the Anschluss and at Munich. As far as he was concerned at the moment he had suffered a set-back in public relations; he did not as yet fully comprehend that the end of appeasement had come. There would be no more cheap victories.

Despite their change of heart, the Allies were still confused and without definite goals; Hitler could probably still have achieved his objectives without going to war if at this point his hitherto infallible sense of timing had not deserted him. From March 1939 on, he abandoned his effective waiting game and became caught up in the frantic escalation of events.

Poland was the obvious choice as his next victim. There was great resentment in Germany toward the Poles who had been given a large tract of East Prussia in 1919. Further,

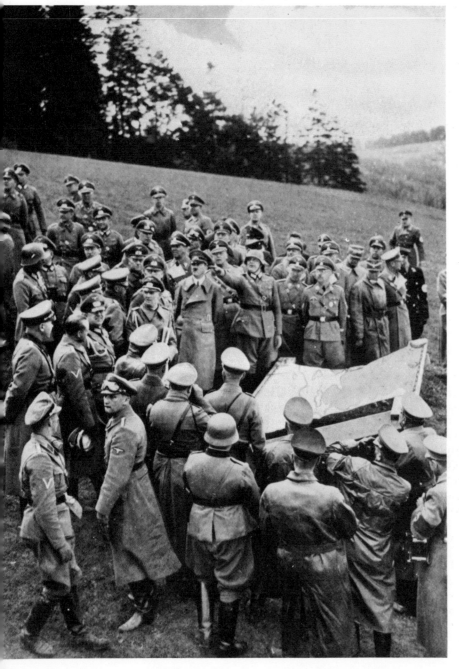

Danzig, though predominantly German, had been made into a Free City to give Poland access to the sea. The Polish Corridor connected it with the rest of Poland, which left East Prussia completely cut off from Germany proper. For the last five years Hitler had been more than friendly to the Poles, as Germany's most suspicious neighbor and France's principal ally in Eastern Europe, he could not afford to antagonize them too soon. Since his long-term plans were directed against Russia anyway, his first option was to convince Poland to join him in an eastward expansion at Russia's expense.

During October and November of 1938 discussions had been held in Berlin between German and Polish officials, with Germany offering eventual compensation in Russia to make up for the Poles' return of Danzig and an extra-territorial road across the Polish Corridor to East Prussia. But the proposal ran counter to one of the fundamental tenets of Polish foreign policy: that friendship with either of its powerful neighbors, Germany and the Soviet Union, was probably at least as dangerous as enmity. If faced with a choice most Poles—who were anti-Communist, anti-Russian and anti-Semitic—would have leaned toward Germany. On the other hand, Germany was greedy and looking for more land and power abroad, while Russia was preoccupied with its own internal power disputes.

The Polish Prime Minister, Josef Beck, managed to keep negotiations open without antagonizing either party until March. But after the occupation of Czechoslovakia, German demands on Poland became more pressing. Finally, on 26 March, the Polish ambassador, Josef Lipski, presented his government's reply: the German demands were unacceptable. Ribbentrop began the usual routine, reminding Lipski of 'certain risky steps' taken by 'another country' (presumably Czechoslovakia) and beginning to mutter about outrages against German minorities in Poland.

Beck replied to the threats by announcing that any attempt by Germany or the Danzig Senate to change the status quo would be considered an act of aggression, and ordered his forces to begin mobilization. He felt in a reasonably strong position since he had received help from an unexpected source. On 31 March Chamberlain, still smarting from his disappointment over Czechoslovakia, had announced to the House of Commons that 'in the event of any action that clearly threatened Polish independence ... HM Government would feel themselves bound at once to lend the Polish Government all support in their power.' In this he was supported by the French.

Hitler flew into a great rage when he heard the news, shouting, 'I'll cook them a stew they'll choke on!' On 1 April, the day after Chamberlain's speech, he issued a dire warning to anyone daring to oppose him. Propaganda releases began to feature England as Germany's most dangerous adversary and negotiations with Poland were broken off. On 3 April a secret directive was issued to the Army, ordering that plans for Operation White (war against Poland) must be ready by 1 September 1939; they were to be made in such a way that they could be executed at any time after that date.

Beck signed a temporary mutual assistance pact in London on 6 April. On the 7th Mussolini moved into little Albania and set up his own protectorate, gaining a good position for moves against Greece and Yugoslavia, and increasing the anxiety of the smaller countries; France and Britain responded by giving guarantees to Greece and Yugoslavia.

Below:
Hitler looks out over Prague from the castle that dominates the city after the German Army had occupied the rest of Czechoslovakia on 15 March 1939. On 16 March he issued a proclamation from Prague saying that Bohemia and Moravia belonged to the German people.

Above:
A week after the occupation of Prague Hitler visited Memel in Lithuania to proclaim its return to the German Reich. The Lithuanian government had been in no position to refuse Hitler and the Memel question aggravated German relations with Poland.

On 15–16 April Göring was in Rome for talks with Mussolini, when a telegram arrived in both the Italian and German capitals from Roosevelt. The American President put his question bluntly: 'Are you willing to give assurance that your armed forces will not attack or invade the territory of the following independent nations [followed by a list of some 30 countries]?' Mussolini declined to reply, but Hitler announced that he would answer the President on 28 April.

He began his two-hour speech, which was broadcast all over the world, in his usual manner—with a detailed explanation of all his foreign policy to date. He then moved on to a denunciation of both the Anglo-German Naval Treaty of 1935 and the German–Polish Agreement of 1934, winding up with congratulations to Mussolini on the takeover in Albania and a celebration of the strength of the Rome-Berlin Axis. At last he turned to Roosevelt's message, demolishing its various points with an irony and heavy sarcasm that was extremely effective, at least with the German audience, at whom his reply was primarily directed. Although it was a great success in Germany, the speech did not have much impact elsewhere; the fact that, for all his rhetoric, he had not answered Roosevelt's question did not go unnoticed.

Following his talks the Führer went into isolation at Berchtesgaden until mid-August, making no attempt to renew negotiations with the Poles. As the excitement died down Britain and France gradually slipped from their warlike

posture and again began thinking of ways to avoid conflict. But Hitler was not idle. Throughout the summer arms were smuggled into Danzig and a continuing series of incidents was staged to keep the Poles on edge. Relations with other nations within the German sphere of influence were strengthened to keep Poland isolated, and Mussolini was finally persuaded to let Ciano and Ribbentrop sign the Pact of Steel. That far-reaching military alliance was formalized in Berlin on 21 May, even though Mussolini was most unhappy about the prospect of war, for which he was completely unprepared.

Both sides had been putting out feelers in Moscow for some time, but though the Allies realized that no collective security system could possibly work without the Soviet Union, their negotiations were hampered by mutual distrust. In addition, the Soviet Union was obviously uninterested in securing the independence of the small Eastern European nations—if anything, the opposite was the case. The prospects for a Soviet–German alliance looked more promising. Although Stalin was well aware of Hiter's eventual goal, he was prepared to ignore it for the moment for two reasons. The first was his fear of a coalition of the capitalist and Fascist powers against the Soviet Union; the second was his own expansionist dream, which could be satisfied first at the expense of Poland and later elsewhere in Eastern Europe.

Though anti-Communism had long been one of Hitler's principal doctrines, he was also willing to forgo principles for the sake of expediency. Convinced that war with the West was inevitable, he had to guard against the danger of a two-front conflict. When he had finished with the Allies, a common frontier with the Soviet Union would give him a springboard to launch an attack in the East. In short, both men were ready, in Hitler's words, to 'make a pact with Satan to drive out the devil.'

Military preparations continued through the summer as well. The seven army divisions that existed when Hitler took over had grown to 30 infantry divisions that included four motorized and three mountain divisions; five Panzer divisions; four light divisions; and 22 machine-gun battalions and they were still growing. The Navy had launched two 26,000-ton battleships, two 10,000-ton armored cruisers, 17 destroyers and 47 submarines. Work was continuing on two 35,000-ton battle ships (the *Graf Spee* and the *Bismarck*), four 10,000-ton cruisers, five destroyers, seven U-Boats and an aircraft carrier. The Air Force, newly created since 1933, consisted of 21 squadrons and 260,000 men. The number of Germans under arms may have been much smaller than the French forces, but they were of a higher caliber.

On 14 June Brauchitsch ordered all units to complete their plans for Operation White by 20

Left:
Hitler receives a Japanese naval delegation. Ribbentrop was in favor of a military alliance between Italy, Germany and Japan but Mussolini did not wish to commit himself until September 1940 when the Tripartite Pact was signed.

Below:
Hitler dines with the List regiment in 1939. Hitler never felt at ease with the members of the German officer class and had a difficult relationship with his generals.

August. The timetable was ready within the week. On the 24th the Army was ordered to work out strategies for seizing bridges over the lower Vistula. Finally, on 27 July, an order for the occupation of Danzig was drafted; the date was not filled in.

Everything depended on negotiating an alliance with Moscow, and the Russians were taking their time. The more Germany pressed for an agreement, the more Vyacheslav Molotov, Russia's Commissar for Foreign Affairs, talked of the need for 'adequate preparation.' When finally the Russian delays threatened to sabotage the entire operation, Hitler swallowed his pride and on 20 August sent a telegram to Stalin, requesting that the Soviet leader receive Ribbentrop on 22 or 23 August. The Foreign Minister, he promised, would have the auth-

ority to draw up and sign both a non-aggression pact and a special protocol covering the division of Eastern Europe. The next 24 hours were an anxious time—the success or failure of all his plans depended on Stalin's decision, for he would not dare move against Poland if there was a chance that while the Allies were moving in on him from the West the Russians were mobilizing in the East. Finally, on Monday 21 August, the reply arrived: Stalin would meet Ribbentrop on Wednesday the 23rd.

At noon on the appointed day Ribbentrop arrived in Moscow and was taken immediately to the Kremlin. Most of the serious business was finished before dinner, and the meeting resumed that evening in a friendly atmosphere, with much clinking of glasses and drinking of toasts. Later both the Non-Aggression Pact and the secret protocol were signed. The latter, which only came to light after the war, divided Eastern Europe into spheres of influence; it clearly demonstrates the shallowness of later Soviet claims that Stalin signed the pact only to give himself some breathing space. In fact Stalin took the agreement quite seriously, unlike Hitler, and as late as June 1941 refused to believe that Hitler was about to attack him.

The Western military mission, also in Moscow to contract a Russian alliance, was left out in the cold. Their protracted negotiations had been hamstrung by Poland's stubborn refusal to let a single Russian soldier set foot on Polish soil—and there was no way that Russia could possibly get at Germany without crossing Poland. When the Poles finally gave in on 23 August it was too late; the Allied mission was politely seen out of Moscow on the 25th.

The Italians were not happy. Count Ciano had visited Hitler earlier in the month, tried without success to change his mind about invasion, and had left feeling completely disgusted with the way Italy was being treated.

News of the expected conclusion of the Russo-German Non-Aggression Pact had reached London on 22 August. Chamberlain, rather than being upset, was rather complacent, now that the Russians had 'shown themselves in their true colors.' He did see fit to send Hitler a letter stating unconditionally that he would support Poland militarily if necessary, but immediately detracted from the strength of the assertion by going on to suggest ways in which negotiations could be begun.

On 23 August Hitler fixed 0430 on Saturday, 26 August as the starting time for his invasion. But during the next three days a number of incidents conspired to move back the time schedule. From London came the news that Parliament was backing Chamberlain in his new, firm stance; Hitler made one last effort to detach England from Poland, but it was not successful. In addition Mussolini, belatedly informed of the plans, made it very clear that he was having no part of any war; although he was ashamed to have to admit it, the Italian forces were in no condition to participate in a major conflict.

Less than twelve hours before the attack was scheduled to begin, Hitler postponed it. He took action just in time; many units were already on the move toward the frontier. Within 24 hours he had set a new and final date: 1 September 1939.

The confused negotiations that followed during the next few days had no effect on the final outcome. Mussolini, after repeating that he was unable to fight, suggested another conference; Hitler declined to accept the suggestion. The pleading of French Ambassador Robert Coulondre and even a personal appeal from Premier Edouard Daladier fell on deaf ears. A series of

hoped to be able either to 'Hacha' the envoy into submission or make the Poles appear as the troublemakers. The Polish government, however, remembered the fates of the Austrian and Czechoslovakian delegations, and refused to send anyone. Britain and France continued to press Warsaw to come to some sort of agreement with Berlin, but did not put pressure on them to send an envoy.

At 1230 on 31 August Hitler signed Directive Number 1 for the Conduct of the War. At 0900 the German radio broadcast a list of Hitler's demands (the Sixteen Points), most of which the Poles had never heard before. The first 'incident' was already being staged: SS Sturmbannführer Naujocks was faking a Polish attack on a German radio station near the frontier at Gleiwitz, leaving behind the bodies of several

proposals and counterproposals traveled back and forth between Berlin and London, through both official and unofficial channels, but came to nothing since all Hitler's terms were based on Britain's looking the other way while Poland was invaded. The Polish government was ordered to send a plenipotentiary with full powers to Berlin within 24 hours; the Germans

concentration camp inmates dressed in Polish uniforms as 'evidence.'

All that night troops and equipment moved toward the border. At 0445 on 1 September the cruiser *Schleswig Holstein* opened fire on a Polish fortress near Danzig harbor. At the same time German troops emerged from their prepared positions. World War II had begun.

VI The Victors

While German troops began their inexorable rush through Poland, supported by wave after wave of Luftwaffe bombers, the streets of Berlin were singularly quiet. In August 1914 cheering crowds had filled the city, jubilant at the prospect of a fight, when the Kaiser made his declaration of war. But at 1000 on 1 September 1939, as Hitler drove through the almost deserted streets to make his speech to the Reichstag, the few people abroad were serious and quiet.

He, too, was serious when he stood up to address the assembled deputies in his tailored field-gray uniform; his speech was quiet and rather flat, and did not sound as if it had been well prepared. In the talk he emphasized his endless patience in the face of constant Polish provocation, and of the new friendship between Germany and the USSR. With some embarrassment he mentioned Italy; Mussolini had reluctantly decided to remain neutral for the time being and Hitler had been forced to send him a telegram formally releasing him from his treaty obligations. His attitude toward the Western Powers was equivocal; since they had not re-

sponded by immediately declaring war, he still hoped to be able to limit the conflict to Poland. On a sentimental note, he announced that if anything happened to him Göring would take over; if Göring were to fall, Hess would be his successor. The fact that such an announcement could be made and accepted without question clearly demonstrated that no German government existed beyond Hitler.

The 1–2 September saw the last, frantic efforts to avoid a global conflict. Mussolini again proposed a conference, hoping to repeat his Munich triumph; but his efforts ran foul of British influence on Hitler's pulling out of Poland altogether, and eventually the notion was dropped. France embarked on a series of evasions and delaying tactics to postpone the inevitable. Britain was more determined: Chamberlain was finally forced to take action alone after trying unsuccessfully to persuade the French to act in concert; Parliament was in an uproar and he was in danger of being forced out of office.

At 0900 on Sunday 3 September Sir Nevile Henderson walked into the German Foreign Office on Wilhelmstrasse. Waiting for him was Hitler's chief interpreter, Dr Paul Schmidt, who had been sent by Ribbentrop to receive what they all knew had to be unpleasant tidings. Henderson delivered his ultimatum: unless Britain received satisfactory assurances by 1100 that morning that the attack on Poland would cease and all troops would be withdrawn, a state of war would exist between the two countries.

Hitler and Ribbentrop were waiting for Schmidt when he arrived at the Chancellery a few minutes later. The interpreter slowly translated the British ultimatum; when he had finished there was complete silence for some moments. After what seemed an age, in which no one moved or spoke, the Führer turned to Ribbentrop who was standing near the window and abruptly demanded with an angry look, 'What now?' The Foreign Minister answered quietly, 'I assume that the French will hand in a similar ultimatum within the hour.'

Schmidt withdrew to the anteroom where he was immediately surrounded by a clamoring crowd, but when he announced that England was declaring war silence fell and faces grew grave. Finally Göring spoke: 'If we lose this war, then God help us.'

Near noon, when the French Ambassador, Coulondre, presented his government's ulti-

matum, Great Britain was already at war with Germany and Chamberlain was speaking to the British people. To the very end the French were not able to bring themselves to use the word 'war'; their ultimatum threatened that unless Germany withdrew its forces at once, they would fulfill 'those contractual obligations which France has undertaken toward Poland.'

Hitler may already have been aware that in the long run he would not achieve victory. Only a few weeks before, on 22 July, he had told Admiral Karl Dönitz that a war with England would mean the end of Germany. Now he had that war, and instead of fighting in the East, as he had been planning for almost twenty years, he was faced with a war in the West.

There is no doubt that Hitler had taken the steps that led to the conflict deliberately; although he had underestimated British determination to fight, he had been fully conscious of the risks he was taking. Why he did what he did when he did it is a difficult and complex question. Germany certainly was not prepared for all-out war. The public mood was not favorable; the great satisfaction over the annexation of the Rhineland, Austria, and the Sudetenland had long worn off. Nor was the people's spirit kindled by the start of the fighting; discontent actually increased, and during the week after Christmas 1939 the police had to be called out to deal with crowds of war protestors.

Economically, Germany still was heavily dependent on foreign countries for vital war materials—tin, copper, oil, rubber and bauxite—

despite the great increases in steel and coal production. Without support from the Soviet Union, Germany could not have survived the British blockade during the first months of the war.

Despite Hitler's prodigious efforts, Germany's military situation was not as impressive as it might have seemed; only half of the Wehrmacht's 100 divisions was ready for real battle, and many of the men were not fully trained. The Polish campaign used up half of the existing ammunition supplies, and stocks of other equipment were dangerously low. The Kriegsmarine was still inferior to even the French Fleet. Only the Luftwaffe, with almost 3300 planes was stronger than the Allied forces.

Weakness, then—not strength—was the starting point for the development of *Blitzkrieg*, the strategic concept which involved striking a series of short, concentrated attacks on individual opponents, wherein surprise and overwhelming force would decide the outcome before the other power could mobilize its troops. Between 1939 and 1941 the world stood in awe of the new method—but it failed, as it was bound to do, as soon as Germany came up against a strong, unified, well-prepared enemy. Hitler, however, persisted in clinging to the concept of Blitzkrieg even when it was obvious that a full-scale, protracted struggle was inevitable—partly because he refused to scrap his own tactics in favor of those advocated by the generals, and partly because of his own experiences in the trenches during World War I.

Hitler lost interest in everything but the con-

Below:
Hitler discusses the situation on the Tenth Army Front in Poland with General Walther von Reichenau. Reichenau was one of the few Army commanders whose loyalty to Hitler and the Nazi Party was certain. Third from the right is General Erwin Rommel who would later lead the Afrika Korps.

Left:
Hitler's armed
bodyguard follows him
on his visit to the Polish
Front.

duct of the war almost immediately. Following receipt of the French and British proclamations of war he took time only to issue a statement to the German people, promising that November 1918 would not happen again, before setting out for the front. There he set up his headquarters in a special train; every morning he would set out in an open car, armed with pistol and whip, to inspect the line while his companions distributed packages of cigarettes to the troops. He immersed himself in every detail of the campaign, taking an interest in the smallest details—even down to the running of the kitchens. One thing that he was most insistent upon was that officers (including himself and his staff) and enlisted men ate the same things.

The German military machine moved across Poland with astonishing speed in this first Blitzkrieg campaign and the Poles—despite their brave and often foolhardy resistance—were doomed practically from the beginning. The Polish Air Force was destroyed within 48 hours; the Army fell within two weeks before the coordinated onslaught. German tanks, including General Heinz Guderian's 2nd Panzer Division, raced forward at a rate of 30–40 miles a day, supported in the air by fighter planes and bombers and followed by a huge army. By 17 September all Poland had fallen but Warsaw and Molna, which were still holding out against incredible odds.

That same day the Soviet Army began its own March through the unfortunate country. The Soviets, although they were taken by surprise by the rapid German success, had hastily organized their own takeover of the territories allotted to them as part of the Non-Aggression Pact; the two armies met at Brest-Litovsk on 18 September. Hitler still needed to remain on friendly terms with the USSR, and Stalin was quick to press his advantage before the Führer changed his mind. He vetoed Hitler's tentative plan for retaining a small, nominally independent Polish state and insisted that the two of them divide the entire country. By careful maneuvering and hard bargaining he managed to make an excellent deal, whereby the Soviet Union got the Baltic States (which provided some protection against a German surprise attack) while Germany obtained control over the great mass of the Polish people (a headache Stalin was happy to forego), along with promises of further Soviet economic assistance. But though on paper it looked as if Stalin had renegotiated the August agreement to Germany's disadvantage, Hitler had nothing to complain about: his main purpose was still to remain free to concentrate on the Western Front, and he also had achieved a common border with the USSR. Besides, he had such a low opinion of the Red Army that he did not mind giving away countries that he could easily regain later by force.

While directing the negotiations concerning the division of Poland on one hand, Hitler was overseeing its 'housecleaning' on the other. On his orders Jews from the Greater Reich were already being collected in several Polish cities in preparation for the 'final solution' – already an open secret among top party leaders. Five *Einsatzgruppen* (Special Groups) were detailed to round up 'carriers of Polish Nationalism,' and some 3500 intellectuals were disposed of in a matter of weeks. In addition 1,200,000 Poles were evicted from their homes to make room for Germans from the Baltic States; the number of those who died that winter from exposure soon topped the total of those on the execution list. Stalin was engaged in similar activities in the West where some 15,000 military and intellectual leaders disappeared. About 4500 of them were found by German soldiers in spring 1941, in a mass grave at Katyn.

The German Navy had swung into action along with the land and air forces; during the first week of the war Raeder's ships sank eleven British ships with a combined tonnage of 64,595. The first, the British passenger liner *Athenia*, went down only ten hours after Britain declared war; 112 people died, including 28 Americans. On 7 September, however, Hitler sent for Raeder and told him to ease up. As far as he was concerned there was no reason to be at war with Britain and France once Poland had been soundly defeated – and in view of the hesitation both countries were showing about making

Above:
Colonel General Heinz Guderian in September 1941. Guderian's Panzer tactics led the German Army to victory in Poland, France and the Low Countries.

Right:
Hitler visits the Polish Front. Second from the right is Lieutenant General Wilhelm Keitel who was Hitler's staff officer.

Above:
Front row, left to right:
General von Manstein,
Heinrich Himmler,
Hitler and General von
Reichenau. Manstein
devised an alternative
plan for attacking
France through the
Ardennes which Hitler
adopted.

a definite commitment, he thought it might still be possible to conclude a peace agreement.

By 20 September the German press and radio were talking openly of peace, and Hitler encouraged Birger Dahlerus—a Swedish friend of Göring's who had played a frantic, if ineffectual part in previous attempts to keep Britain out of the war—to go back to London. Dahlerus had as little success as he had had the first time; finally on 6 October the Führer made a public appeal for peace in a speech to the Reichstag, causing great rejoicing in the streets of Berlin.

Hitler's real desire for a permanent peace is suspect, but a temporary truce would have worked greatly to his advantage, giving him time to re-arm and also the opportunity to drive a deeper wedge between Britain and France. In that sense at least his 'great peace offensive' was sincere. But, he made it very clear that he was not willing to give up anything he had gained. Count Ciano summarized these aims, after a 1 October meeting with the Führer: '... to offer his people a solid peace after a great victory ... perhaps ... still tempts Hitler. But if in order to reach it he had to sacrifice, even to the smallest degree, what seems to him the legitimate fruits of his victory, he would then a thousand times prefer battle.'

Despite a strong antiwar party and much lobbying by members of the government, France responded quickly to Hitler's overture: the next day, 7 October, Premier Daladier announced that the French would never lay down

Above:
A briefing session in the
Führer's headquarters in
1939. From left to right:
Göring, General
Bödenschatz, General
Keitel, Hitler and
Joachim von
Ribbentrop.

their arms until they were assured of a real peace and general security. After a week's delay, on 12 October, Chamberlain issued Britain's reply. In the House of Commons, the Prime Minister noted that Hitler's 'vague and uncertain' proposals contained 'no suggestions for righting the wrongs done to Czechoslovakia and Poland.' No reliance could be placed on the promises of the present German government; if Hitler wanted peace he must show it by 'acts, not words alone'; Britain required 'convincing proof' that he really wanted to end the war.

The news that there was no hope for a negotiated peace shocked the German public, but
Hitler was not taken unawares. As early as 27
September he had informed his Commanders in
Chief that he intended attacking in the West on
12 November. Needless to say, the news threw
the military leaders into a panic – which was not
alleviated on 10 October when they received
Directive Number 6 for the Conduct of the
War, an outline for an invasion through Luxembourg, Belgium and the Netherlands. The
directive was accompanied by a memorandum
that not only displayed the Führer's remarkable
grasp of history, military strategy and tactics,
but also predicted the future course of the war
in the West. Despite the carefully considered
and brilliantly constructed memo, the generals
stalled; virtually all of them were convinced
that they were almost completely unprepared
for war with the Western Allies.

The military leaders began preparing formal
memos themselves, detailing shortages of
equipment to show why they could not possibly
mount an offensive. But all their efforts accomplished was to inflame the Führer even more. As
their frustration grew, plans for *coups d'état* and
assassination plots began to be considered by
several resistance groups within Germany.

As before, the conspirators realized that the
Wehrmacht was the only organization that
could ensure the success of their plans but two
major problems had arisen since the opening
hostilities. First, the enlarged Wehrmacht was
now so packed with fanatical Nazis that it would
be difficult to find a unit that could be trusted to
move against Hitler. In addition, now that the
country was actually at war with Britain and
France, they had to find some way to make sure
that the Allies would not take advantage of
Hitler's removal to impose unacceptable peace
terms on Germany. Negotiations with the
British began, through representatives at the
Vatican and in Switzerland.

Halder, Chief of the Army General Staff, and
Brauchitsch, Commander in Chief of the Army,
were the key military figures in the plot. Halder
however found it difficult to reconcile the contradictions of his situation, believing firmly that
Hitler was leading Germany to disaster yet
aware of his responsibilities as a military commander. Most of his time was spent trying to
pass the buck to Brauchitsch who was even
more irresolute and was also beginning to feel
the strain of his position.

The conspirators were finally prepared, and
received word to hold themselves in readiness
from 5 November onward; on that day Brauchitsch had an appointment to meet Hitler at
the Chancellery in Berlin. His and Halder's final
decision would be based on the outcome of that
meeting. Brauchitsch arrived armed to the
teeth with technical reasons why an attack on
the West was bound to fail. Hitler listened

quietly enough – until Brauchitsch, anxious to
prove his point, began saying that morale in
the infantry was dangerously low. The Führer
flew into a rage, shouting abuse at Brauchitsch
and demanding specific examples (which the
unhappy general, who had deliberately exaggerated the situation, could not supply). Brauchitsch, who was on the verge of a nervous
collapse, crumpled completely, and when he returned to his headquarters at Zossen, was practically unable to speak coherently. With this
the whole conspiracy collapsed – instead of going
ahead with their plans the plotters panicked
and began trying to cover their tracks.

On 8 November the few who had not lost
their heads were startled by the news that
Hitler had narrowly escaped being killed by a
bomb that exploded in the Bürgerbräukeller in
Munich shortly after he had left; the occasion
had been the annual reunion to mark the anniversary of the 1923 Beer Hall Putsch. In fact the
attempt had been staged by the Gestapo in order to raise Hitler's popularity in the country.
Two British secret service men were kidnapped
by the Gestapo in Holland and presented as the
organizers of the plot, which had supposedly
been planned by George Elser – a former inmate
of the concentration camp at Dachau. Though
Goebbels did his best to use the 'miracle' of the

Führer's escape to stir up resentment against the antiwar faction, the plot had been organized a little too well. Most Germans were quietly skeptical. From then on fear of the Gestapo inhibited any plans the conspirators had for a coup.

On the day before the so-called assassination attempt, Hitler had, to the relief of the generals, postponed the attack in the West as a result of the 'meteorological and the military transport situations.' The first directive only moved the date up three days, but the process was to be repeated 29 times before May 1940 when the invasion was finally launched. Perhaps Hitler was deferring to his generals to some extent, though he would never for an instant consider their demands for a long-term postponement.

On 23 November the commanding generals and general staff officers were called to Berlin for a morale-boosting conference. After preliminary talks by Göring and Goebbels, Hitler himself delivered three speeches. He chided the generals for their lack of faith over the years and reviewed the present situation, making it clear that he was determined to 'attack France and England at the most favorable and earliest moment,' and to follow with an attack on the USSR as soon as he was free in the West. Swinging into his grand climax, he proclaimed. 'I shall shrink from nothing and shall destroy everyone who is against me . . . . In this struggle I shall stand or fall. I will not survive the defeat of my people. No capitulations abroad; no revolution from within.'

This meeting, which capped the crisis of the autumn of 1939, marked the final reduction of the military men from professional soldiers to compliant lackeys. To Hitler's eyes, the weakness of the generals had finally been exposed; important decisions would increasingly be made by his special staff within OKW (the High Command of the Armed Forces) rather than by OKH (the High Command of the Army).

The 'Phony War' (or *Sitzkrieg*) dragged on through the autumn and winter of 1940, with no fighting on land. Germany was not ready to move and the French forces, who greatly outnumbered the enemy at the beginning of the war, were content to prepare their defenses and wait. Nor was Britain in any hurry to begin sending men and materiel across the Channel in any quantity. The only military action took place at sea: German U-Boats roamed the shipping lanes of the North Atlantic, while in the South the *Graf Spee* sank nine British cargo ships in three months.

But though there was little fighting, events did not stand still. On 30 November Stalin invaded Finland, putting Hitler in the embarrassing position of having to condone the USSR's unprovoked aggression against a friendly country that had been liberated in 1918 with help from German troops. His unwilling acceptance of the invasion further weakened the already threadbare ties between Germany and Italy. The Pact of Steel had been popular in neither country and Mussolini had been having to cope with an increasing number of anti-German demonstrations. Finally on 3 January 1940 he sent his fellow dictator a long, frank letter, urging him to compromise in the West rather than risk everything, including his regime, in open conflict. But his chief concern was to point out that Germany's relations with the USSR, especially over the war in Finland, were having a disastrous effect on the situation in Italy. Hitler, in no mood to be bothered by his ally's demonstration of independence, set the letter aside; and as Mussolini received no reply, he began slipping back into his old servile role. But the letter had touched a tender point, for both Hitler and Stalin were becoming disenchanted with their new friendship.

Both were doing very well out of the re-

Left:
The 'formidable' West Wall in 1939. This wall was hurriedly constructed in 1936 as an answer to the Maginot Line and was finished in May 1940. However it was not as well built as the Maginot Line and large sections were no more than rudimentary fortifications.

Below:
The Phony War over the Rhine: the slogan reads 'Hitler says "Fifteen days of bombardment and the propagandists will change their tune."'

lationship, however. Hitler had been able to launch his attack on Poland and had even been allowed to use Soviet ports in his fight against the British blockade; Soviet food and oil were essential to Germany's continued survival. Germany had to pay dearly for the goods, and in exchange Stalin wanted machine tools for manufacturing munitions and other war materiel. The USSR was a formidable trader who could not be bluffed or tricked—and through it all Hitler knew only too well that every gun or warplane he sent would be used against him in the future. He still had to guard against the necessity of fighting a two-front war—even though his ambitions in the East had been postponed, not abandoned.

In January 1940 the attack on Belgium and Holland was finally put off until late spring. On 10 January a Luftwaffe staff officer had to make a forced landing in Belgium while carrying Hitler's complete invasion plan. Though he managed to burn some of it, enough remained to necessitate the preparation of a completely new operation. Hitler also finally recognized the fact that it was not feasible to launch an invasion in the dead of winter.

In addition a new project had taken his fancy; its code name was *Weserübung* (Weser Exercise) and its object was the securing of German naval bases in Norway. The original idea had come from Admiral Raeder, who had first raised the matter with the Führer in October 1939. Nothing had been done about it, however, until December when the Soviet invasion of Finland made an Allied move through Norway a distinct possibility, thus threatening Germany's vital supply of iron ore from Sweden. The admiral had already been in touch with Major Vidkun Quisling, leader of the small Norwegian Nazi Party, who was anxious to arrange an Austrian-style takeover with himself playing the role of Seyss-Inquart. On 1 March 1940 Hitler signed

an order for the simultaneous occupation of Denmark and Norway, giving what he termed 'the most daring and important undertaking in the history of warfare' priority even over Case Yellow (code name for the attack in Western Europe).

At long last he turned his attention to placating Mussolini. Sumner Welles, the United States Under Secretary of State, had come to Berlin on a peace-making mission; receiving a cool reception from the Germans, he had gone on to Italy where Hitler feared he would get a more sympathetic response. On 10 March, therefore, Ribbentrop arrived in Rome with an extremely cordial letter from Hitler; by the time he left he had not only calmed Il Duce's fears, but had extracted a commitment from Italy to enter the war. Mussolini's decision was confirmed when the two dictators met at the Brenner Pass on 18 March. Not only was Mussolini completely fascinated by Hitler, but the German was successful in the one area that the Italian respected most—military prowess—and Mussolini had no intention of being left behind in the race for glory. Three months afterward Italy had joined the war.

After his meeting with Mussolini Hitler was able to turn all his attention to the Weser Exercise (a minor operation he had not bothered to mention during their conversation). From the moment the final decision had been made he had taken a close interest in every stage of the planning—the beginning of that personal intervention that was to become more oppressive later in the war and so madden his increasingly distraught generals.

The commander of the expedition, General Nikolaus von Falkenhorst, reported directly to the Führer, and all planning was carried out by a specially appointed group within his own OKW rather than by the OKH. Another of his less desirable traits as Commander in Chief began to emerge in April 1940 as well—his distressing tendency to become overexcited and to blame others for his own mistakes, or for failures resulting from circumstances beyond their control. He was worried about the Scandinavian operations, fearing that if they did not go as planned he would have to postpone his main objective—the attack in the West—once again.

On 2 April, after a long conference with Göring, Raeder and Falkenhorst, the date of the attack was set: it would take place on 9 April, one week later. On Sunday 7 April five German naval groups set out for six Norwegian ports—including Narvik, Trondheim and Stavanger, where German merchant ships lay waiting with combat troops hidden in their holds.

Below Narvik British minelayers were busily at work, for Churchill had finally ordered an Allied landing at the same three ports—Narvik, Trondheim and Stavanger. Although a British ship sank a German troop transport and the

German cruiser *Hipper* saw action with a British destroyer, Hitler's surprise tactics were successful. Even according to Churchill, the British were 'completely outwitted'; Narvik, Trondheim and Stavanger fell on 8 April along with Oslo and Bergen. But thanks to the spirited defense put up by Norwegian soldiers in the fortress of Oskarberg, King Haakon VII (elected to the throne by popular vote) managed to escape with his family, members of Parliament, the gold from the Bank of Norway and the secret papers from the Foreign Office.

The Royal Navy had inflicted some damage, and German forces still had some six weeks of fighting ahead to clear out all of the 13,000 British troops who had managed to land near Narvik and Trondheim. But Denmark had fallen before noon without a fight (the Germans had sustained only twenty casualties), and by the end of April most of Norway was effectively under German control. King Haakon was evacuated by a British cruiser to Tromsö, far above the Arctic Circle, where he established a provisional government; Quisling took control in the central and southern parts of the country.

With his eastern and northern flanks secure, Hitler happily turned to the western offensive. He had not been happy with Brauchitsch and Halder's campaign plan, which was a variation on the old Schlieffen Plan: Army Group B under General Bock would sweep through the Low Countries and descend through northwestern France while General Gerd von Rundstedt's Army Group A controlled the center opposite the Ardennes and General Wilhelm von Leeb's Army Group C held the left wing opposite the Maginot Line. As in World War I, such a campaign was more than likely to degenerate into static trench warfare; quite apart from the fact that he did not have the resources to support such an effort, Hitler was determined not to subject his soldiers to that kind of struggle. In addition, it meant sending tanks over terrain that was cut up by many canals and rivers, and violated the whole principle of Blitzkrieg.

Hitler's preference was for a daring plan conceived by Colonel General Fritz Erich von Manstein, probably the Wehrmacht's most brilliant strategist, who had been Chief of Staff of Army Group A until Brauchitsch relieved him

learned that his plan—using gliders to land a small detachment armed with a powerful explosive on the roof—had worked, he literally hugged himself for joy.

In England Chamberlain was persuaded to resign as Prime Minister and Winston Churchill became the new Prime Minister. While British and French troops were rushing to the defense of the Low Countries, right into Hitler's trap, Army Group A—44 divisions including three Panzer corps commanded by General Ewald von Kleist—quickly made their way through the Ardennes against only nominal resistance. On 12 May they crossed the French frontier by 13 May they were across the Meuse and racing west toward the sea. In fact, they moved so fast that General Guderian's three leading Panzer divisions lost contact with the main unit. Hitler became so nervous that he refused to let them advance further until the motorized infantry caught up with them on the 18th. Soon the British and the best French Army units, still fighting fiercely in Belgium, were cut off in the south; on 20 May the Germans reached Abbeville, on the coast. A week later Belgian King

Left:
General von Manstein was General von Rundstedt's Chief of Staff. His idea for an attack through the Ardennes appealed to Hitler because it was bold and daring.

Below:
The port of Rotterdam goes up in flames.

of his command. His proposal involved shifting most of the Panzer divisions to the center, where the defending forces would be relatively weak. Once the tanks had surmounted the initial difficulties posed by the wooded, hilly terrain, they could sweep across the plains of northern France to the sea, cutting off the Allied Armies which had been lured into Belgium and northwestern France. Hitler had already been thinking along similar lines and eagerly adopted the plan in mid-February—over strenuous objections from the OKH. One of his refinements—the parachuting of small, highly trained units behind the front—was to be a decisive factor in the ultimate victory.

In 1938 the British Intelligence service had purchased a German cipher machine called Enigma from a Polish mathematician for £10,000 and a British passport. The first important news to come from the machine, which had been code named Ultra and set up some 40 miles outside London, consisted of details of Hitler's invasion plan. On 9 May 1940 the Dutch military attaché in Berlin received confirmation of the impending attack from a German friend, Colonel Hans Oster. But as with Norway and Denmark, the Allies refused to listen to the warnings, and when the German attack began shortly after dawn on 10 May, they were taken completely by surprise.

The Germans struck through Holland, Belgium and Luxembourg, overrunning the defenses in their path with ease. In his new headquarters near Euskirchen, not far from the Holland—Belgium borders, Hitler waited anxiously for news of the famed Belgium fortress Eben Emael on the Albert Canal; when he

Above:
Colonel General Heinz
Guderian lead the XIX
Panzer Corps in its
decisive break through
Sedan and across the
Meuse.

Leopold ordered his troops to stop fighting, and the Allies found themselves trapped between Army Group A to the south and Bock's Army Group B to the north.

The Allied forces would have been completely destroyed if Hitler had not ordered Guderian to stop again on 24 May, this time just a few miles south of the port of Dunkirk. The respite gave the Allies the chance they needed, and during the next week nearly 340,000 men were ferried to England with the aid of about 900 fishing boats, private yachts and other small craft. Members of the Führer's entourage have claimed that his order to halt stemmed from admiration of the British and a desire to leave the way open for peace negotiations. More probably the decision—taken in the face of angry opposition from Brauchitsch and Halder—was based on other motives. Hitler was anxious to save his armor for the next stage of the offensive, toward Paris; he was encouraged in this view by Göring who, wanting a bigger share of the glory, promised that his Luftwaffe would transform the port into a sea of flames. Two days later Hitler reversed the order and on 27 May the Panzers were again allowed to move forward. But the British had used the time to strengthen their own defenses and were able to fend off the Germans until the evacuation was completed. It was Hitler's first military mistake, and his failure to wipe out the British Army in Europe was one that would prove to be important.

On 5 June the German Army turned south and 146 German divisions began advancing along the 400-mile front against the 65 French and two British divisions that remained in their way. The much-vaunted French Army had been transformed by defeat into an undisciplined rabble, and the country was on the verge of collapse; even Hitler was surprised by the speed of the advance. During the morning of 14 June German troops began entering Paris. It was more like a parade than a battle, and the first men to arrive at the Arc de Triomphe were met by General Fedor von Bock, who had flown ahead to be able to greet them. After welcoming his men Bock visited Napoleon's tomb before having lunch at the Ritz and doing some shopping on the Champs Elysées. On the 16th Marshal Philippe Pétain was asked to form a new government; his first official act was to ask for an armistice. When Hitler heard the news in his new headquarters at the small Belgian village of Brûly-le-Pesche, he gleefully slapped his thigh and gave a little hop—a spontaneous demonstration of joy that shocked his staff, unaccustomed as they were to such displays. (The Allies later obtained a film of the scene and, by ingeniously 'looping' the frames, transformed the brief gesture into a ludicrous little dance that was used to good effect in Western propaganda films.)

At noon on 18 June, while Churchill was talking of England's 'finest hour' and General Charles de Gaulle was making his first broadcast from the BBC studios, Hitler was meeting with Mussolini in Munich. The Italian dictator was depressed. He had declared war on 10 June against the wishes of his army, industry, even many of his fellow Fascists; Italian troops had attacked the French border town of Menton immediately, but had quickly been brought to a halt. Now Mussolini saw his dreams of glory fading as peace with France grew near.

On the 21st Hitler and his entourage met the French delegation in the woods near Compiègne, where Germany had surrendered to France in November 1918. Hitler stayed long enough to hear Keitel read the armistice agreement before leaving the negotiators to their work. Then he returned to his headquarters to plan his forthcoming visit to Paris. At 1850 General Huntziger signed the peace treaty on behalf of the French government. It was the high point of Hitler's career. He had followed his series of political triumphs with a list of stunning military successes: he had defeated Poland in three weeks; he had overrun Norway, Denmark, Holland, Belgium, Luxembourg and France in two months; and he had driven the British back to their island base. He could not take sole credit for the triumphs, but his ability to apply his knowledge of military strategy and tactics imaginatively had given Germany an important edge over her opponents. Though he was not the only military leader to appreciate the importance of armor, he was the one who had insisted on forming ten armored divisions; his acceptance of Manstein's attack plan was the key to Germany's success in the West; above all, his psychological insight into the minds of his enemies enabled him to analyze situations more accurately than other, more traditional military men. The time when his weaknesses— his monomania, rigidity and gambler's instinct—

would begin to outweigh these strengths was still in the future.

Many Parisians had expected the German occupation to be accompanied by an orgy of rape, theft and murder. But one of Hitler's first orders was to the effect that his soldiers were to behave themselves; anyone caught looting would be shot on the spot. He wanted France to be a productive subject not a resentful one. The German soldiers responded with exemplary behavior that was a masterpiece of public relations; they were quiet and respectful, taking their pictures or conscientiously paying for their purchases in shops and cafés like any other tourist.

For his own visit to the French capital on 28 June, Hitler assembled a group including architects Albert Speer and Hermann Giessler, as well as art expert Arno Breker, to accompany him. His first stop after his plane landed was the Opéra, where he took pride in his ability to guide his companions through the venerable building. Though he did not find Paris as attractive as the Italian cities he had visited, or even as beautiful as Vienna, it was still a sentimental journey; for two days he and his cronies were light-hearted tourists as they visited the Eiffel Tower, Napoleon's Tomb, the Champs Elysées, and Sacré Coeur in Montmartre (which he

Below:
The victorious German cavalry parade down the Champs Elysées on 14 June 1940.

found 'dreadful'). The great parade he had planned for taking possession of the city was canceled to spare French feelings; he made up for it later with a triumphal entry into Berlin— complete with pealing bells, cheering crowds and flowers—when he returned to the German capital early in July for a meeting with Ciano.

When that meeting took place on 7 July the Italian Foreign Minister found the Führer in two minds—not eager to commit himself to further action against England on one hand, but not discounting the possible necessity for further conflict on the other. Since mid-June Hitler had been waiting for some indication from Britain that, with the fall of France, they were willing to begin negotiating for peace. But he had met his match in the new Prime Minister, Winston Churchill, who, far from contemplating a truce, was feverishly working at top speed to organize Britain's defenses against the feared German invasion. On 3 July he had emphasized his intentions by ordering the British Navy to open fire on the fleet of their former allies, the French fleet, in Oran; and on 14 July he made his government's position clear in a speech over the radio from London: 'We shall seek no terms, we shall tolerate no parley . . . we may show mercy . . . we shall ask for none.'

Genuinely astonished, Hitler issued Direc-

ment could hold out indefinitely in the outposts of their far-flung empire. So, while the Wehrmacht and Kriegsmarine quarreled over the number of divisions to be used and the width of the front to be covered, he continued to try to pressure Britain, politically and through 'restricted' military action, into suing for peace.

Since the German Navy was obviously not equal to completing the invasion task as planned, he turned to Göring, who was confident that the Luftwaffe could seriously injure Britain's industrial capacity, destroy the RAF and undermine popular morale. 'Operation Eagle' (to become known as the Battle of Britain) began on 13 August 1940; the first mass raid on London took place on 7 September. On 15 September German planes took off to deliver the *coup de grâce*—but by switching targets from outlying airfields to the city of London they had given the RAF time to recover from the dreadful pounding they had been taking. The Luftwaffe bombers were driven off with heavy losses, and on 16 September bad weather forced an end to Operation Eagle.

Though the bombing of London and other major cities was to continue through the winter, the RAF clearly still controlled the skies, just as the British Navy controlled the sea. Operation Sea Lion, originally set for mid-September, was postponed indefinitely.

During the last half of 1940 Hitler was engaged in a number of indecisive, virtually purposeless political and military moves. In addition to his almost half-hearted plans to conquer Britain by force, he hoped to isolate the country politically by establishing a European bloc under German control. Hopefully a strong united Europe would bring Britain around in time and also ensure the neutrality of the United States. In September 1940 he concluded the Tripartite Pact with Italy and Japan. In October he traveled to Hendaye to meet Franco, followed up with a visit to Pétain and his Deputy Premier, Pierre Laval, in Montoire. In November he even had conversations with Molotov in Berlin, in an attempt to draw the USSR into the alliance.

His efforts bore little fruit, partly because his military successes had made mere political action seem dull and somehow contemptible. He no longer bothered to hide his egotism and thirst for power behind an ingratiating manner and persuasive, if specious, arguments. Both he and Ribbentrop were using the same blustering, transparently self-serving tactics with their friends as they had with their enemies; but without the threat of force to back them up, they had little effect.

General Franco, not at all impressed by the Führer, proved to be a hard bargainer, refusing to ally himself with Germany and take Gibraltar without a substantial commitment from the Germans for large amounts of men and

tive Number 16—an order for the preparation of a landing operation in England, code named Sea Lion. Though Admiral Raeder had been working out various ways to cross the Channel since November 1939, he had never been able to interest the Führer in the project; this was the first time Hitler ever seriously considered the operation. It was a formidable undertaking, and almost immediately reservations began crowding into his mind. Even if the problems of supply and transport could be overcome and the British Isles taken, His Majesty's Govern-

materiel—which he and Hitler both knew could not be met. Although the conversations with Pétain proceeded more amicably, with the two reaching a general agreement on French-German collaboration, there was no real substance to the results. Later Pétain commented to a friend, 'It will take six months to discuss this program and another six months to forget it.'

Mussolini too was showing a distressing tendency to go his own way, in contradiction of the Führer's wishes. Hitler had assigned him the task of invading Egypt, but the Italian forces were making little progress against the British. To recoup his prestige, Il Duce invaded Greece on 28 October—a dangerous step that could easily embroil Hitler in a messy action in the Balkans. Hitler was not informed of the invasion beforehand; his ally was not just anxious for a military triumph of his own, but was determined to give Hitler a taste of his own medicine. 'Hitler always faces me with a *fait accompli*. This time I am going to pay him back in his own coin,' he remarked to Ciano. Hitler could not afford to alienate Italy after his failure to bring Franco in on his side, and had to accept the situation with as much good grace as he could muster.

In the meantime, he had been trying to decide

Left:
Hitler and his adjutant, Lieutenant Schmundt, on a visit to the Western Front in May 1940.

Below:
Hitler leads the Victory Parade in Berlin in June 1940. Note the cameras in the background recording this 'momentous' occasion.

what to do about the USSR. In August 1940 he had ordered the operations staff at OKW to begin planning Operation Barbarossa, giving the Army General Staff similar orders. The USSR had taken advantage of Hitler's pre-occupation with the West to annex the Baltic States and strengthen Soviet influence in Rumania; Hitler began to feel the pressure more and more, though he was not yet ready to break off the continuing round of trade negotiations. Finally he decided that it would not be necessary to defeat Britain before turning to the East. The end of the USSR would force Britain to come to terms with Germany; it would also increase Japan's importance in the Far East and thus divert the United States' attention from European affairs.

By the time he formally declared his intentions to his officers on 18 December, several months of hard planning had already been completed. In addition, troops had been moved to the East, the Economic Section of OKW had set up a special department to survey Soviet industry and natural resources and the operational plan had already been completed and approved. Far from being the result of a whim, the decision was based on a rational assessment of the situation. As Hitler saw it, he had lost his chance to destroy England quickly, and it was obvious that the British would never conclude peace as long as another Great Power existed on the Continent. The longer the war went on the greater the odds that American aid to Britain would increase. It was absolutely necessary to 'remove the Soviet piece from the European chessboard'—and it had to be done quickly, since his only hope of success lay in destroying the Soviet forces before they could withdraw into the depths of the huge country.

Unfortunately Hitler, having reached this point, failed to think it through any further and—typically—departed on wild flights of fancy. Having, in his imagination, brought German soldiers to the Urals by the beginning of winter and reduced Moscow to rubble, he never considered how he would hold the long open frontier against forces that were sure to be mustering against him in the interior.

Once the die was cast he departed to spend Christmas with the troops stationed along the English Channel. The six-month period since the fall of France had been a frustrating one: the defeat of England had eluded him, his allies had let him down, and America and the USSR were becoming increasingly grave threats. At 50, he was already past his prime, both mentally and physically—he had needed glasses for some time, though he would not wear them in public (his secretaries used special typewriters with large print so that he would not need to be seen in them). His ailing health added to his sense of urgency, making him feel the need to accomplish his ends before it was too late. He was not

as sick as he thought he was; complete medical examinations in January and December 1940 both indicated that he was healthy except for high blood pressure (and consequent damage to his heart) and occasional stomach disorders accompanied by flatulence. As he cut himself off more and more from everything not directly connected with the conduct of the war, his relationship with Eva Braun paradoxically improved. He began to spend more time at the Berghof, and abandoned the pretense that they were just good friends. As mistress of the Führer's house, Eva blossomed and her appearance and demeanor improved; she addressed Hitler with the familiar *du* and was in turn called *Chefin* ('Wife of the Chief') by the staff. Their associates from those days claim that as far as they could tell, Hitler's sexual relations with his mistress were normal for a busy 50-year-old man; he even relaxed so much that he would occasionally pat her hand in public.

Before he could embark on his grand Soviet adventure, however, Hitler had to finish a relatively modest one. Mussolini's troops had ground to a halt in Greece and Albania, and the territory had to be secured before the Soviet invasion could safely begin. To get to Greece German troops would have to pass through Hungary, Rumania, Bulgaria and Yugoslavia. The first two had been German allies for some time, while Bulgaria had been pressured into joining the Tripartite Pact in March 1941. But despite Hitler's promises to guarantee Yugoslavia's territorial integrity, Prince Paul (the Yugoslavian Regent) refused to allow German troops to cross his country. In mid-March the government finally decided to sign the Tripartite Pact (still on condition that the German forces would not enter Yugoslavia), but the people rebelled and several Air Force officers overthrew the Regent's government, putting the young heir, Peter, on the throne.

Hitler was congratulating himself on having achieved a happy solution to the problem while getting ready for a meeting with Yosuke Matsuoka, the Japanese Foreign Minister, when he received word of the coup. Disappointment increased his anger; raging at the 'insult' that had just been handed him, he burst in on Jodl and Keitel, vowing to smash Yugoslavia once and for all. Barbarossa would have to be postponed for four or five weeks; Göring was to begin an attack on Belgrade immediately, sending planes 'in waves' from Hungarian air bases; Jodl, as Chief of the OKW Operations Staff, was sent off to work all that day and night on plans for the attack. The German generals would remember that decision bitterly later in the year, when the Soviet winter closed in on troops who were (as the generals saw it) only three or four weeks short of their final objective.

The Führer also took time for two short interviews to enlist Hungary's and Bulgaria's co-

Right:
Hitler met General Franco on the Franco-Spanish border at Hendaye on 23 October 1940. Hitler wished to secure Franco's agreement to a joint attack on the British base at Gibraltar and to other co-operative ventures. Almost a month later Franco gave Hitler a curt rebuff.

Far right:
Paul of Yugoslavia, the Prince Regent, visited Hitler in June 1939. Hitler set out to impress the prince and succeeded in getting Paul to sign a secret pact with the Axis on 25 March 1941 but only a few days later Paul was deposed.

Right:
Hitler addresses the Reichstag on 19 July 1940 to move the acceptance of the administration of the newly-occupied territories.

operation before rushing off to see the Japanese minister, whom he hoped to talk into seizing Singapore from the British. To his visible disappointment the Japanese government (despite Matsuoka's personal inclinations) refused to commit itself to definite action in the near future. Near midnight he dashed off a letter to his Italian ally, telling Mussolini about the Yugoslavian situation and urgently requesting Italy not to carry out any further operations in Albania or Greece.

'Operation Punishment' began at dawn on 6 April with the usual bombing attack by the Luftwaffe, followed by the rapid advance of overwhelming numbers of men and tanks. Belgrade was razed in a 72-hour attack that left 17,000 civilians dead. The Yugoslavian Army finally surrendered at Sarajevo on the 17th. The Greeks, faced with Field Marshal List's Twelfth Army (four armored and eleven infantry divisions), met a similar fate, despite aid from four British divisions that had been hurriedly

Right:
Happier days for Rudolf Hess. In May 1941 Hess surprised everyone by undertaking a secret mission to negotiate peace with England. Hess was arrested in Scotland after he had parachuted out of a plane and spent the rest of the war and his life in jail.

Above:
General Erwin Rommel is greeted by General Gariboldi on his arrival in Tripoli in February 1941.

Above left:
In April 1941 the Deutsche Afrika Korps scored notable successes in the Western Desert and reached the Egyptian frontier.

sent up from Libya. The Greek Armies in the north surrendered on 23 April, and the Germans took possession of Athens on the 27th as the British frantically evacuated their troops. What Mussolini had tried all winter to accomplish, Hitler had finished in three weeks—a public humiliation for the Italian dictator which Hitler emphasized by his unilateral division of Yugoslavia among its neighbors. Only Crete remained in Allied hands, and that British stronghold fell to an airborne assault at the end of May.

Meanwhile, it also had become necessary for Hitler to do something about North Africa, where the Italian Army had been unable to contain the British. Admiral Raeder had been arguing for months that the eastern Mediterranean was Britain's weakest point, and that therefore it was the place where Germany should be concentrating its strength. He was supported in this instance even by Göring, though the two disagreed about virtually every other aspect of the war. But Hitler did not share the German

Navy's natural view of Britain as the main enemy, and was inclined to discount the military importance of North Africa. Reluctantly, he ordered the transport of one armored division from the Balkans and appointed a German officer—the dashing General Erwin Rommel—to lead the combined Italo-German force in the desert.

Rommel, with a total of three divisions at his disposal, was ordered to prepare his plans and submit them for analysis by 20 April. Instead the resourceful tank commander struck on 31 March; by 12 April he had recaptured Cyrenaica, taken Tobruk, and was threatening Egypt from Bardia, only a few miles from the border.

The move took Hitler and the High Command completely by surprise, and left them, though pleased, more than a little embarrassed. Rommel's victory had severely compromised Britain's position in the entire eastern Mediterranean, damaged British prestige abroad and reinforced Stalin in his determination to maintain at least civil relations with Germany. (By this time the Soviet leader was receiving frequent reports about Germany's invasion plans, but he resolutely refused to listen to them—believing them to be lies spread by the British.) But though Raeder immediately began pushing for a strong Egypt–Suez offensive, Hitler refused to consider anything more than a limited action until after the USSR was defeated. His celebrated insight had failed him; it was his third big blunder of the war (the first being his invasion of Czechoslovakia and the second his postponement of Barbarossa for revenge on Yugoslavia).

German forces had been massing in the East since the beginning of the year; Stalin—despite the troop movements, despite frequent violations of Soviet air space by German reconnaissance planes, even despite warnings from his own intelligence service and British Ambassador Sir Stafford Cripps—persisted in the

Below right:
General Keitel, Hitler, Generals von Brauchitsch and Paulus discuss the strategic position in Eastern Europe during the planning phase of Operation Barbarossa in 1940.

Below:
Hitler discusses the progress of Barbarossa with Keitel, whose title was Commander in Chief of the High Command of the Armed Forces, in July 1941.

belief that Hitler would never attack him. But the Führer had succeeded in overcoming his own generals' resistance to the plan, and by early spring, when the attack date was finally set for 22 June, almost all were convinced that 'the Russian colossus will prove to be a pig's bladder; prick it and it will burst.' Most of the Germans felt that the campaign would be over in three months, and Brauchitsch went so far as to predict that the major fighting would take only four weeks. The Germans were so confident of an early victory that only one-fifth of the men were provided with winter clothing.

There were, of course, some major exceptions to the generally optimistic mood in Germany; Ribbentrop and Raeder both thought Barbarossa was a mistake, as did Hess, who was completely opposed to a two-front war. On 10 May Hess—that naïve, shy, rather stupid deputy for whom Hitler felt considerable affection—put into action a plan he had been formulating for several weeks. In a specially outfitted Me-

110 he had managed to cajole from Willy Messerschmitt, the former World War I flying ace survived a hair-raising flight to Scotland and his first parachute jump in order to meet the Duke of Hamilton and attempt to negotiate a peace agreement with Britain. His rather woolly-minded scheme was based on the premise that Hitler could always disclaim knowledge of his dramatic mission if the negotiations failed, and take credit if they succeeded.

Hitler's first reaction was embarrassed anger—Hess' associates were imprisoned and Goebbels' press circulated stories saying that he was mentally disturbed. Later, however, the Führer realized that his loyal deputy had made the flight for him. Hess—who later wrote, 'I was not able to stop the madness of the war and could not prevent what I saw coming ... but it makes me happy to think I tried to do it'—was rewarded by imprisonment, first in the Tower of London and later in Spandau. There he remains today, the last of the Allies' prisoners, still in solitary confinement after more than 30 years.

The generals were becoming increasingly disturbed by Hitler's proposals for administering the conquered territories in the East; the vicious reign of terror imposed by the SS on Poland had already aroused considerable opposition among the professional military commanders. But for the Soviet campaign, Hitler did not make the slightest pretense of deferring to their wishes for an 'honorable' occupation or even of saving their faces. In the first of a series of directives issued prior to 22 June, Heinrich Himmler, the Reichsführer-SS, was entrusted with various 'special tasks,' acting 'independently and under his own authority.' In other words, he and his group of some 3000 security police and SD men were being given a free hand in the USSR and Hitler was making sure that the scruples of the army commanders would not stand in his way. In May another directive made members of the armed forces immune from prosecution for crimes against enemy civilians, and Reinhard Heydrich gave members of the Einsatzgruppen oral in-

structions to murder all the Jews, gypsies, 'Asiatic inferiors' and Communist functionaries they could find. A propaganda campaign against the 'Slavic subhumans' supported orders to enlisted men, telling them to employ 'ruthless and energetic measures' in order to achieve the 'total elimination of all active and passive resistance.'

On 14 June Richard Sorge, the Soviets' crack secret service agent in Japan, sent a terse message from Tokyo: 'War begins on 22 June.' Stalin chose not to listen. On 17 June a defecting German sergeant crossed the Soviet frontier and revealed the date and time of the attack. The commanding general of the Soviet forces did not think it necessary to raise the alarm. On 21 June Sir Stafford Cripps gave the Soviet Ambassador in London one last warning, and Stalin finally agreed to put Soviet forces on the alert.

Right:
Ciano greets Hitler at one of the Führer's headquarters in October 1941.

Below left:
Hitler reviews some troops who fought on the dreaded Eastern Front. The first winter on the Eastern Front was bitter and units spent the coldest season in bastion towns deep in the USSR.

Below:
To keep spirits high on the home front the Wehrmacht put on a victory parade in Berlin in 1941.

By that time more than 3,000,000 German soldiers were in position along the border.

At 0245 on 22 June a disgruntled Mussolini was awakened to receive a long message from Hitler, finally informing his ally of the invasion. While he was still reading the letter, dictated from Hitler's new underground headquarters named *Wolfsschanze* (Wolf's Lair) in East Prussia, the attack had already begun.

In the gloomy, pre-dawn hours—129 years to the day after Napoleon had crossed the Nieman River on his way to Moscow—Hitler's armored, mechanized armies poured across the thousand-mile front which stretched from the Baltic to the Black Sea. Taking part in the great offensive were 153 German divisions, twelve divisions and ten brigades of Rumanian troops, eighteen divisions from Finland, three from Hungary, and two and one-half from Slovakia; later the force would be increased by the addition of three Italian divisions and one from Spain (the 'Blue Division'). Their equipment included 3580 tanks, 2740 planes, 7184 artillery pieces and some 600,000 motorized vehicles. Despite the many warnings, the Soviets appeared to have

been taken completely by surprise. About 5000 Soviet planes (one-half of their Air Force) were destroyed on the ground; as usual, wedges of tanks were driven deep into enemy territory before the pincers closed, encircling whole armies. By the beginning of July Germany had taken some 600,000 prisoners.

In the wake of the armies came the four Einsatzgruppen to set up their own regime in the occupied zones. The leaders set about organizing the mass killings demanded of them with cool efficiency; one of the commanders, Otto Ohlendorff, testified later that in their first year in the USSR his group murdered approximately 90,000 men, women and children. The Jews of Western Russia took the brunt of the SS activities, and conservative estimates place the number of killed during 1941–42 at about half a million. The Germans' job was made easier by the fact that the Soviet people, cut off from the world by Stalin's controlled press, knew nothing of Nazi excesses and in many cases welcomed the Germans as liberators. Heydrich's main problem was not resistance on the part of his victims—who, Jews and Slavs alike, were often calm almost to the point of indifference—but the effect of the program on his own men. They were plagued by nervous breakdowns, stomach ailments and alcoholism; another Einsatzgruppe commander was not exaggerating when he told Heydrich that after their Soviet experiences many of his men would be 'finished for the rest of their lives.' As word of the atrocities filtered back to Germany Rosenberg tried to persuade Hitler to abandon his objective. Far from succeeding, he left the Wolfsschanze on 16 July realizing that Hitler still retained the vision of the Slavs as a lazy, second-class race that he had picked up in Vienna. He had no conception of the structure of the Soviet Union or the psychology of the peoples within it, and was determined to rule with the whip, ruthlessly exterminating anyone who opposed him.

All during the summer the Wehrmacht plunged forward, reaching the Dnieper River in two weeks, by 5 July. By 16 July Bock's Army Group Center had reached Smolensk, just over 200 miles from Moscow and 450 miles from where they had begun. Field Marshal Wilhelm von Leeb's Army Group North was moving up the Baltic States toward Leningrad, while Rundstedt's Army Group South was pushing toward Kiev at the heart of the fertile Ukraine. Hitler was so confident of victory that in mid-July he issued a directive advising that in the 'near future' the strength of the army in the East would be 'considerably reduced' and that emphasis in armament programs would be shifted to submarines and aircraft for the continuing battle against Britain.

But though the Germans were gaining ground rapidly, they were not destroying the

Right:
Field Marshal Fedor von Bock was in command of Army Group Center for Operation Barbarossa. When his armies fell back short of Moscow Hitler dismissed him in December 1941.

Below:
Alfred Rosenberg, Dr Lammers and Hitler discuss problems in Eastern Europe in November 1941. In July 1941 Rosenberg was appointed Minister for the Occupied Eastern Territories. Rosenberg wanted to use disaffected Soviet minorities to fight against the Red Army but the policy never worked because the Wehrmacht had alienated the Russian peoples with its genocide policy.

Soviet armies as Hitler had hoped. However many Soviets were captured or killed, there always seemed to be thousands more in reserve—and the Soviet soldiers were by no means in the 'state of torpor' that Hitler envisioned. On the contrary, they stood their ground and fought fiercely, even when encircled—which greatly surprised the Germans after their easy victories in Poland and Western Europe. Soviet fighter planes, too, kept appearing out of nowhere and the Luftwaffe, without the resources for an all-out war on two fronts, could not maintain their overwhelming air superiority as in the past. Another big surprise was the Soviet T-34 tank which was lighter and more maneuverable than the German Panzers, and so heavily armored that shells from the Germans' 37-mm antitank guns just bounced off it.

Also around the middle of July a great controversy arose between Hitler and his generals, continuing on through August. The Führer wanted to send some of Bock's most powerful armored divisions north to assist in the capture of Leningrad and others south to back up the advance into the Ukraine, so that he could

secure the badly needed agricultural and industrial resources of that region. But his commanders and the Army High Command were unanimous in demanding that they be allowed to concentrate their forces for a drive on Moscow where they were sure they would be able to lure most of the Soviet forces into a decisive battle for the capital. Hitler refused even to consider the notion. His army was being drawn more and more deeply into the Soviet wastes, using much more materiel than had been allowed for; German industry was reaching the limits of its productive capacity; and his supply lines were becoming dangerously attenuated. He desperately needed the rich resources of the Ukraine and Donets Basin and the oil fields of the Caucasus.

In the middle of this bitter dispute the Führer fell seriously ill. His health had been deteriorating for some months, and while some of his problems—notably his stomach problems—may have been psychosomatic, others were probably caused by the large doses of drugs prescribed by Dr Morell; Hitler was taking 120–150 antigas pills a week, along with 10 injections of a strong sulfonamide and as many as four stimulants—a dangerous situation for someone as easily excited and with blood pressure already as high as his. In addition, he was struck down by dysentery at the Wolfsschanze, with its alternating chills and fevers. In late July, during a heated argument with Ribbentrop, he suddenly clutched his chest and staggered backward, finally sinking into a chair; after a few moments he said that he had been afraid he was going to have a heart attack. Morell was so worried by the incident that he sent an electrocardiogram to a colleague, who diagnosed rapidly developing coronary sclerosis. The doctor probably did not inform Hitler of the results; instead, his answer was to prescribe still more drugs.

The medication was beginning to have a noticeable effect. Hitler's behavior would occasionally undergo a complete change, and he would sometimes make thoroughly outrageous remarks; his desire to undertake unreasonable projects became stronger, as his famous memory for technical detail weakened. At about this time, too, more of his confidential associates were told of his plans for the 'final solution' of the Jewish 'problem' in Europe; Adolf Eichmann took steps to halt Jewish emigration from occupied territories, and at Auschwitz he and Rudolf Höss began investigating the most efficient methods of mass extermination.

Hitler's illness was probably one reason why the argument with the generals over basic strategy was allowed to drag on so long. By mid-August when he was on the road to recovery, he put a stop to all discussion and their open rebellion subsided to grumbles and lingering resentment.

At first it looked as if he had been right again; the southern encirclement, which ended with the capture of Kiev, was a great victory that also secured the flank of Bock's central front. Finally, Hitler approved the offensive against Moscow. But he had wasted much valuable time. Already the autumn rains had transformed the Soviet countryside, with its bad roads, into a quagmire which crippled the German vehicles, but which the lighter T-34s negotiated with relative ease. Furthermore, he insisted on diluting the strength of the Moscow offensive by insisting that he could also pursue simultaneous objectives in the north and south; Leeb was ordered to capture Leningrad, while Rundstedt was sent to clear out the Black Sea coast and move east to the Volga and southeast to the Caucasus.

By spreading his forces too thinly along the thousand-mile front, never managing to concentrate them for a decisive knock-out blow and, above all, by underestimating both the numerical superiority and fighting spirit of the Soviet troops, Hitler had fallen into the very trap he had warned the generals about before Barbarossa began—that of allowing the Soviets

Below:
General Gunther von Kluge was Commander in Chief of the Fourth Army during Operation Barbarossa.

to retreat and pull the German Army deep into the depths of the country. When the much-feared winter fell abruptly in mid-November, the Germans were still installed outside Leningrad and Moscow. Ill-equipped for the severe weather (Hitler had consistently refused to order winter equipment, since he remained convinced that there would be no need for a winter campaign), men died of the cold by the thousands, while vehicles refused to run and machine guns stopped firing.

While the Soviet campaign had absorbed nearly all Hitler's attention since it began, it had also encouraged his perception of himself as the man destined to found the new German Empire. His conversation, recorded during this period and subsequently published, clearly shows the exalted mood in which he pursued 'the Cyclopean task which the building of an empire means for a single man.' The same mood was in evidence when he received a visit from Mussolini at the Wolfsschanze on 25 August. The Italian dictator was there to persuade Hitler to let Italian forces take part in the defeat of Communism—but to the Führer it was mainly a propaganda exercise, and Mussolini spent most of his time listening to Hitler expound on his own greatness and the triumphs of the German Army. Before the end of the visit, however, the two dictators had pledged themselves to establish a close, peaceful collaboration among the peoples of Europe. By the time Ciano visited the headquarters in October 1941 the idea had grown, and 'European solidarity' was the new catch phrase among Hitler's entourage. The concept was supported and expanded by the notion of the 'New Germany' in which all class distinctions and privileges had been abolished, a notion Hitler developed in his traditional speech in Munich on 8 November. At the end of November representatives of Italy, Spain, Hungary, Rumania, Slovakia, Croatia, Bulgaria, Finland and Denmark—along with those of Japan and Manchukuo—were invited to Berlin to renew the Anti-Comintern Pact, mainly as a demonstration of European solidarity. What that solidarity meant in operation was another matter; when Ciano mentioned the possibility of severe famine in Greece, Göring not only refused to worry about it, but announced that it was probably just as well, since 'certain nations would have to be decimated' in order to leave enough room for the remainder.

On 1 December when Bock's last all-out attack on Moscow was due to begin, he, along with Hitler and most of the other generals, saw a chance for victory. But though a few units made it as far as the outlying suburbs, not one was able to penetrate the Soviet defenses; by 5 December the German Armies were stopped along the entire front. The next day, 6 December, a relatively unknown commander, General Georgi Zhukov, launched a major

counteroffensive against the German Army. The very existence of his 100 divisions—which consisted of fresh troops who were well-equipped and trained for fighting in the bitter cold—came as a surprise to the German High Command. The threat to Moscow was swept away as the German Army retreated in confusion, their lines continually threatened by Soviet breakthroughs. Hitler was faced with his most important military setback so far in the war, for retreat could easily turn to panic; little but his own determination stood between the German Army and disaster. As if the Soviet situation was not enough, events on the other side of the world were conspiring to draw him into a larger conflict.

The European war turned into a global conflict on 7 December when Japan attacked the American Fleet in Pearl Harbor. The Japanese government had not informed Germany of its intentions, and the news took Hitler by surprise, but he heartily approved of the Japanese tactics even though he himself would have preferred keeping the United States out of the war. Despite Ribbentrop's advice to the contrary, he immediately decided to declare war himself.

The reasons for this action, when common-sense must have dictated letting Japan and America fight it out far away in the Pacific, are complex. For the past two years Hitler had been doing everything in his power to avoid a confrontation, in the face of ever-increasing American aid to Britain. But underneath the conciliatory facade, his resentment—especially of Roosevelt personally—had been growing until it reached the proportions of an obsession. He had come to see the American President (along with Churchill) as the puppet of international Jewry. As he had with the USSR, he tended to underestimate American strength. He simply could not imagine how a country with such a racially mixed and undisciplined population could mount an effective military effort; Japan's easy victory at Pearl Harbor tended to strengthen this conviction. From a propaganda standpoint, he also acquired a powerful new ally, Japan, to help offset the recent setbacks in the USSR. And, finally, he was excited by the concept of a 'war between continents' and the 'historic struggle' that war would entail. On 11 December he convened the Reichstag and formally issued the German declaration of war.

The German generals could spare little time to worry about the implications of acquiring a new enemy, since the Soviet situation was continuing to worsen. Hitler's method for dealing with crisis—ordering his men to stand still and fight to the death—has been criticized. Certainly it resulted in much suffering and hardship. But in this case it did have the desired effect of saving the army from complete destruction; the USSR did not breakthrough that

Right:
At the height of the German successes this painting was exhibited in Berlin. Entitled *The Führer on the Battlefield* it was drawn from his imagination by Konrad Hommel.

Below:
The people of Moscow build a makeshift anti-tank obstacle during the winter of 1941. Until the Soviet counterattack materialized on 8 December it looked as if the German Army would reach Moscow.

winter, and the German line still held, deep in Soviet territory.

Hitler's distrust of his military commanders, which could be glossed over when things were going well, could not be ignored in times of trouble. Convinced that the only person capable of conducting the war was himself, he finally accepted Brauchitsch's resignation on 19 December and announced that he was taking over as Commander in Chief of the Wehrmacht in the field. It would no longer be possible for him to stay in the background; at the very moment when the myth of the invincible German Army was being shattered in the snowfields of Russia, Hitler stepped into the limelight. Henceforth, he would personally be held publicly responsible for whatever happened, for better or worse.

Below:
As casualties mounted,
the German Army had
to rely on volunteer
troops. In this picture
three Caucasians swear
an oath of loyalty to the
Führer.

Far right:
Field Marshal Wilhelm
von Leeb (second from
left) and Lieutenant
General Erich Höpner
(second from right)
were two of the generals
Hitler purged in January
1942.

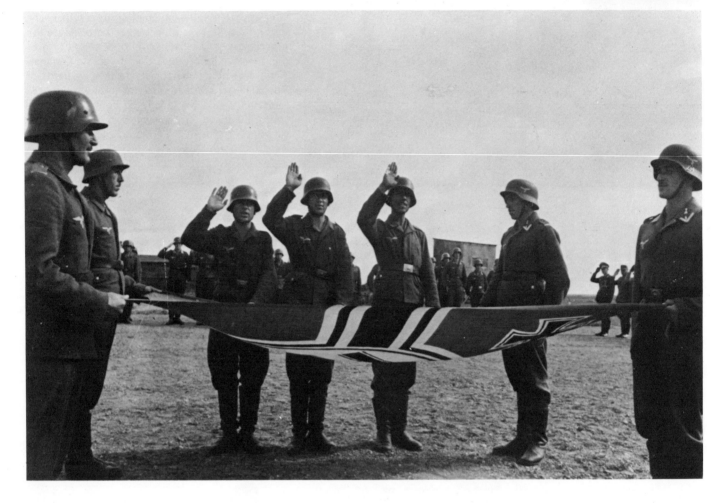

The turning point of World War II is usually said to have occurred in November 1942 when the three great Allied offensives—the landings in North Africa, Montgomery's breakthrough at El Alamein, and the Soviet encirclement of Stalingrad—captured the initiative from the Axis Powers once and for all. But even though as late as the midsummer of 1942 Hitler appeared to be at the height of his power, the seeds of his destruction had already begun to take root in December 1941—with his assumption of complete control over the armed forces, his ever-increasing belief in himself as an infallible military commander, and the entry of the United States into the war.

At the same time Hitler had appointed himself to replace Brauchitsch as Commander in Chief of the German Army, and he had instituted a dramatic shake-up in the entire German High Command which involved many replacements,

recalls and transfers: Bock was relieved as Commander in Chief of Army Group Center and replaced by Field Marshal Günther von Kluge; Rundstedt was replaced by Field Marshal Walther von Reichenau after his retreat from Rostov; the dashing General Guderian was relieved of his command on Christmas Day for retreating without permission; Field Marshal von Leeb, Commander in Chief of Army Group North, voluntarily resigned; General Erich Höpner, an excellent tank commander who had taken part in the assault on Moscow, was cashiered—stripped of his rank and forbidden to wear his uniform; General von Sponeck was actually condemned to death.

Throughout that winter of 1941–42 the German soldiers fought desperately against both the Red Army and the bitter cold; they were allowed to retreat just at the last moment, and then only as far as absolutely necessary. By the

Right:
Stalin and Marshal
Voroshilov of the State
Defense Committee.
Stalin, like Hitler, kept a
tight rein on what his
generals were doing.

160

Götterdämmerung

end of February Germany had sustained more than a million casualties—over 31 percent of the Army in the east. Goebbels visited the Führer's headquarters about this time and found Hitler 'greatly aged'—ashen-faced, serious, subdued and complaining of dizzy spells. The very sight of snow, he said, made him feel physically ill.

As spring drew near, the ground began to thaw and turn into a vast mud-field and both sides—exhausted by the grim fighting—rested, regrouped and planned their summer offensives. Hitler's health improved, along with his self-confidence—after all, he had saved the German Army from Napoleon's fate (even though their plight had been of his making in the first place). However that self-confidence was shaky, and his nerves were still on edge.

Meanwhile the Allies, having gained the United States as an important new partner, were working to establish a unified planning structure, thus avoiding the basic mistake made by the Axis: each of the three partners – Germany, Italy and Japan – pursued its own aims without any co-ordination with the other two. In the 1930s Hitler had enjoyed the advantage of having a definite goal while the Western Powers floundered, often at cross-purposes. Now the tables were turned – it was the Allies who had a concrete goal (defeat of the enemy) and the Axis nations who were separately seeking insubstantial, grandiose objectives.

Though most of his attention was concentrated on the military campaign in the USSR, Hitler had to give some heed to other matters. In December, during the dark struggle with the Soviet Union, he finally ordered the official implementation of the 'Final Solution.' It was a project near to his heart and his decision was taken in the firm conviction that he was doing God's work and cleansing the world of vermin. As long as the killing was done as impersonally as possible, there was no need for him to feel at all conscience-stricken. To the very end he would believe that he was acting for the good of Europe, and that any means he used were therefore justified.

Himmler, always happy to oblige, set his technical experts to devising gas chambers, and began shipping Jews in boxcars to Poland to await completion of the extermination camps. Heydrich began setting up the necessary bureaucracy – though at first many connected with it did not understand the grim reality behind euphemisms like 'deportation to the east.' David Irving's claim that Hitler did not himself realize that mass murder was being planned is patent nonsense: elimination of the Jews and Slavs (the *Untermenschen*, or sub-humans) was of paramount importance to him, and had been for many years – every bit as important as *Lebensraum*. On 23 January, in a conversation with Himmler, he stressed that 'one must act radically'; if the Jews refused to leave Europe voluntarily, there was 'no other solution but extermination.' His major goal was the disappearance of all Jews from Europe. As for the Slavs, they were to be the expendable slaves of the German master race. His view, as transmitted through Martin Bormann to Rosenberg, was that 'the Slavs are to work for us. Insofar as we do not need them, they may die.'

In February 1942 Hitler – whether through good luck or good judgment – made one of the best appointments of his career. On 8 February Fritz Todt – creator of the Autobahn complex and the Westwall – was killed in an air accident; next morning the Führer appointed Albert Speer to take his place as Minister of Armaments and Munitions. Speer, who was not a fanatical Nazi, had already proved himself an able architect – now he showed himself to be a remarkably capable organizer in addition to being objective and retaining a responsible atti-

tude toward his duties. Soon he was being given more and more responsibility, until finally he was in complete control of all German war production. Had war production not increased as much as it did Hitler could never have been able to hold out as long as he did.

The mere fact that he was able to accomplish anything at all is amazing in itself, for on the home front every level of life was riddled with inefficiency and corruption. Loyal Nazis had been given jobs without any regard for their fitness to hold positions of responsibility, from Göring down to the petty, local gangsters who ran nearly every German town. It was little wonder that the black market mushroomed and Nazi officials grew fat on war-profiteering while the number of civil service staff grew to enormous proportions. What saved Germany from total collapse were the regular civil servants, who stolidly continued to do their jobs as best they could under the circumstances.

Hitler, who did not have a systematic mind himself, and who, in any case, preferred to exercise control by encouraging division and inter-departmental rivalry, did nothing to correct the situation. At the end of April, however, he did go to the Reichstag to obtain passage of a decree that gave him not only absolute power, but also placed him and his decisions completely outside the law. Some foreign observers wondered aloud why he even bothered, since he already had more *de facto* power than even Caesar or Napoleon had ever possessed.

During the winter Hitler had been forced to send more troops to the Mediterranean, but he had done so purely as a defensive measure; he still refused to recognize the fact that he was fighting a world war with fronts in the south and west as well as in the east. Furthermore, his experience in World War I, upon which he relied far too heavily, had accustomed him to think in terms of land actions only and to ignore developments at sea and in the air. Thus, though he still enjoyed a superiority in forces and – on the surface at least – still had the initiative, his inability to comprehend the implications of global conflict was already early in 1942 leading him toward the basic strategic mistakes that would in the end destroy him.

Finally, in the spring of 1942 while troops in the East were still waiting for the mud to dry up, Raeder succeeded in getting the Führer's approval for a Middle East offensive that summer. The plan consisted of two parts: Operation Aida (a desert offensive against Egypt, Suez and up through Persia), and Operation Hercules (a plan for the capture of Malta which was seriously threatening Rommel's supply routes). The first part of the plan went well; within a month Rommel had captured Tobruk and was threatening El Alamein. But Hitler continued to postpone the second phase. Refusing to listen to Raeder and Kesselring, he insisted on

trying to starve and bomb Malta out of existence rather than taking the island in an all-out assault. As a result, British bombers, submarines, and battleships continued to play havoc with the German and Italian vessels carrying men and supplies to North Africa, consistently destroying about three-quarters of Rommel's supply ships. Rommel's offensive soon stalled, and by autumn Hitler had lost interest in the project. The Middle East was again relegated to the status of a sideshow, and yet another opportunity had been lost.

By spring plans for Hitler's 'real' war in the USSR were complete; this time, instead of dividing his forces into three groups pursuing simultaneous objectives, he would concentrate them for a drive through the south. Emissaries were sent to Budapest and Bucharest to obtain more Hungarian and Rumanian divisions, and

163

Göring flew to Rome to ask for the Italian troops Hitler had turned down the year before. Before the campaign was due to begin, Mussolini and Ciano were invited to Salzburg, but the visit was not a success. Hitler, whom Ciano thought looked 'tired and gray,' talked and talked and talked, on every subject under the sun, while Mussolini—who preferred to do the talking himself—fidgeted and suffered in silence. On the second day, Ciano wrote in his diary that Hitler talked nonstop for one hour and 40 minutes; his own commanders were so bored that 'General Jodl, after an epic struggle, finally went to sleep on the divan.'

Heavy rains held off the Soviet offensive until 28 June, but once started that action appeared at first to yet again justify Hitler's theories.

Below left:
The defense of
Stalingrad by the Soviet
armies was painful and
heroic. The city was the
focus of fighting on the
southern flank for six
months.

advancing fast enough, and had moved his headquarters to a camp deep in the Ukraine (*Werwolf*). The stifling heat and depressing physical surroundings—a dreary collection of wooden huts in the midst of a huge plain without a hill or tree to be seen for miles—may have exacerbated his always unreliable temper and even affected his judgment. In any case, soon he was making the same mistake as before—overestimating German strength and underestimating that of the Red Army.

General von Kleist later claimed, with some justification, that the Fourth Panzer Army could have taken Stalingrad easily at the end of July 1942. But on 23 July Hitler decided to mount major attacks on both Stalingrad and the Caucasus at the same time, and the tank army

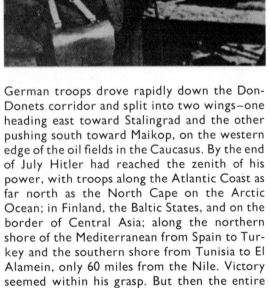

German troops drove rapidly down the Don-Donets corridor and split into two wings—one heading east toward Stalingrad and the other pushing south toward Maikop, on the western edge of the oil fields in the Caucasus. By the end of July Hitler had reached the zenith of his power, with troops along the Atlantic Coast as far north as the North Cape on the Arctic Ocean; in Finland, the Baltic States, and on the border of Central Asia; along the northern shore of the Mediterranean from Spain to Turkey and the southern shore from Tunisia to El Alamein, only 60 miles from the Nile. Victory seemed within his grasp. But then the entire house of cards began to collapse.

Earlier in July the Führer had fired Bock (commander of the southern offensive) for not

Above:
A German aircraft shot
down in Stalingrad.
Göring's Luftwaffe was
not the fine instrument
he claimed it to be. When
at the height of the
fighting Göring said he
would fly in enough
supplies to keep Paulus'
Sixth Army going he was
unable to deliver his
promise.

was shifted south to help with the latter offensive. Two weeks later it was ordered north again—but the Soviets had been given time to prepare the city's defenses, and the Germans were not able to break through. Stalin, who needed the oil fields of the Caucasus as badly as Hitler, was stiffening resistance in the south while both leaders prepared for a battle to the death at Stalingrad, where the city's name and historical associations made it a prize valued far above any real strategic considerations.

Not surprisingly, relations between Hitler and his staff went from bad to worse during that long, hot summer at *Werwolf*. Arguments between the Commander in Chief and Halder became more frequent and acrimonious as the Chief of the General Staff tried to point out the dangers of running simultaneous offensives and the resulting weak position of the northern flank along the Don. All his arguments did, however, was to increase Hitler's distrust of both the commanders in the field and his own staff officers—a distrust which was rapidly becoming pathological.

In late August the discovery of a spy ring, the *Rote Kapelle* (Red Orchestra), confirmed his conviction that he was surrounded by traitors. Even though the *Rote Kapelle* was quickly suppressed, another German spy, Rudolf Rösseler, continued to send important information to Moscow. Much of it was obtained from General Fritz Thiele, second in command of the OKW Signal Corps, and Hitler did not fail to realize that there still was a spy at headquarters. As his

Below right:
A soldier of the Sixth Army advances through the rubble of Stalingrad.

ing began inside the city. The longer the fighting went on, the more depressed Hitler became. Finally, on 24 September, he fired Halder and sent him home, where eventually he was arrested and incarcerated in Dachau concentration camp to await the coming of the Allies—along with fellow prisoners like Schuschnigg and Schacht. His replacement was Karl Zeitzler, a young, relatively inexperienced major general, whose first address to the other officers made it clear that he expected them all to exhibit absolute confidence in the Führer.

Relieved, Hitler left the headquarters and traveled to Berlin to make a speech on 30 September in the Sportpalast. The talk was short and rather dull, but it left many in the audience feeling slightly uneasy; underneath the usual

suspicions increased the generals came under even more fire. On 9 September Field Marshal Wilhelm List, Bock's replacement as commander of Army Group A, was sacked; Hitler took personal command of the group. By this time he was avoiding all contact with his staff. Any necessary conferences took place in an icy atmosphere, with a secretary ostentatiously taking notes. Hitler even ate alone, with only his Alsatian dog Blondi for company, and would leave his blockhouse only after dark. For several months he even refused to shake hands with meek General Jodl.

In mid-September when the fall of Stalingrad was expected momentarily, Soviet resistance suddenly stiffened. Reinforcements began pouring over the Volga, and bitter street fight-

Above:
Soviet tanks on the Southwestern Front complete the encirclement of the Sixth Army in the autumn of 1942.

tirade against the Jews Hitler was announcing to those in the know that the 'Final Solution' was proceeding on schedule. In fact, during the previous spring six extermination camps had been put into operation in Poland, and since early summer they had been receiving a steady flow of victims—many through the auspices of Jewish Councils (the leaders in the Jewish community) set up to discourage resistance.

All through October the desperate battle raged in the streets of Stalingrad as Paulus' Sixth Army fought grimly for every house, every yard of rubble. Foot by foot the Soviets were being pushed back, but only with a tremendous expenditure of German men and materiel. Finally, on 25 October, Paulus radioed that he thought they would be able to complete the

occupation by 10 November. The news cheered Hitler enormously; the Sixth Army and Fourth Panzer Army were ordered to push south and north along the Volga as soon as Stalingrad had finally fallen. By this time even Zeitzler was suggesting that the long northern flank along the Don, thinly held by Rumanian troops, was in a dangerous situation. But though the Führer was worried, he did not consider the possibility of a Soviet breakthrough serious enough to warrant substantial reinforcements. He and his staff left *Werwolf* and returned to *Wolfsschanze*, for he was convinced that any winter offensives would take place in the northern and central sectors.

In November 1942 the decay that had been growing beneath the surface finally became evident; the three Allied offensives in that month took the initiative from the Germans and they were never to regain it. On 2 November General Montgomery broke through the German-Italian positions at El Alamein; early in the morning on 8 November British and American troops landed along the coasts of Morocco and Algeria, moving rapidly to occupy all of French North Africa as far as the Tunisian border; and on 19 November three Soviet Army groups broke through the German lines north and south of Stalingrad to encircle within five days 22 German divisions—about 220,000 men, 100 tanks, 1800 guns and 10,000 vehicles—between the Don and the Volga.

Hitler had trouble recognizing the importance of the events that took place in November. Worse, his only solution—as in the USSR during the previous winter—was to stand firm at all cost. Rommel had already begun withdrawing toward Fuka when the order came: 'Victory or Death.' Reluctantly, and against his better judgment, the general decided to obey orders. But with no reserves of any kind, and with the RAF in complete control of the skies, he could not hope to stop the Allied advance. Within 15 days he and the remnants of the Afrika Korps had been forced back some 700 miles, beyond Benghazi.

On 3 November, while Rommel was fighting for his life in Egypt, the OKW had received word of a huge Allied armada gathering at Gibraltar; the news did not upset the Führer, who thought that it was probably just another convoy bound for Malta. By 7 November it was clear that the ships were headed for North Africa, but Hitler was still more concerned about the speech he was due to deliver to party comrades on the nineteenth anniversary of the Beer Hall Putsch. On the 8th, while British and

Above:
As Hitler's strategy on the Eastern Front failed the Axis Armies in North Africa were forced to retreat into Tunisia. An Italian column retreats from the battle of the Kasserine Pass.

Right:
For the first time in World War II the American Army intervened in the European War in North Africa. Although US troops were inexperienced it was the American intervention which turned the balance against Hitler.

American troops were still hitting the beaches, Hitler was proclaiming to his audience that, unlike Wilhelm II, he would never capitulate.

Later that evening, when news of the landing became too grim to be ignored any longer, he summoned Laval and Ciano to Munich for a conference. The former was informed that Tunisia and the rest of France would be occupied without delay. Ciano would have been pleased under ordinary circumstances, but at this point he was not in the mood to be happy about anything; it was only too obvious what the Allies' target

would be after North Africa. Nearly 250,000 German and Italian troops were rushed to Tunisia to hold the bridgehead between Tunis and Bizerta. A small fraction of that number could have assured Rommel's victory two months before; now they were being thrown away. All would be lost before the next summer.

From Munich Hitler went to the Berghof at Berchtesgaden, where he spent more time musing contentedly on the fact that all those great forces had been mobilized against *him* than he did on organizing defensive measures. His intellect was beginning to decay and his sense of proportion vanishing. He honestly believed that he could simultaneously occupy or control some twenty European countries, defend North Africa and Crete, and defeat the combined forces of the United States, Great Britain

Above:
The commanders of the Soviet Sixty-Second Army, from left to right: Major General Krylov, Lieutenant General Chuikov, Lieutenant General Gurov and Major General Rodimtsev.

Above left:
Despite having been made a field marshal by Hitler only the day before, Paulus surrendered to the Soviets on 30 January 1943 and the bitter battle for Stalingrad was over.

and the Soviet Union. Rumors that he was mad began to filter back to Berlin.

On the 19th the Soviets, commanded by Generals Vatutin, Rokossovsky and Eremenko, began their huge encircling movement; by the 23rd, when Hitler finally returned to *Wolfsschanze*, the ring was already closing tightly around the city of Stalingrad. Angrily, the Commander in Chief refused to listen to Zeitzler's pleas that he order an immediate break-out: the men were to stand firm and die fighting. On the 26th he was persuaded to let Field Marshal von Manstein, who had devised the western invasion plan, try a relief operation with a newly formed force, Army Group Don.

But the force could not be assembled quickly, and it was 12 December before it finally set out toward Stalingrad. Inside the city the defenders

Paulus' chief of staff, Major General Arthur Schmidt, looked out his window on the 31st and saw a large group of German and Soviet soldiers smoking cigarettes and chatting around a fire, he realized it was all over. Within an hour the two leaders were in a car heading for General Shumilov's Sixty-fourth Army Headquarters, and the next day, 1 February, Moscow announced the Sixth Army's surrender. Hitler, of course, was furious and indignant at Paulus' betrayal—more so because he had just promoted the General to Field Marshal in an at-

waited anxiously, but never saw the tanks they were looking for; Manstein could not get through. Meanwhile, Hitler kept on refusing to consider a break-out by the Sixth Army. Paulus, though he was prepared by the end of December to disobey the Führer's orders, did not have enough tanks, fuel or ammunition to attempt an escape in any case.

The situation worsened during January, and by the end of the month the Sixth Army was in a hopeless position. The Luftwaffe had been unable to airlift sufficient supplies to the city; food, ammunition and medical supplies were gone. To Paulus' requests to be allowed to surrender, Hitler still had but one reply: 'The Army will hold its position to the last man and the last cartridge.' Soon isolated groups of Germans began surrendering on their own. When

Above right: Paulus directs operations outside Stalingrad.

tempt to ensure loyalty. The commanders should have shot themselves, he declared, rather than surrender. In all the suffering he had inflicted on the thousands of men he had sent to death or captivity at Stalingrad, he could see only a personal affront.

The Allies had begun 'terror bombing' the German civilian population on 26 March 1942 with an RAF raid on Lübeck that completely destroyed that historic city. When Hitler retaliated with a 200-bomber raid on the old English cities, the British were able to come back on 30 May 1942 with the first thousand-plane raid of the war, on Cologne. From 1943 on, British and American Air Forces subjected Germany to a constant, round-the-clock air offensive which the Luftwaffe could not begin to handle along with its responsibilities on the other fronts.

As the bombing of German industry and the increasing losses of men and equipment continued, demands on the eastern territories for raw materials, food, machinery and labor mounted. Men, women and children were rounded up and shipped *en masse* to Germany where they were forced to work under terrible conditions. By the end of 1944 there were almost five million foreign workers in Germany: practically two million Soviets, over 800,000 Poles, 764,000 French, 274,000 Dutch, 230,000 Yugoslavs and 227,000 Italians.

After Stalingrad, Hitler gradually began to come out of his self-imposed isolation, although he was still only comfortable with his secretaries and adjutants – with whom he took on the role of a fond uncle. But as his natural suspiciousness deepened into paranoia he was gradually emptying the space around him; by the end of the war he would have quarreled with all but a very few of his military leaders, both in the field and at headquarters.

Physically he had aged fifteen years since the beginning of the war; the enormous number of drugs prescribed by Dr Morell (sometimes as many as 28 at a time), combined with the lack of exercise during his caveman's existence in his headquarters, his vegetarian diet, his irregular hours and the stresses involved with his position, were all taking their toll. He stopped striking poses and moved wearily, his shoulders slumped and one foot dragging, his left hand trembled slightly, his face was pale, his eyes dull. More and more he had to depend on drugs to stimulate him to action.

His intellect, too, was affected: his monologues at dinner now were always the same as he reverted more and more to discussing events from his earlier life in Vienna, World War I, the years of struggle; other times he would deliver long lectures on Aryan prehistory, the degeneracy of modern life, his hatred of Christianity and – as always – the Jews. Even his manner of expression grew cruder and more elemental – something better suited to a student agitator or even a flophouse debater than to one of the world's most powerful military leaders and statesmen. His military decisions began to be based more and more on his World War I experiences; his interest in weapons was restricted to traditional systems, and he showed little concern for advances in new fields such as radar, heat-seeking ground-to-air rockets or atomic weaponry. He blocked the manufacture of the first jet plane, the Messerschmitt 262, until 1944, and then against all advice ordered that it be used as a bomber, not a fighter.

His withdrawal from reality continued with the aid of Martin Bormann who, as the Führer's secretary, helped him stave off the real world and at the same time created for himself one of the strongest power bases in Nazi Germany. It was Bormann who handled the routine adminis-

Above:
The damage at the base at Peenemünde following an Allied bombing raid on the night of 18 August 1943. The Allied strategic bombing offensive at the time was directed at industrial and military targets. Toward the end of 1943 German cities were bombed more intensively but instead of leading to defeatism the bombing stiffened German morale.

Right:
The bombing of the ball-bearing factory at Schweinfurt on 14 October 1943.

trative work, decided who would or would not see Hitler, pushed through appointments or eliminated rivals in government. Bormann encouraged Hitler in the life of a recluse, which began to reach pathological proportions after November 1942. Blackout curtains covered the windows of his conference room 24 hours a day. He traveled in a curtained railroad car, at night when at all possible. He insisted on remaining aloof from the German people, and was to deliver only two more major public speeches – he realized that he had lost the knack of arousing the masses and refused to confront them, despite the fact that without his constant presence the people were losing much of the spirit of energy and self-sacrifice he had been able to instill. Increasingly the Führer preferred to inhabit magnificent imaginary worlds where he thought in terms of centuries and continents, and where the purified Aryan race ruled 'the class of subject alien nations ... the modern slave class.'

His obsession with the annihilation of the Jews and the enslavement of the Slavs began to intrude more and more on his thoughts, draining his energies still further for the conduct of the war. In the extermination camps in Poland – Auschwitz, Belzen, Kulmhof, Maidenek, Sobibor and Treblinka – hundreds of thousands of Jews were herded to an ignominious death. In the concentration camps, formerly used for the 'protective custody' of opponents of the regime, the number of Jews and

Left:
Albert Speer was
Hitler's Armaments
Minister and was
responsible for seeing
that German industry
was rationalized and
dispersed so that
production could be
maintained in spite of
the Allied bombing.

suspicious of his professional soldiers, mainly because of their objectivity, he tried even harder to wage war without them.

For the first few months after the fall of Stalingrad the situation did not appear to be too grave. The German front held firm and the army in the Caucasus was not cut off. When the spring thaw came the Germans were still deep in Soviet territory, and in North Africa Axis troops still held Tunisia. Hitler spent most of April at the Berghof, which most of his entourage found a welcome change from their gloomy, spartan existence at *Wolfsschanze*; the round of military conferences was punctuated by tea parties, and by Hitler's birthday celebration on 20 April.

In Italy, however, there was trouble brewing. The Fascist regime was crumbling fast. In Milan and Turin workers struck for 'bread, peace, and freedom'; Mussolini himself was ill and disillusioned; and it was obvious that all the Italian people wanted was to get out of the war. When Ciano left the Foreign Ministry and took a post as ambassador to the Vatican, Germany suspected he was trying to negotiate a separate peace.

In mid-April Hitler invited Mussolini to Salzburg again, to 'push him back on the rails'; the Italian sat silently through the new round

resistance fighters from occupied countries rose steadily. In 1942 Himmler obtained permission to use concentration camp inmates as a labor pool for the munitions factories, and several classes were identified as being suitable for literally working to death. Many were put to other, more macabre uses, the most revolting of which included being used as subjects for 'medical experiments' by SS doctors. It is possible that the great mass of the German people remained ignorant of the worst excesses of the Nazis, and probably only a relatively few high-ranking officials had any idea of the scope of the extermination program. But a woman who lived as a child in a small town near Mauthausen, a concentration camp in Austria not far from Linz, recalls how the smell of burning bodies permeated the town—and how the children would follow trucks from the camp to pick up any bones that fell off, until the authorities discovered what was happening and changed the route. In all, possibly between 4,200,000 and 4,600,000 Jews were to lose their lives at the hands of the Nazis, not to mention the millions of Slavs and other non-Jews who were murdered in the course of the war. To his generals it appeared as if Hitler's internal stabilization system had given way—he was increasingly irritable and unpredictable, and his ostentatious pose of calm in the face of crisis would unexpectedly be broken by violent fits of rage (when he would berate his commanders as 'cowards, liars and idiots') or by maudlin demonstrations of self-pity. As he became more

Above:
King Boris III, King of
Bulgaria, visited Hitler
in Vienna in 1943. Shortly
after this visit Boris died,
probably from a heart
attack. At the time it
was thought that the
strain of the interview
with Hitler had led to
Boris' death.

of interminable monologues and left, looking more cheerful but still a defeated man at heart. On 7 May the Allies captured Tunis and Bizerta, and within a week all Axis forces in North Africa had been captured; it was obvious that the next target would be Italy itself. There were only two questions to be answered: where would the landing take place (Mussolini thought Sicily while Hitler opted for Sardinia) and would the Italian Army actually put up a fight? Soon after the Allied Armies successfully landed (on Sicily) on 10 July, Hitler received reports that the Italian Army was in a state of collapse. On the 19th the two dictators met again, this

Above:
Hitler visits an armaments factory on the occasion of his birthday, April 1943. His public appearances after this date became more and more rare.

Below:
Marshal Pietro Badoglio led the anti-Mussolini coup.

time at Feltre in northern Italy, and again Hitler delivered his monologues, while Mussolini listened. During the meeting, word arrived of the first daylight air raids on Rome.

The end came on 24 July 1943 when the Fascist Grand Council met for the first time since 1939 and violently criticized Mussolini's conduct of the war. The next evening Il Duce received a summons from the King, who peremptorily dismissed him and sent him off, under arrest. Marshal Pietro Badoglio formed a non-Fascist government, the Fascist Party was dissolved, and Fascist officials were dismissed. Hitler was deeply shocked at the news of his friend's fall, and ordered that the German people be told he resigned 'for reasons of ill-health.'

Hitler's main concern, however, was saving his military position; as he told the generals only a few hours after Mussolini's arrest, it was obvious that while Badoglio's government was proclaiming their loyalty to the Axis they would secretly be negotiating an armistice with the Allies. For his part, he was prepared to pretend to go along, all the while building up his forces in Italy for the inevitable takeover. His first idea was to stage a putsch, taking Rome with the 2nd Parachute Division and the 3rd Panzer Grenadier Division; he even contemplated occupying the Vatican, to 'get that bunch of swine [the Diplomatic Corps] out of there.'

By 26 July he had come up with four plans to present to the rest of the Nazi leaders. First,

Eiche ('Oak') provided for rescuing Mussolini. Second, *Student* dealt with the occupation of Rome and restoration of the Fascist government. *Schwarz* ('Black') was a plan for the military occupation of Italy, while *Achse* ('Axis') outlined the capture and/or destruction of the Italian fleet.

Luckily for Hitler, the Allies delayed making peace with the Italian government for six weeks; by the time the armistice was announced on 8 September, Germany was in a much stronger position. The sixteen German divisions in Italy were able to disband all the Italian troops and take control of Rome and other important positions without any serious trouble. Kesselring, commander of the German forces in Southern Italy, was further cheered by the fact that the Allies chose to land on the mainland at Salerno, much further south than he had anticipated. Though command headquarters where Rommel was installed as Commander in Chief was located in the mountains north of Florence, Kesselring was able to halt the Allied advance to a line not far north of Naples—leaving more than two-thirds of the peninsula, including all the industry, in German hands. The Allies would not make it to Rome until June 1944.

Mussolini was finally rescued by an SS detachment led by the famed commando Otto Skorzeny from a small hotel on the Gran Sasso, high in the mountains of Abruzzi. Listlessly Il Duce, now a broken man, allowed himself to be made a puppet dictator, leaving most decisions to his ministers, and even ceding Trieste, Istria, South Tyrol, Triente and Laibach to Germany without a murmur. He even was forced to hand his son-in-law, Ciano, over to the Germans and to see him shot in January 1944 by a German firing squad acting on orders he had signed. But though he had come to hate the man who once fascinated him, he still had to pay the price for that fascination; his end would come two days before Hitler's on 28 April 1945, when he and his mistress Clara Petacci would be caught by partisans in the tiny hamlet of Mezzagra, summarily executed, and their bodies displayed on a makeshift gibbet in Milan's Piazzale Loreto.

At the end of 1943 Hitler's position in the south–though weakened–was not yet lost. In addition to retaining control of most of Italy, Germany had taken over the Italian-held portions of the Balkans, Yugoslavia, Albania and Greece. But the fact remained that the war was now being fought on the European mainland; it could only be prolonged, no longer won.

In the other major land action, in the east, things were going less well. After a successful offensive against the Red Army in March 1943 Hitler ordered a new assault for July, in the German salient around Kursk. In what has

Above:
Hitler, with Martin Bormann standing behind him, greets Nazi leaders in his headquarters on the Eastern Front. At this point Bormann was Hitler's personal assistant, and tried to shield Hitler from reality.

become known as the greatest tank battle in history, 17 Panzer divisions (equipped with new Tiger tanks and some half a million men) were launched against the Soviet lines. Not only were they stopped, but on 12 July the Soviets began their own offensive further north. Despite Hitler's usual orders to stand and fight to the last man, the German Armies were forced back, until by the end of the year they were practically at the Polish and Rumanian frontiers.

In the west, where most of the action was taking place at sea and in the air, the picture was even more dismal. Admiral Dönitz, the U-Boat specialist who had replaced Raeder as Commander in Chief of the Navy in January, was unable to stop Allied shipping in the North Atlantic, and had finally been forced by the enemy's antisubmarine measures to withdraw his U-Boats entirely from the area in May. Though they returned in September they had little more success; for all intents and purposes the Battle of the Atlantic was over by the end of 1943.

The war in the air struck closer to home, as the RAF and the American Air Force maintained an almost constant offensive against Germany. The carpet bombing of Hamburg in late July–early August reduced that city to a blazing 600-acre mass of ruins and left more than 70,000 dead. After the attack Hitler was furious, Goebbels in a panic, and Göring–for the first time–was near collapse from despair. Most worrying to Hitler, however, was not the loss of life (he had long since removed himself from such human concerns) but rather the effect of the Allied bombings on German war production. The relentless attacks, coupled with Germany's inferiority in natural resources and the pressure of the blockade, soon resulted in ever more serious shortages of everything, from food to oil and armaments.

During the summer and fall of 1943 the Soviet Union, fearing that the United States and Britain were trying to promote a war of attrition that would leave the USSR too weak to defend itself, put out tentative feelers about a negotiated peace. It is not certain just how serious Stalin was, but the question does not really arise since Hitler was uncompromising in his refusal to consider the matter. At one point, when Ribbentrop was trying to persuade him to respond to the overtures, he remarked with a shrug, 'You know, if I came to an agreement with the USSR today, I'd attack her again tomorrow–I just can't help myself.'

Christmas 1943 was a gloomy affair at the *Wolfsschanze*; Hitler would not even allow a Christmas tree, and completely ignored the holiday. The first six months of 1944 were merely a repetition of all the earlier problems, as the Allies pressed their assault on Fortress Europe. By the spring thaw, at the end of March, the Soviets had crossed the Polish and Rumanian borders. In March American planes made their first daylight air raid on Berlin; in May Kesselring was forced to begin a retreat; by 4 June the Allies were entering Rome. That same morning Rommel, who had been transferred to build up the Channel defenses at the end of 1943, set out for Germany–ostensibly to visit his wife, but really to try to persuade Hitler to divert more men and equipment to Normany. He was still at home at dawn on 6 June when a

Right:
Colonel Otto Skorzeny was ordered by Hitler to rescue Mussolini from captivity in September 1943. He accomplished this with his special commando unit and Hitler was so pleased he allowed Skorzeny to expand his unit.

young paratrooper named Murphy dropped into the backyard of a school teacher in Ste Mère Eglise. The D-Day invasion had begun.

It took several days to finally convince Hitler that Normandy represented a real invasion, and not just a feint; even after he accepted the fact he refused to give his field commanders, Rommel and Rundstedt, a free hand–thus ensuring the Allies' success in establishing their beachhead. Finally, on 12 June, he ordered the begin-

Above:
Stalin, Roosevelt and Churchill attend the Teheran Conference in December 1943. This conference set a date for Overlord because Stalin was very anxious for the Western Allies to open a second front and relieve the pressure on the Eastern Front.

ning of the V-1 rocket campaign against London (which, though damaging, had no effect on the Normandy situation), and on 17 July he drove from Berchtesgaden to a village near Soissons in France to meet the two Field Marshals. In the face of Hitler's tendency to blame his commanders for the Allied success, Rommel tried his best to convince him of the seriousness of the situation–but to no avail. Hitler remained as unmoved by Rommel's plans for a strategic

Right:
Rommel inspects troops on the Atlantic Wall in May 1944. Hitler sent Rommel to France to prepare against the Allied invasion and his strengthening of coastal defenses made the Allied landings more difficult.

Below:
Landing craft bring troops to the Omaha Beach in Normandy on D-Day, 6 June 1944.

retreat as the Field Marshal was by the Führer's promises of rocket bombs and 'masses of jet fighters.' Finally, in a thoroughly bad temper, Hitler set off home to the Berghof, announcing that Rommel had lost his nerve and become a pessimist. Two days later, however, he gave the defenders of Cherbourg permission to pull out 'at the last possible moment' to prevent their being encircled.

For some time after the Normandy invasion Hitler, who thrived on crisis, seemed calmer and more in control of both himself and the situation as a whole. He even listened to criticism with equanimity–from Admiral Dönitz, General Dietl, even his adjutants and secretaries. But though he listened, he never changed his mind, stubbornly refusing to consider anyone else's suggestions.

Ever since it had become obvious that Hitler's plans were going awry, resistance to the Nazi regime had been forming throughout Europe–including Germany itself. The German opposition was by no means a unified group; rather, it consisted of several small units with no linking organization, motive or purpose. The Army was, as usual, the center for most of the conspiracies but here, as before, it was difficult for the officers to overcome the notion that they were courting treason and personal dishonor for violating their oaths of allegiance. Every value they held dear cried out against a coup, while every ounce of commonsense they possessed was in favor of it. Thus we see the history of the German opposition as a series of mix-ups, contradictions and misdirected scruples. The conspirators' position was not improved by the fact that Franklin Roosevelt refused to recognize or assist them, in line with the Allies' insistence on unconditional surrender. If they succeeded they would be on their own–and with the Red Army on their doorstep, this was not an attractive prospect.

There were three major opposition groups in Germany in 1943–44. One was the so-called Kreisau Circle, named after Count Helmuth von Moltke's Silesian estate. This was mainly a high-minded discussion group which was not concerned so much with removing Hitler as with the economic, social and moral bases of the society that would follow him. Von Moltke was arrested and the Kreisau Circle broken up in February 1944–and it should be noted that the count died bravely, holding to his principles.

Above:
Field Marshal Gerd von Rundstedt was Commander in Chief of the West at the time of D-Day and his troops were caught unprepared.

Below:
German prisoners are rounded up on Omaha Beach.

The next important group, which consisted of conservatives and nationalists led by General Ludwig Beck and Karl Gördeler, favored the establishment of a right-wing, authoritarian regime. Their first attempt on Hitler's life was made on 13 March 1943, when General Henning von Tresckow and one of his lieutenants, Fabian von Schlabrendorff, placed a time bomb in Hitler's plane. The bomb (which was hidden in a package of brandy bottles) failed to go off, and Schlabrendorff had to fly quickly to the Führer's headquarters and retrieve it. Six more

questions; as Stauffenberg once told a new recruit to the cause, 'With all the means at my disposal I am practicing treason.' Operation Valkyrie—a plan for the Home Army to take over the emergency measures necessary to run the country—was worked out in detail, ostensibly in reaction to rumors of a foreign workers' uprising.

By good fortune Stauffenberg was promoted to full colonel at the end of June 1944 and named Chief of Staff to the Commander in Chief of the Home Army—a position that gave him

attempts were planned for the end of 1943, but all of them came to nothing, either because of technical failures or simple bad luck. Despite their amazing slowness in tracking down the conspirators, the Gestapo finally began closing in; in December 1943 General Hans Oster, a key figure in the *Abwehr* (Intelligence Bureau), was forced to resign after an exhaustive investigation. With exposure now a constant threat, Gördeler and Beck wavered. In April 1944 they made one last attempt to get support from the United States. When they received no reply, they stopped making specific plans.

At this point a group of younger officers took over, led by Klaus Philip Schenk, Count von Stauffenberg. In contrast to the Beck-Gördeler group, the younger men were more inclined to the left than the right and thought in terms of a *rapprochement* with the Soviet Union rather than the United States. They were also more inclined to action and less to debating moral

frequent access to Hitler himself. After two assassination attempts on 11 and 15 July, neither of which could be consummated, he resolved to make his third, decisive try on 20 July. That morning he flew to the Führer's headquarters in East Prussia, a time bomb in his briefcase among his papers. Mussolini was visiting, and a conference had been called for 1230.

The subsequent events have been described many times. Stauffenberg's luck was bad from the beginning: the meeting was suddenly moved to barracks with thin walls that did not contain the blast; he was actually seen before the meeting setting the time fuse; his briefcase was kicked up against a table leg which absorbed much of the explosion; and when it came Hitler was leaning over the heavy table looking at a map. As a result he was not badly hurt, aside from a blackened face, a few bruises and some splinters of wood in his legs. The Führer's first reaction was one of relief—once again he had been miraculously saved from his enemies.

Stauffenberg, meanwhile, had left the area before Hitler emerged from the bunker, supported by General Keitel. Believing the Führer had been killed, the colonel flew back to Berlin only to find that Operation Valkyrie had not yet been put into motion. By the time he got things underway it was too late—Hitler was known to be alive and the entire scheme was in shambles. That night began a wave of arrests and executions that would continue through April 1945 and include many suspected enemies of the regime, whether or not they had any connection with the coup. Stauffenberg and three companions were shot without ceremony in a courtyard at OKW, while Beck tried twice to shoot himself and finally had to be finished off by a fellow officer; every member of Stauffenberg's family, from a three-year-old child to an 85-year-old patriarch, was arrested with the families of other conspirators; Rommel, who had been drawn into the plot early in the year, was permitted to commit suicide. In all, official Gestapo records list 7000 arrests, and one source quoted at Nuremberg puts the number of executions at almost 5000.

Meanwhile, in Poland, Jews continued to die by the thousands, depite the efforts of the 'Bloodhound Judge,' Konrad Morgan, who had embarked on a one-man crusade to root out corruption in the extermination camps (he had no power to touch the actual work of the camps, since they had a direct mandate from the Chancellery). Others were dying too—not just Slavs, but Jehovah's Witnesses (who had been among Hitler's most obdurate opponents from the beginning), gypsies and many ordinary citizens of Western Europe who were victims of the mass executions that usually followed acts of rebellion or sabotage. As it became clear that the Nazis' New Order was merely a euphemism for complete political and economic domination, the resistance movement grew—and Nazi oppression and brutality increased proportionately. But still, the masses did not rebel; the desire to survive was stronger than any other motivation, and most ordinary people simply tried to get on with their lives as best they could.

In Germany, Stauffenberg's attempted coup did more than give Hitler an excuse to rid himself of 'all those "vons" that call themselves aristocrats,' whom he had hated for years. It also gave him an incentive to tighten up on the Home Front, which Goebbels had been pressing him to do for months. Schools and theaters were shut down; embargos and restrictions were increased; military leave was canceled; compulsory labor for all women under the age of 50 was introduced; and on 24 August total mobilization was announced. Shortly thereafter, in October, all fit men (that is, practically everyone who could walk) between sixteen

and 60 were drafted into the new *Volkssturm* (Home Guard) under Himmler's command. The Waffen SS was made an equal partner with the Army, Navy and Air Force to complete the generals' humiliation.

By this time Goebbels' propaganda campaign was openly using fear to impel the German people to one last effort, painting a grim picture of the extermination and enslavement that awaited them at the hands of the Allies. To emphasize the regime's demand for total commitment, it was announced that families of deserters would be shot.

With the new measures, Speer managed to achieve an astronomical rise in armament production, but it was a last-ditch effort—its only long-term result was to use up irreplaceable resources at a faster rate. Eventually the production of aircraft fuel dropped from 156,000 metric tons in May 1944 to 10,000 in September; fighter planes with empty tanks lined German airfields.

While his enemies converged on Germany from every side Hitler retired to his bunker, refusing to leave the stuffy, fetid rooms for even a breath of fresh air. He suffered from headaches, an attack of jaundice, a series of problems with his teeth; his ears had been damaged in the

Wolfsschanze explosion and he was in great pain. In mid-September, shortly after Allied troops crossed the German border, he was felled by a heart attack; for a time he seemed to have lost all desire to live and lay shivering on his bunk. Then, suddenly, he began to pull himself together for the final effort. He was still obviously ill; his back was stooped, his face pale and puffy, his hands trembled, his left arm twitched, he dragged his left leg as he walked, and had trouble keeping his balance. But he recovered his spirits and had one last trick up his sleeve.

During the last months of 1944 there was a curious lull in the fighting. By the end of September the Allies, who had moved rapidly through France, were poised just west of the Rhine. But the German Army's resolve had stiffened as they approached their homeland. Their determined defense (orchestrated by Field Marshals von Rundstedt and Model), along with increasingly bad weather, Allied supply and transport problems, and differences of opinion among the Allied High Command, all combined to halt the advance. Kesselring had stopped the Allies in Italy south of the Po River; the Soviets had been held up at the Vistula in Poland. Danger still threatened from the southeast, where a strong Soviet offensive was steadily pushing Germany out of Rumania, Bulgaria and even Hungary, and where the British were liberating Athens.

Hitler's plan, however, was to pay scant attention to the threat in the southeast and mount an offensive in the west, where he hoped to take the enemy by surprise and regain the initiative. If it worked he would have some time to rearm, and perhaps even be able to take advantage of the inevitable split between the Allies. Although his decision represented a tacit abandonment of the principle of a 'battle against Bolshevism,' the west was in fact the logical place for an offensive. There he would have shorter distances to cover (without vast expanses of territory behind the front where whole armies could be lost), as well as the Westwall fortifications (which were a natural pushing-off place). Also, despite Goebbels' propaganda campaign, fear of the Soviets was still greater than the fear of the Western Allies; the soldiers on the Eastern Front could probably be relied on to resist more fiercely than those on the Western Front.

The objective of the plan, which Hitler worked out with Jodl that autumn in 1944, was to drive through the Ardennes, cross the Meuse and recapture Antwerp, the most important Allied supply port. In addition the move would split the Allied forces and trap the British troops between the Meuse and the Rhine. As the idea developed, it soon expanded in his mind to become comparable to the great advance of 1940; events would lead naturally to

Left:
Hitler confers with Himmler in October 1944. The assassination attempt in July 1944 increased Hitler's distrust of the Army and made him rely more and more on his inner circle and especially on Himmler.

Right:
Karl Wilhelm Krause (center) served as Hitler's valet. He is seen here with friends after he had been personally presented with a Gold Cross by Hitler in September 1944.

Above:
Speer (left) and Admiral Dönitz (center) were some of the few whom Hitler trusted until the end. In his final testament Hitler named Dönitz as his successor as Head of State.

Above:
Hitler's last gamble in
World War II was the
Ardennes Offensive
which became known as
the Battle of the Bulge.

another Dunkirk—but now the British would not get away.

Although it was a good plan (the unsuspecting Allies had their weakest troop concentrations in the Ardennes sector), seeing it as a repetition of 1940 was completely unrealistic. Even if Germany had been able to take Antwerp, there was no way it could be held. In addition, the Eastern Front was being seriously weakened, and all the reserves were being thrown away on one last desperate gamble. As usual, the generals tried to point out the ultimate futility of the operation, and as usual Hitler would not be dissuaded; even General Guderian (who had been recalled after the assassination attempt and made Chief of the Army General Staff) could not make an impression. The Führer's headquarters were moved to Bad Nauheim near the Western Front so he could keep a tighter control over the situation; the orders sent to Rundstedt, which covered the smallest details of the operation, carried the warning, 'Not to be altered.'

On 16 December the offensive began along a 75-mile front with elaborate precautions to preserve secrecy: low-flying planes drowned out the noise of men taking up positions; some equipment was moved with horses; deceptive radio messages were sent to fool the Allies. The Germans even had a stroke of luck when the low-hanging clouds grounded the enemy Air Forces. As a result their opponents were taken completely by surprise, and for the first few days the German Army made rapid gains. But they never had a hope of reaching Antwerp for their supplies ran out almost immediately—one tank group found itself stranded just a mile from an American supply dump containing three million gallons of gasoline. By Christmas the weather had cleared and Allied planes began blasting the German lines; for all intents and purposes the Battle of the Bulge was over.

In the east the Soviets began preparations for their own offensive. Guderian tried twice to persuade the Führer to transfer troops from the hopeless cause on the Western Front over to the Eastern Front, but Hitler angrily refused to countenance the suggestion. The Soviets were bluffing, he asserted—and furthermore, it was still possible to win in the west. Finally, in June, the whole front collapsed. Model's second attempt to reach the Meuse failed, while a new attack into northern Alsace fell short of Strasbourg; on 8 January Hitler was forced to order German armor back from the front, and by the 16th his forces had been pushed back to their original starting point. In the meantime, on 12 January, the Red Army had begun their offensive, and the huge avalanche of men and machines was rolling easily over German lines along the entire front. By the end of the month Marshal Zhukov was only 100 miles from Berlin.

Soon after the beginning of the Soviet offensive Hitler left his headquarters in the west and returned to the Reich Chancellery in Berlin, now an island in a sea of rubble and ruined buildings. Strangely, the wing in which his own apartments and offices were located was still undamaged, but the constant air raids soon forced a more or less permanent move into a massive concrete bunker built 24 feet below the Chancellery garden. Once installed, he left the deep shelter less and less; the cave-like existence fitted perfectly with the withdrawal from reality and paranoia that had taken possession of his mind. From dreams of grandiose victory and world domination, his thoughts now turned to visions of magnificent destruction. In Hitler's hands the 'scorched earth policy,' which had been used to good effect by the USSR earlier in the war, soon degenerated into destruction for destruction's sake. In addition to industrial complexes, he ordered that all communications, food and sewage systems were to be demolished. When Speer ventured to remonstrate with him, pointing out that people still had to live in de-

Above:
US soldiers dig up the bodies of their friends who died on 17 December 1944.

Left:
Americans surrender during the first phase of the Battle of the Bulge.

feat, he was told, 'If the war is to be lost, the nation also will die.'

His physical condition mirrored his mental disintegration. One staff officer remembers him during this period as a 'dreadful sight': he appeared to drag himself around by willpower alone, he had lost his sense of balance, and his once hypnotic eyes were glazed and bloodshot. His face was gray with red blotches. Often saliva dripped from the corners of his mouth, and his clothing was frequently spotted with food stains. He developed an obsessive appetite for chocolate and cake.

On the outside the Allies were closing in. In February the Yalta Conference healed the split in the Grand Alliance, at least for the time being; at the end of the month the Red Army broke through to the Baltic; early in March the Allies overran the Westwall, captured Cologne, and established a bridgehead on the east bank of the Rhine. In Hungary the Soviets chased the elite Waffen SS units out of the country, while Tito's army of Yugoslav partisans opened its own offensive.

Opposite top:
This is a photomontage of Hitler and Eva Braun dining in the Führer bunker. The join in the center is clearly visible.

Opposite bottom:
Stalin attends the Yalta Conference and talks through an interpreter to Harry Hopkins (turning away from the photographer). Hopkins was one of Roosevelt's special advisers and was very concerned about the fate of Europe after the war was over.

Below:
Toward the end of his life Hitler drew hope from the story of Frederick the Great who was saved from disaster when the Tsarina Elisabeth died. He kept a portrait of the Prussian monarch, in the background here, with him wherever he went.

But within the bunker Hitler retained some of his old power to create his own reality in the minds of the people with whom he was in contact. Though formality decreased as the months went on, his staff unquestioningly accepted the increasingly transparent fantasy world that existed only in his imagination. There was little attempt to challenge his authority, even after he had lost the power to enforce it. One of the few who tried was Albert Speer; in February, having failed to convince Hitler by logical means that the war was lost, he had devised a plan for introducing poison gas into the ventilation system of the bunker. At the last minute the air shaft had to be reconstructed and the plan was scrapped. Hitler's phenomenal luck in avoiding serious bodily injury still held. In March Speer personally traveled to the front, convincing local officials not to obey Hitler's orders for total destruction, and even issuing submachine guns to people in charge of factories so that they could defend their buildings against demolition squads. When Hitler found out he not only demanded that Speer stop, but insisted on an admission that the war was not yet lost—

but Speer managed to avoid doing either, at the same time delivering such a convincing declaration of personal loyalty that Hitler, touched, actually restored some of his former powers.

Roosevelt's death on 12 April raised Nazi spirits for a moment, but it was soon obvious that it would have no effect on Allied military operations. By mid-April the mighty Third Reich was reduced to a narrow strip hardly 100 miles wide through the heartland of Germany.

A few days later Eva Braun appeared unexpectedly, in defiance of Hitler's orders, announcing that she did not intend to leave his side. On 20 April Hitler's birthday was celebrated in the bunker by the leaders of the now defunct regime—Bormann, Goebbels, Göring, Himmler, Ribbentrop and Speer—along with the military commanders. The Allies celebrated in their own way, with another thousand-bomber raid on Berlin. Most of his companions in the bunker were trying to persuade Hitler to leave immediately for Berchtesgaden, but Goebbels took the opposite view—the Führer should stay in Berlin and make it an end in the grand historic tradition. That night the exodus began, as Himmler, Ribbentrop, Speer and Göring began preparing to move south. But Hitler still hesitated, unable to make up his mind.

His grasp on reality was almost completely gone; few of his generals even attempted to give him a real picture of events outside the bunker during the conferences which were still held daily. On 21 April he issued orders for a major attack against the Soviets who were already within the city limits. 'You will see,' he told Karl Koller (chief of staff of the Luftwaffe), 'the Soviets will suffer the bloodiest defeat in their history at the gates of Berlin.' But the orders he issued were so confused that before SS General Felix Steiner could begin mounting the offensive the Soviets had broken through the German lines and penetrated the city.

The realization that his last card had been played threw Hitler into a fury that led to a three-hour denunciation of everyone in sight. With fists raised and tears running down his cheeks, in a voice suddenly grown strong again, he accused everyone in the room of being cowardly, treacherous, incompetent and corrupt. This was the end. He could bear it no more. They could leave if they wanted, but he would stick it out in Berlin and die on the steps of the Chancellery. Telephone calls from Dönitz and Himmler trying to recall him to a realization of his duties as Commander in Chief had no effect. Petulantly he refused to change his mind, and that evening dictated a radio message announcing that he had personally taken over the defense of the city and would stay there until the end. That evening he invited Goebbels and his family to join him in the bunker.

For the last week, then, the inhabitants of the Berlin shelter were Hitler; Eva Braun; Goebbels, his wife Magda, and their six children; Hitler's valet, Heinz Linge; his SS adjutant, Otto Günsche; his two secretaries, Gerda Christian and Traudl Junge; his surgeon, Dr Ludwig Stumpfegger; his cook, Fräulein Manzialy; and Goebbels' adjutant. Bormann, Generals Krebs and Burgdorf, Artur Axmann (leader of the Hitler Youth), and a number of SS guards, liaison officers, etc occupied nearby shelters and were frequent visitors.

On the 23rd a message arrived from Göring who, having heard secondhand that Hitler had designated him to negotiate with the Allies, was requesting confirmation. But his hated rival, Bormann, managed to turn the request for information into an announcement of a *coup d'état* and Hitler—whose moods had become, if anything, even more unstable—railed loudly against his old comrade, stripping him of all his offices. Later, however, slumped exhausted in a chair, he remarked in an off-hand way, 'All right. Let Göring negotiate the surrender. . . . It doesn't matter who does it.'

Next day he sent an urgent message to General Ritter von Greim, ordering him to come immediately from Munich to Berlin, to be appointed Göring's successor. Greim arrived in the beleaguered city on the 26th, after a difficult journey accomplished with the aid of a young woman, Hanna Reitsch—one of Germany's best test pilots, who had been involved in testing Willy Messerschmitt's first jet planes. Greim's right foot had been seriously injured in a dogfight before they reached the city, but Reitsch managed to get them both in, by flying very low and landing on the broad street that runs through the Brandenburg Gate, then commandeering a car and driving through the flames and rubble to the Führer's bunker. That night the first Soviet shells began hitting the Chancellery.

The next day, 27 April, Greim attended a series of military conferences, while Reitsch spent most of her time in Goebbels' suite. She thought Goebbels himself was too theatrical, and considered Eva Braun a shallow woman who thought of little beyond her clothing and appearance. But she greatly admired Magda, who always managed to keep up a cheerful façade for the children and whose greatest fear was that she would weaken and be unable to 'help them

Above:
General Alfred Jodl signs the German surrender at Rheims on 7 May 1945.

Opposite top:
Soviet tanks drive through the center of Berlin in May 1945.

Opposite bottom:
The signing of the formal ratification of the Third Reich's unconditional surrender: General Zhukov sorts through the papers as Air Marshal Sir Arthur Tedder looks on.

out of this life' when the time came. Reitsch tried to give her some time to herself, amusing the children with stories of her flying experiences and teaching them songs. In Italy, meanwhile, Mussolini and his mistress had been captured by the partisans—they would be killed the following day.

During the evening of 28 April Hitler received the final blow—from a brief news report he learned that Himmler had contacted Count Bernadotte, a Swede, to negotiate peace terms. The news of his deputy's treachery left Hitler resigned to his fate; he was finally determined on a mass suicide in the bunker, an idea with which he had been toying for some time. But first he dispatched Greim and Reitsch with orders to fly out of Berlin and arrest Himmler at all costs. The two were driven in an armored car to the Brandenburg Gate, where an Arado 96 training plane was hidden. Reitsch taxied down the broad avenue and took off in a hail of bullets; soon she had climbed above the searchlights and flak explosions and was heading north, leaving behind a sea of flame.

Just before midnight on the 28th Hitler took time for some personal matters. First he called Traudl Junge and dictated both his political and personal wills; then the entire entourage assembled in the map room of the bunker. Eva had been the one person who had remained loyal to him through thick and thin, and now—at the end of their lives—she would have her reward. The two were married in a brief civil ceremony, with Goebbels and Bormann as witnesses. The 29 April passed slowly. The Soviets were only a mile away as copies of Hitler's personal and political testaments were entrusted to several emissaries for delivery to his successor, Admiral Dönitz, and the new Commander in Chief of the Army, Field Marshal Schörner. At 1800 the usual group assembled in his study, where he passed out phials of poison and thanked his staff for their devotion and courage. Word of Mussolini's end in the gas station in Milan had arrived, and the agitated Führer ordered that his body be burned, so that he would not be subjected to similar indignities. Later, at the final briefing, General Wiedling informed him that the city would fall within 24 hours.

During lunch with his secretaries and cook on 30 April (Eva had kept to her room), Hitler chatted as if it were just an ordinary meal. But immediately after he had finished eating he fetched Eva, who was wearing his favorite black dress, and said farewell to his assembled staff. Taking Günsche aside he gave him his final order—to find enough gasoline to burn both bodies after their deaths. He did not want to be 'put on exhibition in a Soviet wax museum.' He and his wife returned to their suite, and at 1530 a single shot rang out. When the little group outside the door entered they found Hitler sprawled on a blood-soaked sofa, shot through

the right temple. Beside him was Eva, also dead, her nostrils discolored by cyanamide.

The Führer's instructions were followed to the letter: the bodies were removed from the bunker and set alight in a sandy depression near the ruined Chancellery. In the midst of a Soviet barrage the adjutants kept watch; finally, after several hours, the charred remains were collected in a canvas bag and buried in a shell hole.

For the next two days Goebbels and Bormann attempted unsuccessfully to negotiate with the Soviets. Finally, on 1 May, Goebbels released news of the Führer's death—then returned to the bunker where he gave poison to his children, then shot both his wife and himself. Bormann slipped out of the bunker; for many years it was not certain whether he escaped or not, but in 1973 it was proven, conclusively to most, that he was killed not far from the shelter.

The German Army in Italy had already surrendered; on 4 May the German forces in northeast Europe capitulated; and on the 7th, at Rheims, General Jodl and Admiral Friedeburg unconditionally surrendered to representatives of the United States, Great Britain, the Soviet Union and France. The Third Reich, which was to have lasted a thousand years, had survived Hitler by only a week.

Epilogue

It has not been the purpose of this book to present Hitler as a hero, monster or madman, for he was all and yet none of these. Chance played a part in his success, as did the disorganization and disagreement of his opponents. But his own talents were of significance: his insight into both the moods of the time and the minds of his critics, his sense of timing and spectacle, his willingness to break out of traditional molds and take chances, and above all, his consistent pursuit of a single, clearly-defined goal.

In his pursuit of this, one should not underestimate the scale of Hitler's very real support from the German people. Although he never gained a constitutional majority in the Reichstag, some 13,000,000 people voted for National Socialism in 1933. Indicative of the weakness of democratic forces in Germany and the strength of the fear of Communism, supposedly threatening to overturn the Western World, was the fact that Hitler was appointed Chancellor in 1933 according to legitimate process—though giving the persuasive force of the SA their due.

However, the seeds of Hitler's destruction, as with his success, lay within himself. Hatred and the urge to dominate governed all his actions; the man who found a sense of purpose in armed service in the Kaiser's war, sought his ultimate goal in the accumulation of personal power. Eventually these emotions were to lead to a loss of perspective and failure. Internally, plots against Hitler were to develop out of the various agencies of power which he had set up to offset each other, in order to leave ultimate control in his own hands. Abroad, his overambition in war was to suffer defeat under the combined forces of the Allied powers.

Below:
The Führerbunker in Berlin in 1945.

Why read yet another book about Adolf Hitler? For some, the fact that this one man may be judged responsible for redirecting the course of the twentieth century would be justification enough. There are other reasons.

It has often been said that Fascism was a purely German phenomenon – the result of a peculiarly German set of historical events that made it possible for one man, with a certain combination of qualities that mirrored the neuroses of his age, to seize power and exploit circumstances to his own ends. However, it could be said that many of the factors which fostered the success of National Socialism – from psychological distress and frustration in defeat to economic privation – contributed to the rise of dictatorial governments in other countries at the time, such as Italy and Hungary. Fascist powers gave lip-service to different philosophies, but all could be described as movements of the extreme Right, strongly nationalistic and anti-Communist with a reverent belief in the healing powers of the 'leader.' Der Führer was but one manifestation of this phenomenon.

He gave Germany a sense of direction and unity when it was on the verge of collapse, and in many ways the National Socialist regime improved the life of the German people; from providing employment and food to the now ubiquitous Volkswagen. Decades later it is easy to deplore his rise to power. Without the benefit of hindsight it is impossible to know if we would have acquiesced, as most Germans did, under a devotion to duty and loyalty to the homeland, or perhaps underestimated – even ignored – the intentions of a political force, as the powers of Europe and America did by their signal failure to check the ambition of Hitler until he had already begun to help himself to the cake.

The threat of overweening power looms in every age. The rise and fall of Adolf Hitler is a case in point that we ought not to forget.

Index